D1711616

LIBERTY, EQUALITY AND EFFICIENCY

Also by J. E. Meade and of related interest

PLANNING AND THE PRICE MECHANISM
THE CONTROL OF INFLATION
THE INTELLIGENT RADICAL'S GUIDE TO ECONOMIC POLICY
STAGFLATION
Volume 1: Wage Fixing
Volume 2: Demand Management (*with David Vines and Jan Maciejowski*)
ALTERNATIVE SYSTEMS OF BUSINESS ORGANISATION AND
  WORKERS' REMUNERATION
DIFFERENT FORMS OF SHARE ECONOMY
MACROECONOMIC POLICY: Inflation, Wealth and the Exchange Rate
  (*with Martin Weale, Andrew Blake, Nicos Christodoulakis
  and David Vines*)

Liberty, Equality and Efficiency

Apologia pro Agathotopia Mea

J. E. Meade
Emeritus Professor of Political Economy
University of Cambridge

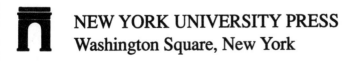

NEW YORK UNIVERSITY PRESS
Washington Square, New York

338,9
M481L

Copyright © J. E. Meade 1993
Chapters 4 and 5 © The David Hume Institute 1989
and revision © J. E. Meade 1993

All rights reserved

First published in the U.S.A. in 1993 by
NEW YORK UNIVERSITY PRESS
Washington Square
New York, N. Y. 10003

Library of Congress Cataloging-in-Publication Data
Meade, J. E. (James Edward), 1907–
Liberty, equality and efficiency : apologia pro agathotopia mea /
J. E. Meade
p.   cm.
Includes index.
ISBN 0–8147–5491–0
1. Economic policy.   2. Monetary policy.   I. Title.
HD87.M42   1993
338.9—dc20   92–34923
                                                    CIP

Printed in Great Britain

MB

To
Edwin Morley Fletcher
who led me to Agathotopia

University Libraries
Carnegie Mellon University
Pittsburgh, Pennsylvania 15213

Contents

Acknowledgements

Part I of the present book consists of a reprint of a book published in 1964 by George Allen & Unwin, entitled *Efficiency, Equality and the Ownership of Property*. This is reproduced without revision except for an addition to footnote 19 on page 80 of the present book.

Part II covers four recent Agathotopian Papers. 'Can We Learn a Third Way from the Agathotopians?' was first published in *The Royal Bank of Scotland Review*, September 1990, and subsequently presented at an International Economic Association Conference on 'The Economics of Partnership' in September 1991, the proceedings of which conference were published in 1993 as *Alternatives to Capitalism*, edited by Anthony B. Atkinson (Macmillan).

'Agathotopia: The Economics of Partnership' is a revised version of Hume Paper No. 16, published by the Aberdeen University Press for the David Hume Institute, 1989. The sections in the original edition (on the Removal of Conflicts of Interest between Labour and Capital; Discrimination: The End of 'Equal Pay for Equal Work'; The Effect of Discriminating Labour-Capital Partnerships on the Distribution of Income between Labour and Capital; Alternative Treatments of Retiring Worker Partners; The Renegotiation of Share Holdings; The Treatment of Undistributed Revenue; and the Treatment of Capital Gains) have all been completely rewritten in order to embody a new analysis of the far-reaching effects of alternative definitions of an enterprise's current revenue. I owe the idea behind these changes to a comment on my work by Professor E. Fehr of the Technical University of Vienna for which I am most grateful.

'The Building of the New Europe: National Diversity versus Continental Uniformity' was published in 1991 by the David Hume Institute, as Hume Occasional Paper No. 28, and was presented in January 1991 as a special lecture at a University of Rome Conference on 'Building the New Europe', the proceedings of which conference were published in 1992 as *Building the New Europe, Volume 1: The Single Market and Monetary Unification*, edited by Mario Baldassarri and Robert Mundell (Macmillan).

'In Praise of Slowth: or The Agathotopian Treatment of the Environment as a Common National Asset' is a paper written in 1991 but not previously published.

Christ's College
Cambridge   J. E. MEADE

1 Introduction[1]

All the items in this book deal in one way or another with the choice of economic policies and institutions designed to cope with the inevitable clashes between three basic economic objectives: first, citizens' freedom of choice in markets for jobs and for the satisfaction of their wants (Liberty); second, avoidance of any resulting intolerable contrast of poverty side by side with great riches (Equality); and, third, the use of available resources in ways which will produce the technically highest possible average standard of living (Efficiency). But there is one particular clash of objectives in this general category which binds all the items in this book particularly closely together, namely the problems raised by the fact that the setting of money prices and in particular of money wage rates has very strong effects both upon the distribution of income and also upon the effectiveness of the economy in finding the most efficient levels of employment and of outputs of various goods and services.

It is arguable that ever since the end of the Second World War the greatest domestic economic problem in the United Kingdom – and to a lesser extent in all free-enterprise industrialised countries – has been the resolution of the clash between the use of money wage rates as instruments for the distribution of the national income and their use as instruments for guiding resources into their most efficient employments. After the war there was a general consensus in favour of a Keynesian financial policy for the management of the total demand for goods and services so as to maintain a high and stable level of employment. Keynes himself had grave fears that such a policy might well be frustrated by excessive wage claims which would cause any expansion of money expenditures to lead to an inflation of money costs and prices rather than to an expansion of output and employment at uninflated prices. And so it turned out to be the case. For two decades after the war the Keynesian policies were remarkably successful with low rates of unemployment combined with reasonably low rates of inflation. But gradually, as in our imperfectly competitive society separate groups learned to press their monopolistic bargaining powers to obtain each for itself the best possible share of the available income, the system broke down. The consequential abandonment of Keynesian demand management and its replacement by a restrictive monetary policy reduced markedly the rate of price inflation so long as the restrictive policy was effectively applied, but it did so at the cost of a much higher level of unemployment.

1

We have now been living in a world of fairly rapid price inflation for many years and as a result have learnt to take an expected rate of future price inflation into account in our commercial calculations. A group of workers who seek a 5 per cent rise in their real rate of pay over the coming year and who expect a 10 per cent rise of prices and so of the money cost of living over the same period will seek a 15 per cent rate of rise in their money rate of pay. A creditor who is lending £100 for a year and who seeks a 5 per cent per annum real rate of return on his wealth will similarly demand a 15 per cent per annum money rate of interest on his loan if he expects a 10 per cent rise in the cost of living.

The rate of rise in their real rate of pay at which workers aim will in part at least depend upon the level of activity in the economy as a whole. With a high level of demand for the products of industry unemployment will be low; employers will be seeking workers rather than workers seeking employment; and it will be easier for workers to strike a bargain for a higher real rate of pay and for employers to face the higher rate of real labour costs. Conversely in a slump with low demand for goods and services and heavy unemployment wage bargains will be settled for lower rises in real rates of pay.

Suppose that any any one time there were an average rate of growth of labour productivity of, say, 3 per cent per annum and that at the same time there were a level of economic activity and of unemployment which resulted in wage bargains aimed at a 3 per cent rise in the real rate of pay. This level of unemployment, at which the bargained rate of rise in real rates of pay is equal to the existing rate of rise in labour productivity, may be called the 'equilibrium' level of unemployment. It is then easy to show that, if expansionary financial policies (low rates of interest, low rates of tax, high rates of governmental expenditures) are adopted to increase the demand for goods and services and so to reduce unemployment below this equilibrium level, there will be a continuing rise in the rate of price inflation. Conversely if restrictive financial policies are adopted to maintain unemployment above its equilibrium level, there will be a continuing decline in the rate of price inflation. The following example may help to explain these relationships.

Suppose the current and expected rate of price inflation is 10 per cent per annum, that the current rate of increase in the productivity of labour is 3 per cent per annum, but that the rate of unemployment is kept below its equilibrium level so that current wage bargains aim at a 5 per cent per annum rise in real wage rates. Wage bargains will be set at 15 per cent increases in money wage rates (10 per cent to offset the current rate of inflation of the cost of living plus 5 per cent to represent a rise in real wages). But with labour productivity rising only by 3 per cent, money wage costs and so also selling prices, set at a fixed mark-up on costs, would be rising by 12 per cent (i.e. by the 15 per cent rise in money wage rates less the 3 per cent rise in labour productivity.) But money wage bargains would now rise from 15 per cent to 17 per cent (12 per cent to offset the rate of price inflation plus 5 per cent for the planned increase in the real wage rates). This would lead to 14 per cent rises in money wage costs and prices (i.e. 17 per cent in money wage rates less 3 per cent increased output per head) which in turn would lead to 19 per cent rises in money wage claims (i.e. 14 per cent to cover inflation plus the 5 per cent for increased real wages) and so to 16 per cent rises in money wage costs and prices (i.e. 19 per cent in money wage rates less 3 per cent in increased output per head). And so on in a never-ending upward movement of the rate of price inflation, which will accelerate in speed as people begin to take into account in their transactions not only the current rate of price inflation but also the expectation of a continual increase in that inflationary rate.

By a similar process of analysis it can be shown that if restrictive monetary and fiscal policies are used to keep unemployment above its equilibrium level, the result will be an ever declining rate of price inflation.

Once an upward boom or a downward slump of this kind has been set in motion there are a large number of dynamic repercussions in the economy which will intensify the swings in activity and will complicate the problems of monetary and fiscal controls in ways which the above analysis does not take into account. But the above analysis does explain an underlying structure of relationships which is of central importance for the issues discussed in this book and from which we may conclude:

(1) that one can temporarily reduce unemployment below its equilibrium level by expansionary financial measures which will, however, threaten to lead in the end to an intolerable hyperinflation of prices, unless one reverses the financial policies as soon as any further rise in the rate of inflation becomes intolerable and has to be prevented;

(2) that one can reduce the rate of inflation to a newly desired low level by restrictive financial measures but only at the expense of a rise in unemployment above its equilibrium level while the process of reduction of inflation is taking place; and

(3) that one can achieve a permanent and lasting reduction of unemployment only by reducing the equilibrium level of unemployment. This involves a reform of wage-setting and price-setting policies and institutions in order to increase the levels of economic activity and employment at which demands for increases in real rates of pay do not exceed actual increases in labour productivity.

Recent experiences in the United Kingdom appear to illustrate the truth of these conclusions. It is possible to reduce the rate of price inflation from a high to a low level, but only at the expense of a protracted period of heavy unemployment well above the equilibrium level. There is an obvious cost involved in the loss of real output experienced during the period while unemployment is above the equilibrium level; this loss does not take the form simply of a temporary reduction in the standard of living during the process of adjustment; in so far as it takes the form of a diminished incentive to invest in new capital equipment during the period of temporary depression it involves entering the future post-adjustment period with a permanently diminished capital structure for the economy.

There is, moreover, a second reason for moderating the country's efforts to lower the rate of inflation, a reason which is especially relevant for the main issues discussed in this book. It is of course unquestionably desirable to pursue a sufficiently restrictive set of monetary and fiscal policies to prevent an ever rising rate of inflation; or in other words no attempt should be made by financially expansionary measures to hold the level of unemployment below the equilibrium level. But price inflation at a constant moderate rate, while it may involve some costs in commercial transactions to make sure that contracts are taking it properly into account, will at the same time help to make the economy more flexible and efficient. Suppose, for example, that for one reason or another the demand for labour is falling off in region or occupation A and is rising in region or occupation B. As will be argued later, efficiency requires the price of labour to go down in A relatively to its level in B in order to stimulate demand and restrict supply of labour in A with the reverse effects in B. But wage contracts are fixed in terms of money. It will be much easier to raise the money wage rate in B than it is to lower the money wage rate in A. A moderate rate of overall average price inflation will thus enable relative money costs and prices to be adjusted more readily by relying on some extra rises in the absolute level of money wages in the expanding sectors of the economy than by negotiating absolute reductions in money wage rates in the contracting sectors of the economy.

But to return to the main theme, the general level of unemployment cannot be satisfactorily or permanently reduced simply by expansionary financial policies leading to an increased demand for goods and services. It requires a change in basic wage-setting institutions to enable an explosive runaway rise in the rate of inflation to be avoided at a lower rate of unemployment in the economy. What are the basic changes in wage-setting institutions necessary for this purpose?

Suppose that we start with an equilibrium unemployment percentage of 20 per cent in the following conditions: (i) there is a price inflation of 5 per cent per annum, (ii) there is an increase in labour productivity of 3 per cent per annum, and (iii) there is an 8 per cent per annum rise in money wage rates, yielding a 3 per cent (8 per cent less 5 per cent) rise in real wage rates. The question which arises is simply: Why can we not reproduce exactly these same three figures with the unemployment percentage reduced from 20 per cent to 10 per cent? We have so far given the following answer to this question. If the demand for goods and services were so expanded that unemployment was reduced from 20 per cent to 10 per cent, the bargaining strength of the workers would be improved. In consequence they would no longer be content to aim at the 3 per cent per annum rise in their real wage rates which matched the 3 per cent per annum rise in labour productivity; they would therefore demand increases in money wage rates above the previous level of 8 per cent to offset the 5 per cent rise in the cost of living; and this would set off the process of explosive price inflation which we have already examined.

But, alas, there is an even greater difficulty to be faced. It would be necessary for the workers in the new position not merely to refrain from aiming at a higher rate of rise of their future real wage rate in spite of a stronger bargaining position; they would have also to accept a lower absolute real wage rate as the starting base from which the 3 per cent increases were bargained. In any given situation with a given set of real resources, capital equipment, and technical knowledge to expand the labour force by 10 per cent or more would lead to an increase in total output; but it would almost certainly involve a reduction in average output per head. More labour would be crowded on the same equipment or older and less productive machinery would have to be recalled from idleness for use by the new workers. Or workers would have to be set to produce less valuable services in addition to those which were already being produced. The new workers would probably be of less skill or ability or resident in the less appropriate localities or trained in the less needed occupation. There could be some offsetting advantages in economies of larger-scale production. But in general in any given situation in which there was not an initial marked surplus of capital productive capacity, a marked expansion of labour intake would reduce average output per head. Employers would be prepared to absorb the additional labour only if the real wage of labour was reduced.

In so far as this is the case, we must conclude that to reduce significantly the equilibrium level of unemployment requires basic changes in wage-setting institutions and policies which make acceptable real wage rates which are much more sensitive to the supply – demand conditions in the labour market, allowing adjustment in money wages to be made on principles which produce employment opportunities for unemployed workers.

It is suggested that the best combination of financial and wage-setting institutions and policies should be designed on what may be called New Keynesian lines. In this case the full panoply of Keynesian demand-management weapons (rates of interest, rates of tax, rates of government expenditures) should be used to control the level of total *monetary* expenditures on home-produced goods and services (the money GDP) on a moderate inflationary growth path, leaving it to the design of institutions and policies for the setting of wage-rates and selling prices to enable this moderate and steady expansion of selling markets to lead to the greatest possible expansion of *real* output and employment instead of merely to rising money prices and costs.

This may be contrasted with what can be called the structure of Orthodox Keynesian policies under which the financial policies were to be designed to control the total demand for *real* goods and services at a Full Employment level, backed so far as necessary by policies and institutions to control *money* wages and prices (incomes policies) so as to prevent this from leading to a runaway inflation.[2] New Keynesianism may be claimed to have two important advantages over Orthodox Keynesianism. It avoids the impossible task of trying to estimate appropriate levels of output and employment (either in the form of Full Employment or Equilibrium levels). It employs a more natural division of tasks between the controlling instruments, with monetary and other financial instruments controlling monetary inflation and with price-setting policies and institutions making the best adjustments between supplies and demands in the various markets for real goods and services.

So far the emphasis in this Introduction has been on the waste caused by mass unemployment. This emphasis may be excused because it has for the time being become the predominant issue. But it should not be forgotten that inefficiencies due to the use of wages as a main instrument of distributional policy are not confined to the general level of unemployment which such a policy may involve. The so-called 'micro' problems of flexibility of particular wage rates and prices relatively to each other are in fact just as important as the 'macro' problems concerning the setting of the general average level of wage rates and prices throughout the economy. Efficient free-market use of resources requires that differential prices for labour should be charged according to the relatively scarce, or relatively plentiful, supply of particular groups of workers according to their particular skills or lack of skills and their particular locations in depressed or active regions of the country. Relatively high or low rates of pay are needed to induce employers to produce goods of a kind, and by methods, and in localities, which economise on scarce resources and to encourage workers by choice of training and residence to move from positions of excess to positions of deficient supply.

The post-war history of attempts to control wage rates or otherwise to make rates of pay more flexible by the outlawing of monopolistic methods of wage bargaining suggests that there is no possibility of seriously reducing the reliance on rates of pay as a major instrument for the distribution of income unless some alternative means can be found for ensuring a fair and acceptable distribution of income.

Any alternative method of affecting the distribution of income must necessarily imply that individuals receive income which, in some form or another, to a greater or smaller degree, is not related to the pay which they receive from their work. For this to be effective in reducing the distributional importance of their pay the reduction in the amount which is directly tied to pay and/or the increase in the amount of income which is not directly tied to pay must be on a substantial scale. If, however, the divorce between pay and income is carried too far it will clearly have a disastrous effect on the incentive to work. If there were no pay for the amount and quality of work done there would be no commercial incentive to work at all.

This is a vital consideration in the clash between the distributional and the efficiency aspects of variations in rates of pay. Clearly any policy for the divorce of distributional aspects from the setting of rates of pay must not go too far. The question arises whether it can go to any length which is sufficient to have an appreciable effect on reducing the importance of distributional considerations without having so great a disincentive effect as to do more harm than good.

There are a number of important reasons for not exaggerating the inefficiencies introduced into the system by such disincentive effects.

In the first place it must not be forgotten that there are important improvements in the efficient use of labour to offset any loss of work through any disincentive effects. If the policy does in effect allow rates of pay to be used more flexibly and with less regard to their distributional effects, this, as has already been argued, may allow involuntarily unemployed workers to be taken on in less well paid extra jobs. The decrease in involuntary unemployment may well outweigh any increase in voluntary leisure due to any decreased attractiveness of work.

Moreover any policies which make rates of pay more flexible and thus make differential rates of pay more responsive to supply and demand conditions in the various labour markets would also, as has already been argued, enable a more efficient use to be made of the workers who are in employment. This constitutes a further and very important source of greater efficiency to be set against any undesirable increase in voluntary leisure.

The extent to which any policies of divorcing distributional aspects from wage-setting policies and institutions will reduce incentives to work will depend not only upon the scale on which any such innovations are imposed but also upon the form in which such policies are designed. Indeed as will be argued later it may be possible to devise systems of pay which reject the egalitarian distributional principle of Equal Pay for Equal Work and thereby at the same time improve both incentives and, paradoxically, the overall degree of equality in earnings.

There are two forms of redistributive policy which take the form of redistribution of 'unearned' income from property. The first (which may be called the Property-Owning-Democracy method) operates through measures devised to increase the widespread and more equally distributed ownership of private wealth and so of the income received from holdings of wealth. Such income is independent of the owner's earnings from work and thus diminishes the relative importance of earned incomes. The second (which may be called the Social Ownership of Property method) produces indirectly a similar effect by arranging for a considerable proportion of what would have been privately owned wealth to pass into ownership of the State; and the income accruing from such property can be distributed in some forms of social benefit payable to the generality of citizens without regard to their individual earnings from work.

Both these methods merely redistribute any disincentive effects – those individuals who as a result of the redistribution hold less wealth having a greater incentive to earn while those who receive more 'unearned' income have less incentive to work. It is, of course, possible that the disincentives to work of the latter more numerous group may exceed the increased incentives to work of the former less numerous group. But there will certainly be some offset of the disincentives of the latter group.

In addition to these two methods which rely simply on the redistribution of existing sources of income which are unrelated to rates of pay there is a third method (which may be called the Welfare State method). This method converts income from pay into income unrelated to pay by raising the rate of tax on existing incomes and using the revenue to pay out to the generality of the citizens social benefits of one kind or another which are unrelated to the level of the earnings of the individual citizen.

This form of tax-cum-social-benefits is most frequently used also as a means for helping to equalise incomes – the taxes being levied on the rich and the benefits being paid to the poor. That is another matter, to which we will return. Our present concern is a different one which can be illustrated by considering the case of a representative citizen who receives as a social benefit which is not related to his income from other sources exactly the same amount as he pays in tax on this other income. It is clear that this will reduce his incentives to earn income. His fixed social benefit will make him need less income from work and at the same time the tax on what he earns will mean that he would have to work harder than before to earn the same post-tax income. This Welfare State method will without doubt have a marked disincentive effect on work, and it is most probable that any really effective scheme will have to rely in part at least upon this Welfare State method.

From the point of view of the amount of effective work done there is thus a balance of forces to be considered. If – and as will be argued later it is an important 'if' – an alternative scheme for affecting the distribution of income does have an appreciable effect in allowing rates of pay to be used more flexibly to promote greater and more effective employment, this increase in effective employment can be set against the disincentives to work of those who are in employment. Will the gains offset the losses in promoting effective employment?

Clearly the scheme – and particularly any Welfare-State element in the scheme – must not be carried to excess; we have already argued that as the proportion of income derived from earnings fell towards zero, so any purely commercial motive to work would disappear entirely. But long before such an extreme decision was reached there would be a net loss of effective employment.

It is, however, important to realise that even if there were some moderate reduction of effective employment, the scheme might still be welcomed. There are two quite different possible reasons for this.

In a highly populated, highly industrialised rich economy increases in economic activity are likely to take the form of the production of luxuries rather than necessities. Increased production may entail greater congestion and greater strains on the environment, and the increase in these social costs may not enter into the calculations of the individual producers and consumers of these goods. At the same time the total size of the economy's market may be so large that there are no economies to be gained from an enlarged scale of production. In such circumstances a policy which increases the attractiveness of increased leisure relatively to that of increased income may actually be socially desirable.

The second reason why a policy which actually reduces the total of effective employment may in fact on balance be socially beneficial is quite different. The change may be welcomed in spite of its having a deleterious effect on economic Efficiency because it has a still more marked desirable effect upon economic Equality. In this Introduction we have started this whole analysis from the assertion that the use of wage-setting for distributional purposes makes it a very bad instrument for efficiency purposes, leading to the question whether one can improve its efficiency effect by divorcing the distributional effects from its use. One could equally well have started the analysis from the assertion that the use of wage-setting for efficiency purposes makes it a very bad instrument for distributional purposes, leading to the question whether one can improve the distributional results by divorcing distributional policies from wage-setting arrangements. One might then well find that measures which greatly improved the distribution of income had some moderate net deleterious effect upon the efficiency of the economy, but that the distributional gains outweighed the efficiency losses. The distributional effects of the three methods of Property Owning Democracy, Social Ownership of Property, and the Welfare State are discussed in some detail in the main texts of this book. Their effects on incentives and on the net efficiency of the economy are discussed in less detail. The emphasis put on these incentive effects in this Introduction may in part help to restore the balance. It is possible, as has been argued above, that the design of a separate set of policies and institutions for the promotion of Equality may actually be compatible with a resulting concomitant increase in the Efficiency effects of wage-setting. But there may remain an inevitable and unavoidable clash, in which case one must judge whether any improvement in Equality outweighs any loss of Efficiency.

These and other clashes between Liberty, Equality and Efficiency are the subject matter of the main text of the present book.

The 1964 book *Efficiency, Equality and the Ownership of Property*, reproduced in Part I of the present book (Chapter 2), was devoted wholly to a discussion of the clash between the distributional and the efficiency effects of wage-setting institutions and policies and to a description of some ways in which the distributional objectives could be achieved by other means. In the 1964 book all three available methods were mentioned: (i) the taxation of the rich in order to pay social benefits to supplement the incomes of the poor (the Welfare State method), (ii) fiscal and other measures designed to lead to a more equal distribution of the private ownership of wealth so that a greater equality of distribution of income from property could be achieved (the Property-Owning Democracy method) and (iii) measures which would result in the transfer of ownership of property from private ownership to ownership by the State – expressed in particular through a reduction of the National Debt – so that income from capital wealth could directly or indirectly be more equally distributed (the Socialist

State method). The 1964 book merely mentioned the Welfare State method in passing and concentrated its attention on the two other methods which are aimed directly or indirectly at offsetting greater inequalities in 'earned' incomes by means of greater equality in 'unearned' incomes. In particular the book discussed in great detail the problems involved in achieving a Property-Owning Democracy. It paid little attention to possible disincentive effects, which may be partly explained by its not having been concerned with the Welfare State method.

The later four Agathotopian papers which are included in Part II of the present book cover a much wider range of topics; but these are all centred round the clash between the distributional and the efficiency effects of wage-rate adjustments. The main ways in which these papers enlarge the scope of the discussion are as follows:

(1) A main feature is the proposal for replacing the familiar capital company and the ordinary labour-owned cooperative by what are called Labour-Capital Partnerships, in which both labour and capital share the risks and the rewards of the enterprise. The historical reason for the great emphasis put on this new structure for business enterprises is explained in the Preface to the main tract on 'Agathotopia: The Economics of Partnership' (Chapter 4 of the present book). The change may be welcomed as having great merit in itself – perhaps for the promotion of Fraternity. But it is also of great importance for the solution of the central problem of using flexible rates of pay to encourage effective employment of labour. It is proposed that in exceptionally successful labour-capital partnerships the terms offered to new worker-partners should not necessarily be as favourable as those already enjoyed by the existing worker-partners. The employment of additional labour could then be on terms which were attractive to the new workers without threat to the incomes of the well-paid existing workers. This would be a method of introducing a much more flexible use of rates of pay for the employment of labour in efficient uses at the margin. The employment of additional 'outsiders' would no longer be a threat to the pay of the existing 'insiders'.

Paradoxically the abandonment of the rule of Equal Pay for Equal Work might well result in a net increase in overall Equality. Consider two groups of workers: the high earners in the successful partnerships and the low earners in unemployment or in the less successful enterprises. The proposed change of institutions would lead to a shift of some of the low earners into an intermediate group, earning less than the existing high earners but sufficiently more than the unemployed and the lower earners to attract them into their new employments in the successful enterprises. The terms offered by the high earners to attract the new intermediate group would probably not absorb the whole of the additional revenue generated by the newly engaged workers. In this case some rise in the earnings of the high earners would be combined with a reduction in the number of the lowest earners and their transformation into a better paid intermediate group. Thus net overall Equality would not necessarily be diminished. Indeed it might well be improved, while Efficiency and the average standard of living would certainly be raised by the shift of workers into more productive uses.

(2) The Agathotopian papers deal at length with the Welfare State solution. They propose the introduction of the payment of a tax-free basic income to every citizen and discuss at some length the ways in which this might be financed. In this connection much attention is paid to various possible disincentive effects.

(3) One of the Agathotopian papers (Chapter 6 of the present book) discusses the conditions in which some disincentive to work and preference for leisure arising in a Welfare State economy might in fact be a blessing in disguise for environmental reasons.

(4) The Agathotopian papers do not discuss the problems of establishing a Property Owning Democracy in the great detail in which the matter is discussed in the earlier 1964 book. But they do draw attention to the proposal that the institution of taxation on the holding and the transfer of capital wealth should be combined with an exemption of personal savings from direct taxation. This would make it easier for citizens with little wealth to accumulate more wealth, while at the same time reducing the possibility of accumulating or inheriting excessive holdings.

(5) Great stress is put on the distinction between State management of business concerns and State beneficial ownership of capital wealth. State beneficial ownership without State management could occur if the State owned (directly or indirectly through investment trusts and similar financial intermediaries) shares in various companies on just the same terms as many private rentiers now invest directly or indirectly in privately managed companies. What amounts to this distinction between social management and social beneficial ownership appears in one short footnote in the earlier 1964 book; but it plays a central role in the Agathotopian papers (Chapters 3 and 4 of the present book) which (in the interests of Freedom and Efficiency) put more stress in general on the desirability of maintaining free-enterprise management and competition in all possible suitable cases.

(6) A main argument against lowering money wage-rates as a means of reducing the cost of labour and so encouraging greater employment is that the effect on expectations may cause it to have exactly the opposite effect on employment. Cuts in money wage costs may give rise to reductions in money prices; and the expectation of falling money prices may in turn give

rise to the postponement, and so to the reduction, of money expenditures on goods and services. Such reductions in demand may be on such a scale as to cause a reduction in the amounts of goods and services which are demanded. It may thus intensify a trade recession by leading to a reduction rather than to an increase in output and employment. This may well happen in the absence of any other offsetting measures. But the Agathotopian papers make it clear that flexibility of money wage rates as an instrument for promoting the efficient use of labour must be combined with what may be called a New Keynesian financial policy, namely a set of monetary and fiscal policies which will keep the total of money expenditures on domestically produced goods and services (the money GDP) on a steadily growing path. In such conditions, so long as any unemployed resources remain available, a reduction of money wage costs and prices would certainly lead to an increase in the total quantities sold. Any depressing effects on total expenditures due to the expectation of lower future prices would be offset by New Keynesian monetary and fiscal measures to stimulate expenditures. The need for such a New Keynesian financial policy is tacitly assumed in the earlier 1964 book, but it is expressly argued in the Agathotopian papers (Chapters 3 and 4 of the present book).

(7) The Agathotopian paper on 'The Building of the New Europe: National Diversity versus Continental Uniformity' (Chapter 5 of the present book) raises and discusses in great detail a central problem which is not mentioned in the earlier 1964 book. How far could a single country carry out experiments in Agathotopian policies and institutions in a world economy without introducing a wide range of controls over its international trade and payments?

Finally the question remains whether there are any lessons to be learned for application in the real world from the examination in the present book of a set of ideal economic policies and institutions. Or is the whole enterprise a waste of time in the construction of a dream world which one could never in fact realise? Agathotopians unlike many Utopians recognise that in the real world in which we live it is impossible to build a perfect society and that the search must always be confined to the attainments of a workable compromise between Freedom of Choice, Fairness of Distribution, and Promotion of a High Standard of Living. To aim for completely unrestricted personal freedom, exact equality of real incomes and the highest technically conceivable standard of living would be a complete waste of time. The proposals in the present book claim only to have sought a good working compromise between Liberty, Equality and Efficiency for a world in which individual citizens strive selfishly in the market place to do the best they possibly can for themselves and for their close relatives and friends.

Yet, it must be admitted, there is a large element of the unrealistic ideal in the background against which such feasible economic solutions are examined in the present book. Thus, it is tacitly assumed:-

(1) that citizens who operate selfishly in the market place nevertheless cast their votes in the democratic ballot box for a government which will seek the common good rather than the satisfaction of the voter's own special interests;

(2) that the members of the governmental machine are themselves devoted, wise, and incorrupt in their search for feasible means of promoting the common good;

(3) that the individual citizens are all law-abiding and operate in the market place strictly within any restrictions laid down by the governmental authorities; and

(4) that if it were possible to design an effective alternative method of influencing the distribution of income, it would be possible largely to ignore the distributional effects of changes in money rates of pay.

In fact, none of these four propositions can be safely assumed to be wholly valid, and indeed over recent years a large body of important work has been done by economists, especially by Professor James Buchanan, in assessing the implications for economic policies and institutions of the failure of the first three of these background assumptions. In particular this work has provided a strong additional argument in favour of using, as far as possible, the free-market competitive price mechanism instead of the method of central planning for determining the allocation of resources as between different uses. The analysis in this book argues the case for the free-market mechanism in the direct interest of the two basic objectives of Liberty and Efficiency. These arguments are reinforced by the realisation that this would also reduce the importance of the first three of the basic background propositions. The smaller the role of government interventions, the less important it is to ensure that the government is made up solely of philosopher kings and that society is composed exclusively of law-abiding citizens who vote altruistically at the ballot box. Such considerations are of essential importance for the formation of final decisions in the choice between different economic policies and institutions.

On the other hand little or no work has been done on the problems involved in connection with the fourth of the basic background assumptions. In the present book it is taken for granted that the discovery of some alternative distributional method is a necessary condition for seriously diminishing the importance placed on the distributional effects of wage-setting policies and institutions. If that be the case, it is not a waste of time to consider whether a feasible alternative method can be devised.

But this does not, of course, imply that the adoption of an alternative distributional mechanisms would alone be sufficient to shift the emphasis adequately from the distributional to the efficiency effects of adjustment of rates of pay. It would seem probable that the institution of the alternative methods proposed in this book would have some more or less automatic effect in the desired direction; but it would seem equally probable that any such automatic effect would be inadequate and that a great deal of political argument about, and actual experience of, the effects of various fiscal and other measures would be necessary. Continual political debate about the best levels of basic incomes for different categories of citizens (old, young, single-parents, disabled, etc.), about the best forms and levels of various taxes (surcharges on low incomes, progressive rates on high incomes, exemptions of savings from direct taxation, levies on investment incomes, charges on holdings and/or transfers of wealth), and about various changes in structures for setting rates of pay might have considerable effect in diverting attention away from wage costs on to the other means of adjusting the distribution of income.

There are serious difficulties; but they should not deter us. In fact in all liberal societies there is already an element of truth in each of the four ideal background assumptions, the degree of validity of each assumption varying from society to society. One of the tasks of building a good society is to discover how to promote the attitudes and behaviours of members of society which are in harmony with the demands of these basic background assumptions. The sort of analysis carried out in the present book of what could be done if the background assumptions were fully valid is an essential step in the process of building the good society. It provides a vision of the direction in which one should aim to mould attitudes and customary behaviours and to reform economic policies and institutions in so far as the validity of the background assumptions will at any one time allow.

The changes of policies and institutions which are proposed in the present book cover a very wide range of markets and are designed in such a way that their combination constitutes a single coherent whole. It should not, however, be argued from this that there must be a single grand once-for-all revolution in which all changes take place simultaneously so that their various effects may properly interlock. Gradual changes can be made in each of the various markets – for example, in experimentation with individual labour-capital partnerships, in exempting different forms of saving from income tax, in the reform of death duties, in the redemption of the National Debt, and so on. The purpose of the complete analysis of the final ideal interlocking of all of the changes is to provide a vision of the future which allows one to judge whether each individual current change is in the direction which the final structure demands. Special occasions may from time to time occur when a big revolutionary step can be taken, such as a large Capital Levy to redeem a large sector of National Debt in a reconstruction programme after a major war. But in general a gradual process of reform is in any case to be preferred; and this is especially true in the inevitable absence of any certainty about the degree to which the proposed changes will in fact have their desired effects on the economy and in conditions in which in any case a considerable period of political debate and experience of new methods is necessary to engender the changes of attitudes and behaviour which will be necessary to shift the emphasis significantly away from the distributional effects of rates of pay.

I am saddened that so many of my professional colleagues seem at present to be so exclusively engaged in discussing how best to design fiscal, monetary, foreign-exchange and wage-setting policies and institutions so as to get the best pay-off between inflation and employment, given the present combination of distributional and efficiency objectives in setting rates of pay. This work is very important and very valuable. But I appeal to some of them to divert some of their attention away from making the best of the present bad job and on to the design of a better job. They may well not accept Agathotopia as the best possible model for this purpose, in which case I challenge them to produce a better one. But whatever its precise structure, a model of an Agathotopian kind is needed during a process of gradual change as a means of judging whether each small change represents a movement towards or a movement away from an ultimate goal and as laying the ideological foundation on which a new political consensus might be built.

Notes

1. In writing this Introduction I have had great help from comments by Professor Frank Hahn, Mrs Miriam Camps, and Mr Martin Weale.
2. In terms of our earlier terminology one might describe Orthodox Keynesianism as maintaining by monetary and fiscal means an independently chosen Full Employment level of real economic activity and then using wage-setting policies to force the 'equilibrium' level of unemployment down to correspond with this predetermined level and thus to prevent a runaway inflation. On the other hand New Keynesianism employs financial policies to maintain the inflation of total money incomes at a predetermined rate and thus avoids a runaway explosive inflation and then uses wage- and price-setting policies to reduce the 'equilibrium' level of unemployment to the lowest possible level.

Part I

2 Efficiency, Equality and the Ownership of Property*

PREFACE

This chapter is based on lectures given to students of the University and of the Business School in Stockholm in May 1964. I would like to thank these two institutions for the invitation to lecture and the British Council and the Council of Europe for making my visit possible. I would like also to thank the editor of the *Economic Journal* for permission to incorporate certain passages from my article 'Mauritius: A Case Study in Malthusian Economics' published in the *Economic Journal*, September 1961. The arguments in section V of this chapter have been much influenced by a thesis (alas, still unpublished) by Mr D. G. Champernowne on the causes of economic inequalities. I am also much indebted to my wife for suggesting a number of improvements in my exposition.

The subject matter of these lectures is of great and (with the development of automation) of growing importance; but it is strangely neglected – particularly in the United Kingdom. In Sweden there is (i) a progressive tax on capital gains, (ii) a progressive annual tax on total personal wealth, (iii) a progressive tax on gifts *inter vivos*, and (iv) a progressive tax on individual bequests. I implore any of my fellow countrymen who read this chapter not to object: 'It can't be done.'

J.E.M.

Christ's College, Cambridge
May 1964

---

* Originally published by George Allen & Unwin, 1964.

I ECONOMIC EFFICIENCY AND DISTRIBUTIONAL JUSTICE

The following pages are an exercise in the analysis of the dual function of the price mechanism. The price of a commodity or of a factor of production is a determinant both of the use which will be made of that commodity or factor of production and of the real income which the owner of the commodity or factor of production will receive as a result of its sale. These we will call the 'efficiency' and the 'distributional' aspects of the price. As is well known to all professional economists, relative prices properly used either in a competitive market or else by a planning authority can help to guide the economic system to an 'efficient' use of resources, that is to say, to a state of affairs in which resources are so used that it would be impossible to make one citizen better off without making any other worse off. For if a high price is charged for scarce resources and a low price for plentiful resources, their users will always try to satisfy their needs in 'efficient' ways which use relatively little of the scarce resources and relatively much of the plentiful resources; and this will be true whether the users be entrepreneurs buying materials and other factors of production as inputs into some productive process or whether they be housewives buying consumption goods and services. But such an 'efficient' system may, of course, lead to a very undesirable distribution of real wealth. If citizen A owns nothing except a factor (e.g. his own unskilled labour) whose price is low and needs for his family's welfare goods whose price is high, he will be very poor, as compared with citizen B who happens to own a factor (e.g. a scarce natural resource) whose price is high and who happens to need for his family's enjoyment goods which are very cheap.

It is not, of course, my contention that a policy of *laissez faire*, leaving everything to be determined by the free play of market forces, would alone lead to a fully efficient use of resources. Professional economists are well aware of the obstacles to such a solution which must be overcome by various acts of governmental policy.

(1) Total effective demand for goods and services must be controlled by monetary and budgetary policy to maintain full employment and a background for economic growth.

(2) Forecasting and planning *à la française* or in the mode of the United Kingdom's National Economic Development Council is necessary so that the many independent decision-making units may have a better and more consistent set of views about what future conditions will be like.

(3) Monopolistic powers and market imperfections will cause discrepancies between prices and costs. Legislation against restrictive practices, control of prices, greater freedom for the import of competing products are among the measures which may be appropriate to deal with some of these problems. In other cases socialisation and central public management may be the appropriate remedy.

(4) There are innumerable cases of external economies and diseconomies (such as the congestion, noise, and stench of motor traffic in our cities) where government taxes and subsidies or other regulations are needed to bring private and social interests into harmony. In many cases such as police, defence, and justice the social concern is so predominant over the private interest that the activity is best conducted directly by the public authority.

(5) Consumers are ignorant and gullible. It is, therefore, desirable for the State to discourage private commercial advertisement and to foster disinterested consumer research and information services.

And so one could go on. But these are matters with which it is not my intention to deal on the present occasion. My present point is simply that even when the State is doing all that it should to make the system work efficiently, it will still be necessary to use the price mechanism as a guide to efficiency. In a modern complex economy the State must set the background of institutions and policies which will enable the system to harmonise social and private interests; but it is still necessary to attach price tags to the various factors of production and to the various final goods and services in order to guide those who have the day-to-day decisions to make (whether these be private entrepreneurs, the servants of public authorities, or individual housewives) as to what is plentiful and what is scarce. But prices used for this efficiency purpose may result in a very undesirable distribution of income and wealth.

There are many instances of this dilemma. A good example is the international market for primary products. It may often happen that a low price of a plentiful primary product is needed on world efficiency grounds to make the fullest use of this plentiful resource, but the producers of the primary product may be among the poorest citizens of the world. In a paper on 'International Commodity Policy'[1] I have tried to devise a policy which would divorce the 'efficiency' from the 'distributional' effects of the prices of primary products.

In these pages I am going to attempt the same task in a rather more elaborate manner for another and perhaps even more basic price. The price with which I shall be concerned is the wage rate of labour, the level of which can have most important 'efficiency' and 'distributional' effects. The policy measures and institutional reforms with which I shall primarily be concerned are those which influence the ownership of property. Such reforms have recently been strangely neglected by economists and politicians; but it will be my purpose to suggest that they might offer in the long run the principal means for reconciling the desired 'efficiency' and 'distributional' aspects of the level of the real wage rate.

The dilemma in the case of the real wage rate presents itself at present in its starkest form in some of the overpopulated underdeveloped countries of the world. In an article published in 1961[2] I have already tried to outline the nature of this price dilemma in the case of one such economy – that of Mauritius, which can be taken as a microcosm typical of the many and large underdeveloped countries of the world in which there is a population explosion.

Mauritius is a small sugar-producing island in the Indian Ocean with a high and very rapidly increasing population. It is the outstanding example of a monocrop economy with 99 per cent of its exports and 40 to 50 per cent of its national output consisting of sugar. The big sugar factories and the greater part of the best land are owned by rich estate owners, mainly persons of French origin. The sugar estates are worked by comparatively poor workers mainly of Indian origin. In 1946–7 malaria was eliminated. The death rate fell from about 44 to 14 per thousand and the birth rate did not fall. The population began to grow at 3 per cent per annum. Since all those who will be of working age in fifteen years time have already been born, it is possible to calculate that, whatever may now happen to the birth rate, the working force in 15 years time will be 50 per cent greater than it is now. Thus the pressure of population upon resources which is already great is bound to become much more intense in the future.

Let us consider what classical economic analysis would have to say on this issue. Mauritius will be an economy in which unskilled labour is extremely plentiful and land and capital equipment are scarce. Such a situation would be one in which, in the classical competitive economy, the rent of land and the rates of profit and interest would rise and the real wage rate would fall. This would give every incentive to private producers as well as to public authorities to go in for the production of things which required much labour and relatively little land and capital for their production and, in the production of any product or service, to choose those processes and techniques of production which used much labour and little land and capital.

The ultimate purpose is, of course, not to give employment, but to obtain the largest possible output from the community's (scarce) resources of land and capital and (plentiful) resources of labour. And this is what the classical price mechanism might be expected to bring about. A rise in rent and interest and a fall in wage rates will induce producers to employ more labour with a given amount of land and capital if, but only if, a larger output can thereby be produced. No entrepreneur will take on more labour with a given amount of land and capital in order to produce a smaller or less-valuable total output. Indeed, it is one of the main merits of this use of the price mechanism that it will not choose inefficient techniques in order to make work for work's sake.

There can be little doubt that this principle is of the utmost relevance in an economy such as that of Mauritius. A few examples must suffice. In cane-fields weeding can be carried out either by hand, or else, in part at least, by the use of imported chemical herbicides. Which method it is profitable for the sugar estates to use depends essentially upon the wage and availability of labour. Another example is the handling of sugar when it has been produced. With the labour-intensive method, sugar is put into bags at the factory on the sugar estate, transported by rail or road to Port Louis, and carried by hand on to the ship, where the bag is opened and emptied into the ship's hold. The alternative capital-intensive method of bulk handling is to load the sugar automatically into special containers on road vehicles at the factory, to discharge the sugar from these vehicles automatically into silos at the quayside and to discharge the sugar automatically direct from the silos into the ship's hold at the quayside. This method economises much labour in stevedoring at Port Louis, in handling the sugar in the factory and in the growing of the hemp and the manufacture of the hemp into bags, which is done at present at a government factory in Mauritius. On the other hand, it involves very heavy capital expenditure on the new road vehicles, on deepening the harbour to bring the ships to the quayside, on the new equipment at the port and so on. Whether or not it is the cheaper method depends essentially upon the wage rate of labour compared with the cost of acquiring the necessary capital.

A further example is given by the problems involved in the establishment of a tea industry in Mauritius. Tea is a rather labour-intensive crop and needs a higher level of employment per acre than sugar. There are prospects that Mauritius might be able to produce good-quality tea. Just because tea is a rather labour-intensive crop it is very appropriate as a way of saving land and using labour. But just because it is a labour-intensive crop the wage element in its cost is of great importance. At present the wage rate in

Mauritius is significantly higher than in Ceylon and East Africa, with whose teas Mauritian tea would have to compete. The success of this new avenue for employment will be greatly affected by the cost of labour in Mauritius.

Mauritius will be able to find productive employment for a greatly increased working force only if she can establish and expand some manufacturing industries. She cannot rely on finding employment for a greatly increased population in her present staple industry, namely sugar. The sugar industry is a highly progressive one in which output per worker employed is constantly rising. The world market for sugar is at present strong; but even if the market for Mauritian sugar expands as rapidly as the output of Mauritian sugar, there is a strict limit to the amount of land on which sugar can be grown, and this must set a strict upper limit to employment in the sugar industry in Mauritius. Other lines of agricultural production are capable of some significant expansion; but in the end limitations of land will make it impossible to find sufficient employment in these lines of agricultural production.

Mauritius must develop some industries. But in manufacturing industry the island starts with many disadvantages. She has little technical knowhow in manufacturers or experience, outside the sugar factories, in the conduct of industry; she has little technical training; she has few raw materials; she is not rich in capital; and her domestic market alone will not provide a sufficient market for large-scale production. She must emulate in a minor way economies such as Hong Kong, Jamaica, Japan and the United Kingdom, where raw materials are imported to be made into manufactures for export. But can Mauritius establish such manufactures except on the basis of cheap labour? Initially, at least, plentiful labour will be her one comparative advantage.

While the simple classical answer would be to reduce the wage rate in Mauritius, in fact in recent years exactly the opposite has happened. After a considerable period of stability, both of the cost of living and of the money wage rate, between 1956 and 1959 the wage rate in the sugar industry (which sets the pattern for the rest of the island) went up by some 45 per cent, while the cost of living remained constant. Here in a most marked form is the basic economic dilemma or paradox of such communities. The sugar industry was certainly very prosperous in the sense that the big sugar estates were making very good incomes from rents and profits, and the political awakening of the underdog in Mauritius has not unnaturally been associated with aggressive trade-union action, which has pushed up the wage rate in the sugar industry as a method of redistributing part of the wealth of the island. But from the point of view of getting the best use of resources in Mauritius there is little doubt that the wage rate ought to be very low.

Moreover, the effect of the wage rate on the level of rents and profits in an economy like that of Mauritius will affect the rate of economic development in another way. In Mauritius the big sugar estates do in fact plough back a large part of their profits for the expansion of the sugar industry; the rate of profits tax is high, the rates of personal income tax on the higher incomes are high and progressive, and these direct taxes are collected by an efficient tax administration. The result is that a substantial part of the high gross profits and rents either goes direct into the capital development of the sugar industry or goes to swell the Government's budgetary revenue, from which capital development outside the sugar industry is largely financed by the State. A high wage rate is also, therefore, liable to reduce the rate of economic development by reducing the sources of private and public capital accumulation.

This is perhaps the basic economic conundrum of such overpopulated underdeveloped countries. Let us take an extreme example and consider a country which is so overpopulated that if all available labour were employed the marginal product of labour would be zero. Then to get the most out of the country's resources and to maximise its national income labour should be free to all who want to use it. But, of course, if the wage rate is set at zero, while the national income may be maximised it will all go in rents, interest, dividends and profits to the owners of property, and none of it will go to labour. If the wage rate is set at a level which gives labour a reasonable share of the product, then there will be under-employment and unemployment; foreign capital will not be attracted as it might be by the high rate of profit which would result if the labour which it employed were freely available to it;[3] traditional labour-intensive processes and products will be discouraged; engineers and technicians, who in any case will normally have been trained in developed countries where the need is to save labour rather than capital, will not be encouraged to apply new scientific knowledge in devising new ways to enable much labour to work effectively with little capital equipment; the economy will not be able to compete as it should with foreign producers of labour-intensive products; and the sources of capital accumulation, and so of economic growth, may be dried up.

An underdeveloped economy like that of Mauritius with scarce resources of land and capital but threatened with intense overpopulation presents the conflict between efficiency and distribution in its most dramatic form – for economic efficiency labour should be treated as if it cost nothing, but a zero wage rate would allot nearly all of the Mauritian national income to a few 'sugar barons'.

Up to this point I have spoken of the efficiency of an economic system in very static terms, that is to say, as if it were simply a question of using today's resources in such a way that it would be impossible to make anyone better off today without making someone else worse off today. But in fact, of course, much productive activity today will be making capital equipment which will be used to enhance someone's final consumption of goods and services tomorrow or the next day or the day after that. It would always be possible to make some citizens better off today without making any others worse off today by using more resources to produce for today's consumption and less resources to produce capital goods today which will be useful either to produce consumption goods tomorrow or to produce capital goods tomorrow which will be useful to produce consumption goods the day after tomorrow – and so on. If we consider an economy moving through time, we can say that it behaves in an efficient manner only if at each point of time it would be impossible to make some citizen better off at that point of time without making someone worse off at that same point of time or at some other point of time.

At any one point of time each individual producer in our economy will be faced with a set of prices at which he can sell any consumption goods (bread and shirts) which he chooses to make and a set of prices at which he can sell any capital goods (ploughs and looms) which he chooses to make. At the same time there will be a certain amount of resources (land, men, existing capital equipment) available to produce these various outputs – bread, shirts, ploughs, looms. Competition among the individual producers for the use of the available resources will bid up the price of each resource until it is profitable to use it only in the most efficient ways in the most productive uses. This will maximise the value of total output at the given selling prices of the various products. The competitive bidding up of the prices of the available productive resources will raise the cost of production of each product up to its selling price. It will be possible to produce £1-worth more bread only if £1-worth less shirts or ploughs or looms are produced.

The consequent use of resources will be a fully efficient one *provided that the future course of market prices and of technical production possibilities is correctly foreseen*. It is not possible to give on this occasion a precise proof of this formidable proposition; but it can be intuitively demonstrated in the following way.

As far as goods for immediate consumption are concerned (bread and shirts), the current market prices will measure their importance to consumers. It will not therefore be possible to make present consumers better off by producing £1-worth more shirts and £1-worth less bread or *vice versa*; they could only be made better off by producing less ploughs or less looms for future use, i.e. at the expense of citizens in the future.

It remains only to ask whether some future citizen might not be made better off without any other being made worse off by altering the composition of today's output of capital goods. Suppose, for example, that one plough costs the same to produce as one loom and that one more plough and one less loom were produced today for future use. This would alter the future flow of consumption goods onto the markets, more bread and less shirts being made available. Suppose that it were possible by such a change to keep all consumers at every point of time equally well off (the increased supply of bread having the same price at each future point of time as the decreased supply of shirts) except that at one point of time some one consumer could be made better off without any one else being made worse off (the increased supply of bread having at that point of time a higher price than the decreased supply of shirts). Suppose further that these market conditions and technical possibilities were correctly foreseen. Then an entrepreneur today would be prepared to offer a higher price for a plough than for a loom, because there would be a prospect of a higher return on the former than on the latter. More ploughs and less looms would be produced. The current use of resources would be drawn away from its inefficient pattern.

Thus in order to set today's prices in a pattern which will act as a guide to an efficient use of today's resources, one must know future technical production possibilities and the pattern of future prices. This requirement can, of course, never be perfectly fulfilled, though systematic cooperation (for example, in the National Economic Development Council) in comparing, coordinating, and assessing individual plans for future development may help to achieve more accurate expectations about future market conditions.

But in any case it remains true – and that is the essential point for our present purpose – that there may be most important divergences between the 'efficiency' and the 'distributional' aspects of pricing. The fact that an economy is developing through time complicates, in the way which we have just examined, the use of prices for efficiency purposes; but it in no way ensures that the prices which we reckon today to be the best guide to an efficient use of today's resources will result in a desirable distribution of today's income and wealth.

I have explained at some length what must be the characteristics of an economy which is moving efficiently through time. But such an efficient time path must be distinguished from what may be called the optimum time path. A time path is, as we have seen, efficient if as time passes it is always impossible to rearrange today's use of resources so as to make some future consumers better off without making any other present or future consumers worse off. Suppose that the situation is continuously efficient in this sense. It still remains an open question whether it would not in fact be desirable to make future consumers better off even though this must be at the expense of present consumers. This could always be done by increasing today's savings so that less was spent by today's consumers on today's consumption goods and services and more was invested by today's citizens in new machines and other items of real capital equipment to be available to serve tomorrow's citizens. The optimum time path is that one among the infinite number of possible efficient time paths which provides the most desirable distribution of real consumption between the consumers of different years.

In reality in the choice of economic policies there are four basic *desiderata* to be borne in mind:

(1) First, it is desirable that resources should not be wasted in involuntary unemployment. Monetary policy (by making more difficult or more easy the terms on which money can be borrowed for the purchase of capital goods) and budgetary policy (by raising or lowering the amount of private spending power taken away in taxation or by lowering or raising the level of governmental expenditure on goods and services) can be used to reduce or to raise the level of total money expenditure on goods and services, so that the general level of demand for economic resources is kept in balance with the supply of such economic resources.

(2) Second, it is not only desirable that all scarce resources should be used to produce something that is wanted. It is also desirable that they should be used in a fully efficient manner in the sense already explained at length in this chapter.

(3) Third, it is desirable that there should be an equitable distribution of income and wealth between the citizens in the community at any one point of time.

(4) Fourth, it is desirable to achieve an optimum level of savings at each point of time, that is to say, as we have already explained, to achieve the most desirable distribution of real consumption as between the citizens of successive time periods in the economy's development.

This chapter is essentially concerned with possible clashes between *desiderata* (2) and (3) in the above list – between the use of the price mechanism to achieve economic efficiency and its use to achieve distributional justice. Throughout the rest of this chapter I shall simply assume that monetary and budgetary policies are in the aggregate so used that full employment is maintained. *Desideratum* (1) is simply assumed to be achieved.

Many of the measures which will subsequently be discussed in these pages will affect the level of savings. We cannot, therefore, simply neglect *desideratum* (4), even though there will be no systematic discussion of the optimum level of savings in this chapter. There is indeed some reason to suppose that individual citizens left to themselves will save less than is socially desirable, partly simply because they are shortsighted and partly because individuals, unlike the State, are mortal and do not give as much weight to the interests of future generations as they do to themselves. We shall, therefore, in what follows occasionally make incidental references to the effects of various policies upon the level of savings, counting it as a loss if any policy tends to reduce the proportion of the national income which is saved and invested in capital equipment for the use of future generations.

We are now in a position to return to our main theme – the problem of the possible clashes between the 'efficiency' and the 'distributional' aspects of prices and, in particular, of the real wage rate. The possibility of such a clash in an economy which is developing through time can be clearly seen by considering a highly developed economy such as that of the United Kingdom. The clash may not be quite so stark as in an overpopulated underdeveloped economy such as that of Mauritius; but it exists none the less. In such an industrialised country at any one time there is an existing array of natural resources and fixed capital equipment – land of various qualities and situations, plant and machinery of various forms, some new, some old, some rigidly designed for one use in one industry, some flexible general purpose tools, and so on. At the same time there is an existing array of workers in the labour force some old, some young, some highly educated, others with little education, some rigidly trained for one purpose only, some with a general-purpose training, some unskilled, some clever, some stupid, some strong, some weak, some tied to one locality, some mobile, and so on. Given the relative demands for the products of the various activities (including as we have seen the present demands for capital goods as determined by what we hope are correct anticipations of future conditions) efficiency requires that the existing array of workers be spread over the existing array of land and capital equipment in such a way that the value of the additional product due to the use of a worker at one point is not less than the value of the additional product due to his employment at any other point in the system. Efficiency does not require that literally all existing acres and machines be necessarily used. If labour is scarce and land and machines plentiful, it may be desirable to use the limited labour only on the most efficient and productive acres and machines. A high wage rate which measures the shortage of labour will make it impossible to work the other acres and machines without making an out-of-pocket loss. The land is sub-marginal; the machines are obsolete. Perfection will, of course, never be reached. But a reasonable approach to this pattern of efficient use of men, machines, and natural resources requires the setting of today's prices or wage rates for the various broad categories of labour at levels which will guide the various employers, public and private, to the most efficient use of the available labour.

As time passes some capital equipment will depreciate physically as a result of ageing and of wear and tear. Other and new equipment will have been built. Improved technical knowledge will have affected the capabilities of the new equipment and, to a lesser degree, of some of the old equipment as well. The size of the working population may have changed and the amount and quality of educational effort invested in the new members of the labour force may have increased. The efficient spreading of the new array of workers over the new array of equipment may well require some change in the level and pattern of real wage rates.

In a highly industrialised developed economy this process will generally entail a continuous rise in output per head. Net capital accumulation means that the machinery and plant which is newly installed will exceed the machinery and plant which is physically worn out; technical progress will raise output per worker employed; and increased investment in training and education will also raise the workers' productivity. Unless there is a very rapid rise in the size of the new working population to be spread over the new array of equipment, real output per head is likely to be higher. But as every professional economist knows, output per head (the average product of labour) is not the same thing as the addition to output which is due to the employment of an additional amount of labour (the marginal product of labour). It is the latter and not the former which is relevant to the use of the real wage rate as a guide to the efficient use of resources. Indeed this is the very heart of our dilemma. It is the value of the additional product which could be produced by taking on a little more labour which should on efficiency grounds be related to the real wage rate; it is the value of total output per head which will determine the total real income available for distribution among all citizens. If the marginal product of labour is low but its average product is high, wages paid on our efficiency basis will represent only a small proportion of total real income, the remainder accruing to the owners of property in profits and rent.

In the highly developed industrialised countries a substantial proportion of the real product does accrue to the owners of property and property is very unequally owned. There is already, therefore, a problem. The pattern of real wage rates which is required on efficiency grounds may lead to a very high level of real income per head for the small concentrated number of rich property owners. And it is possible, though not certain, that this problem will become more acute as a result of automation.

To the engineer automation in industry means the incorporation into a productive process of a particular type of control mechanism. In the economists' jargon this implies, I suspect, a high rate of technical progress with a marked labour-saving bias in it. Automation will certainly increase the output per head which will be produced by the aid of the new automated machinery. But it could conceivably reduce so much the amount of labour needed with each new machine of a given cost that the total demand for labour was actually reduced. This could happen if, in spite of the net accumulation of capital equipment, the new labour required with the new automated machines was actually less than the growth of the labour force plus the labour made redundant by the scrapping of physically worn-out old machinery. In such a case to absorb the new and the redundant workers in the next best uses (for example, on machinery previously considered obsolete or in uses which need no machinery such as domestic service) might require an absolute reduction in the real wage rate on efficiency grounds. Even if this extreme case were avoided, it is clear that automation might well cause output per head to rise relatively to the marginal product of labour. In this case efficiency pricing would require that an ever-increasing proportion of output accrued to property owners and the distributional dilemma would to this extent be intensified.

Most discussions about the social and economic problems which will arise in an automated world run in terms of the rise in real output and real income per head of the population. What, we ask, shall we all do with our leisure when we need to work only an hour or two a day to obtain the total output of real goods and services needed to satisfy our wants? But the problem is really much more difficult than that. The question which we should ask is: What shall we all do when output per man-hour of work is extremely high but practically the whole of the output goes to a few property owners, while the mass of the workers are relatively (or even absolutely) worse off than before?

II   THE PRESENT POSITION IN THE DEVELOPED COUNTRIES

The problem is already a very real one in the highly industrialised developed countries in many of which there is a really fantastic inequality in the ownership of property. As the figures in Table 2.1[4] show, at the end of the

Table 2.1   Distribution of Personal Wealth in the United Kingdom

Percentage of population	Percentages of total personal wealth			Percentages of personal income from property (before tax) 1959
	1911–13	*1936–38*	*1960*	
1	69	56	42	60
5	87	79	75	92
10	92	88	83	99

1950s in the United Kingdom, in spite of some marked equalisation since pre-First World War, the ownership of private property was still extremely unequal. For example, no less than 75 per cent of personal property was owned by the wealthiest 5 per cent of the population. Moreover, the rich obtain a higher yield on their property than do the poor, presumably partly because they are better informed through financial advisers but partly because with larger properties risks can be taken and spread more easily so that the average yield is higher. The result is that the concentration of income from property is even more marked than the concentration of property ownership itself, and in 1959 no less than 92 per cent of income from property went to 5 per cent of the population.[5]

What effect this concentration will have upon the distribution of total incomes between persons will depend upon two other proportions. (i) The first of these is the proportion of total personal incomes which is made up of income from property; if this proportion is small, then a very unequal distribution of property will not in itself lead to any great inequality in the distribution of total income; it is when 'efficiency' demands that only a small proportion of income should be paid in wages, leaving much to accrue in profits, interest, and rents, that the inequality in the ownership of property causes great inequalities in the distribution of income. (ii) The other factor is the distribution of earned incomes; if the rich owners of property cannot earn more than the average wage per head, earned incomes will reduce the inequalities due to property incomes; but if the earnings of the rich are also as concentrated as their unearned incomes, there will be no diminution of inequalities of income from this source.

The interaction between these various factors can be shown by a set of formulae of the following kind:

$$i_1 = p_1 \ (1 - q) + l_1 \, q$$
$$i_5 = p_5 \ (1 - q) + l_5 \, q$$
$$i_{10} = p_{10} \ (1 - q) + l_{10} \, q$$

Let q represent the proportion of total personal income which is paid in earnings so that $1 - q$ represents the proportion going in income on property. If p_1 represents the proportion of total income from property going to the 1 per cent of the population who receive the largest total incomes and l_1 represents the proportion of earned incomes which are received by the same 1 per cent of the population with the highest total incomes, then $p_1 (1 - q)$ will represent the proportion of total personal incomes which accrues to this group in the form of unearned incomes and $l_1 q$ will represent the proportion of the total of personal incomes which accrues to this group in the form of earnings. Thus $p_1 (1 - q) + l_1 q$ or i_1 will equal the proportion of total personal incomes accruing to the 1 per cent of the population with the highest total incomes. Similarly i_5 and i_{10}, p_5 and p_{10}, and l_5 and l_{10} represent these proportions for the richest 5 per cent and the richest 10 per cent of the population.

For the United Kingdom in 1959 we can very roughly estimate the p's and l's as is done in Table 2.2.[6] For the reasons given in Appendix I it is more difficult to estimate the relevant value for q, but the last three columns of Table 2.2 give the values of i which would result if q were 95, 85, or 75 per cent respectively. These figures give some indication of the importance of q in determining the distribution of total personal incomes. Thus with q equal to 85 per cent the richest 5 per cent of the population would receive 24 per cent of total personal incomes, made up of 66 per cent of total personal incomes from property and 17 per cent of total incomes from earnings. The distribution of earned income is much more equal than that of income from property. If q were lowered by automation from 85 to 75 per cent, then the richest 5 per cent of the population (with the same distribution of income from property and the same distribution of income from earnings, i.e. with the p's and l's unchanged) would receive 29 per cent instead of 24

Table 2.2   Distribution of Personal Incomes from Property and Earnings, United Kingdom, 1959

Percentage of population	Percentage of personal incomes from property (p)	Percentage of personal incomes from earnings (l)	Percentage of total personal incomes (i)		
			$q = 95\%$	$q = 85\%$	$q = 75\%$
1	47	6	8	12	16
5	66	17	19	24	29
10	73	27	29	34	38

per cent of total personal incomes. The unequally distributed incomes from property would have become more important relatively to the less unequally distributed incomes from work.

The above account is in one way very incomplete, if not positively misleading. Earning power depends upon education and training, and education and training involve the investment of scarce resources in those who are educated and trained. This represents an important form of capital and of property; and a considerable part of the earnings of the educated and trained is in fact a return on the capital invested in their education. This form of capital is not recognised in Tables 2.1 and 2.2 above, where personal property includes only the tangible marketable assets of a person and excludes the intangible unmarketable value of his education and where earned income includes all the increase in earnings which are due to the capital invested in education and training. In a highly developed industrialised country the total value of the capital sunk in the education of the population can be very great, as is illustrated by the figures in Table 2.3[7] for the United States of America.

The figures in lines 2 and 3 of this table measure the value of the resources (teachers' salaries, costs of running the schools, etc.) directly used up in the past education of the existing citizens of the country. They also include, as they should, in the case of the later stages of education, the wage earnings foregone by the students as a result of staying on at school or university instead of earning their living more promptly. Such is a true capital investment; immediate income is sacrificed for future benefit. When earnings foregone are thus included in the capital cost of an education, the total cost of the later stages of education is greatly increased. From Table 2.3 it can be seen that in 1957 the capital sunk in the education of the total population represented 40 per cent of the total of physical tangible capital plus intangible educational capital.[8]

Table 2.3   The Stock of Tangible and Intangible Capital in the United States, 1929 and 1957

| | 1929 | 1957 |
	($000,000,000 of 1956 value)	
1. Reproducible tangible wealth	727	1270
2. Educational capital in population as a whole, of which	317	848
3. Educational capital in labour force	173	535

Of course expenditure on education cannot be treated simply as any other form of productive capital investment. It confers benefits quite apart from the fact that it increases the future commercial earning power of the educated. It enables the educated person to enjoy a fuller life quite apart from any increase in his money income which it may bring; and it has further social advantages in that in many ways it is better for his neighbours to live with him as an educated rather than as an uneducated fellow citizen. But education does undoubtedly have value to the educated person as a straightforward commercial investment. It increases the productivity and economic value of the person educated. There is considerable evidence that, even if we make no allowance for the general cultural and social advantages of education, the return on it as a purely commercial proposition is very high, particularly in the case of the spread of elementary education among a previously largely uneducated community.[9]

There has in the last half century been an enormous increase in the amount of education per citizen in the developed countries of the world.[10] To what extent this is a force equalising the ownership of property and earnings depends upon two factors: (i) Has the additional educational investment been received by those who are already wealthy or by those who are poor? (ii) Who has provided the cost of the education invested in these persons?

There can be no doubt that the great expansion of the first stages of education in the last half century has been an equalising factor of the greatest importance. It has been financed by taxation which has fallen presumably at least somewhat more heavily on the rich than on the poor and it has been open without direct charge to the poor. If the figures of personal property and of income from personal property in Tables 2.1 and 2.2 could be recast to include the intangible stock of educational capital invested in each person and that part of his earnings which was a return on this investment, there would have been revealed undoubtedly a greater movement away from extreme inequalities in property ownership and in incomes from property.

But we cannot in fact arrange our figures in such a way as to include educational capital in personal property; and educational capital has so many peculiar features that we should perhaps in any case not wish to do so. In what follows we shall consider personal property as referring only to tangible assets and we shall treat educational investment in a special category as something which has a special effect upon the capacity to earn income.

We have already noted that the ratio q, namely the proportion of the national income that accrues to wages is an essential factor which decides the importance of the distribution of property ownership in determining the distribution of income. The really overpopulated underdeveloped economy is one in which on efficiency grounds q should be practically zero, in which case income distribution would be wholly determined by the distribution of income from property. In the United Kingdom at the present q is perhaps about 85 per cent and the distribution of income thus depends much less on the distribution of property and much more on the distribution of earning power.

But what of the future? Suppose that automation should drastically reduce q. The country would tend to become a wealthy edition of Mauritius. There would be a limited number of exceedingly wealthy property owners; the proportion of the working population required to man the extremely profitable automated industries would be small; wage-rates would thus be depressed; there would have to be a large expansion of the production of the labour-intensive goods and services which were in high demand by the few multi-multi-multi-millionaires; we would be back in a super-world of an immiserised proletariat and of butlers, footmen, kitchen maids, and other hangers-on. Let us call this the Brave New Capitalists' Paradise.

It is to me a hideous outlook. What could we do about it? The rest of these pages will be devoted to a discussion of four possible lines of attack which we may summarise as the replacement of the Brave New Capitalists' Paradise by

(1) A Trade Union State.
(2) A Welfare State.
(3) A Property-Owning Democracy.
(4) A Socialist State.

I shall deal with the first two of these very briefly and cursorily because the problems connected with them are familiar to most economists. My present purpose is to recommend for much closer attention and study the last two modes of a Property-Owning Democracy and of a Socialist State.

III   THE TRADE UNION STATE

By trade union action or by legislation a minimum real wage might be set for all work done. The outstanding disadvantage of this form of action is that it would reduce the volume of employment that it was profitable to provide with a given amount of real capital equipment. It is possible, but not certain, that automation involves not only (i) a rise in output per man and

(ii) a reduction in the relative importance of men to machines but also (iii) a reduction in the elasticity of substitution between men and machines. If this is so, the direct damage done by the pushing up of the wage rate in any one automated industry would be limited; if a fixed number of men is required to look after each automated machine, a rise in the real wage will cause a fall in profits without much affect on employment per machine.

But this does not mean to say that the damage done to the economy as a whole would be slight. Automation is a matter of degree. There would be many industries where the ratio of men to machines was neither rigid nor low. In industries in which the ratio of men to machines was not rigid the 'inefficiently' high real wage would restrict the demand for men per machine, and in industries in which the ratio of men to machines was not low the cost of the product would rise relatively to the cost of the fully-automated machine-intensive products. The labour-intensive industries (including of course above all the occupations for personal service) would be contracted relatively to other industries. The total demand for labour would be reduced.

There would then be three possibilities.

(1) The first possibility is that the minimum wage arrangements are in fact operative only in a limited number of fully automated industries and occupations. Society would then be divided into three economic classes: the very wealthy property owners, the privileged workers who were lucky enough to get the limited number of available posts in the protected occupations, and the underprivileged workers whose wage would be extremely low as they competed for the remaining jobs. The minimum wage protection in the privileged jobs would reduce not only the profits of the capitalists but also the real wages of the unprivileged workers in so far as it led to any restriction of the number of jobs in the protected occupations; for this would increase the competition for jobs in the unprotected occupations.

(2) The second possibility is that the minimum wage arrangements would be effectively extended to cover all occupations. By this I mean not merely that a given minimum *money* wage rate is extended throughout the economy, but that this minimum money wage rate effectively represents a minimum real wage rate. This means, of course, that we must abandon our present monetary and budgetary policies for full employment. The trade unions push up money wage rates on equity-distributional grounds. That is their basic *raison d'être*. They succeed in pushing wage rates up more quickly than the rise in labour's marginal productivity. At present our financial authorities, in the interests of full employment, allow an expansion of total demand so that selling prices chase costs up in a vicious spiral of inflation. Real wage rates are not in fact raised more quickly than marginal

productivity; but employment is maintained. This combination of policies would have to be abandoned. When money wage rates are pushed up, monetary demand must not be expanded by monetary and budgetary policy so as to maintain full employment; for we must avoid the raising of money selling prices of goods and services which would merely reduce the real wage rate again to the extent necessary to provide full employment. In other words the possibility which we are now examining involves the employment of a limited number of the working population at what is regarded as a fair real wage rate and the acceptance of unemployment for the remainder. This unemployment might be designated as the technological unemployment due to automation and labour-saving inventions.

(3) The third possibility is that an effective arrangement for the universal application of a minimum real wage should be combined with an effective limitation of the amount of work which any one individual citizen might do. Such work-sharing – or might one not more appropriately call it such unemployment-sharing? – might be effected partly by preventing some potential workers (e.g. the young, the old, and the married women) from working at all, partly by limiting the number of hours which any worker might work, and partly by a network of trade union restrictive practices which spread each job over an unnecessarily large number of workers – the modern form of Luddite activity. This possibility would certainly be better than those previously described: it could in the conditions envisaged effectively raise the incomes of workers relatively to those of property earners without creating an underprivileged class of deprived workers or a solid mass of unemployed workers. But it is nevertheless an inefficient system and might turn out to be a very inefficient system. For it means partly that an artificial technical inefficiency is created by various restrictive practices and partly that there is an artificial edict against the provision of those labour-intensive products and services which workers (who are by hypothesis being forced to work less than they would like to do at the current wage rate) would like to produce for other workers (who would buy these services if only they were cheaper).

IV THE WELFARE STATE

By this I mean the taxation of the incomes of the rich to subsidise directly or indirectly the incomes of the poor. I shall not describe the many possible variants of this principle. The whole system is one which is much discussed these days and with which we are all fairly familiar. In my view it could have one great and decisive advantage over the Trade Union – Minimum-

Wage method. It could be combined with a real wage rate which was as low as considerations of efficiency demanded, so that labour-intensive activities were in no way inhibited; but at the same time the gross inequalities of income that would otherwise result would be avoided. There would remain, however, two defects in the system, (i) one from the point of view of efficiency and (ii) the other from the point of view of distribution.

(i) If, in the automated world we are envisaging, a really substantial equalisation of individual incomes is to be achieved solely by redistributive income taxes and subsidies, the rates of income tax would have to be quite exceptionally progressive; and such highly progressive income taxation is bound to affect adversely incentives to work, save, innovate, and take risks. This subject is a controversial but nevertheless familiar one. I do not wish to develop it in these pages. The system unquestionably involves inefficiencies, though it may be debatable how great those inefficiencies would be.

(ii) The system could be used to equalise incomes; but it would not directly equalise property ownership. Extreme inequalities in the ownership of property are in my view undesirable quite apart from any inequalities of income which they may imply. A man with much property has great bargaining strength and a great sense of security, independence, and freedom; and he enjoys these things not only *vis-à-vis* his propertyless fellow citizens but also *vis-à-vis* the public authorities. He can snap his fingers at those on whom he must rely for an income; for he can always live for a time on his capital. The propertyless man must continuously and without interruption acquire his income by working for an employer or by qualifying to receive it from a public authority. An unequal distribution of property means an unequal distribution of power and status even if it is prevented from causing too unequal a distribution of income.

V   A PROPERTY-OWNING DEMOCRACY

Let us suppose that by the wave of some magic wand – the nature of which we will examine later – the ownership of property could be equally distributed over all the citizens in the community. What a wonderful culture could now result from our future automated economy! Imagine a world in which no citizen owns an excessively large or an unduly small proportion of the total of private property. Each citizen will now be receiving a large part of his income from property. For we are assuming that for society as a whole the proportion of income which accrues from earnings has been greatly reduced by automation. Institutions in the capital market would no doubt need to be appropriately developed so that a very large number of moderate private properties could be pooled through insurance companies, investment trusts, and similar intermediaries so that risks were spread and the ultimate investments chosen by specialists on behalf of the man in the street.

The essential feature of this society would be that work had become rather more a matter of personal choice. The unpleasant work that had to be done would have to be very highly paid to attract to it those whose tastes led them to wish to supplement considerably their incomes from property. At the other extreme those who wished to devote themselves to quite uncommercial activities would be able to do so with a reduced standard of living, but without starving in a garret. Above all labour-intensive services would flourish of a kind which (unlike old-fashioned domestic service) might be produced by one man for another man of equal income and status. Play-acting, ballet-dancing, painting, writing, sporting activities and all such 'unproductive' work as Adam Smith would have called it would flourish on a semi-professional semi-amateur basis; and those who produced such services would no longer be degraded as the poor sycophants of immoderately rich patrons.

Let us turn our attention therefore to the questions why in the sort of free-enterprise or mixed economy with which we are familiar we end up with such startling inequalities in the ownership of property, what changes in our institutional or tax arrangements would be necessary substantially to equalise ownership, and what disadvantages from the point of view of efficiency these reforms could themselves have.

I shall consider these matters in three stages. First, I shall assume that we are dealing simply with a number of adult citizens who have presumably been born in the past but who do not marry or have children or die or even grow old in the sense of experiencing diminished ability or vigour as time passes. I shall at this first stage examine the effects upon property distribution as these citizens work, save, and accumulate property. I shall assume that the State taxes neither income nor property and does not interfere in any way with this process of private capital accumulation.

At a second stage I shall introduce the demographic factors – births, marriages, deaths – and will examine the way in which they are likely to modify the pattern of ownership that would otherwise be developing.

At the third stage I will introduce the State. At this stage we shall be concerned with the ways in which economic and financial policies might be devised to modify the economic and demographic factors in such a way as to lead to a more equal distribution of property.

For the first stage I will employ a method which has been pioneered for another purpose by my colleague Dr L. Pasinetti.[11] Consider two personal properties, a small one (K_1) and a large one (K_2). Will the small property be growing at a smaller or a larger proportional rate of growth than the large property? If the small property is growing at a greater proportional rate (say, 5 per cent per annum) than the large property (say, 2 per cent per annum), then the ratio of $\dfrac{K_1}{K_2}$ will be becoming more nearly equal to unity. In this case *relative* inequality will be diminishing.[12] We are concerned then at this first stage of our enquiry with the factors which will determine the proportional rate of growth of different properties.

These proportional growth rates (which we will call k_1 and k_2) for our two properties may be expressed as

$$k_1 = \frac{S_1(E_1 + V_1 K_1)}{K_1} \text{ and } k_2 = \frac{S_2(E_2 + V_2 K_2)}{K_2}$$

respectively, where E_1 and E_2 represent the earned incomes or wages of the two property owners and V_1 and V_2 represent the two rates of profit earned by the two owners on their properties K_1 and K_2. Thus $V_1 K_1$ and $V_2 K_2$ represent the unearned incomes of the two property owners and $E_1 + V_1 K_1$ and $E_2 + V_2 K_2$ their earned and unearned incomes. If S_1 and S_2 represent the proportions of these incomes which are saved and added to accumulated property, then $S_1 (E_1 + V_1 K_1)$ and $S_2 (E_2 + V_2 K_2)$ are the absolute annual increases in the two properties and these, expressed as a ratio of the two properties measure their proportionate rates of growth.

In these pages I can do little more than enumerate the various influences at work. Some of them, it will be seen, tend to make $k_1 > k_2$ (these are the equalising tendencies), and some tend to make $k_2 > k_1$ (these are the disequalising tendencies). There is undoubtedly at work a large element of these latter disequalising tendencies – what Professor Myrdal has called the principle of Circular and Cumulative Causation – the 'to-him-that-hath-shall-be-given' principle. On the other hand, trees do not grow up to the skies, and there are some systematic equalising tendencies. It is the balance between these equalising and disequalising factors which results in the end in a given unequal, but not indefinitely unequal, distribution of properties. Let us consider in turn the influences of E, V, and S upon the rate of growth of property k.

(1) The influence of earned incomes, E, must be an equalising factor so far as two properties at the extreme ranges of the scale of properties are

concerned. We can see the point this way. If K_1 were zero, citizen 1 would have only an earned income E_1. If he saved any part of this, his savings would be $S_1 E_1$ and his proportionate rate of accumulation of property would be $\frac{S_1 E_1}{0} = \infty$. Consider at the other extreme a multi-multi-multi-millionaire. Now earning power, E_1 may well be enhanced by the ownership of property, but not without limit. In the case of our multi-multi-multi-millionaire, E_2 will be negligible relatively to K_2. If $\frac{E_2}{K_2}$ were for practical purposes zero, k_2 would equal $\frac{S_2 V_2 K_2}{K_2} = S_2 V_2$. As between the extreme ranges then, we have $k_1 > k_2$ and there is bound to be equalisation. This is perhaps the basic reason why our measure of relative inequality $\frac{K_1}{K_2}$ can never reach zero or infinity. In the intermediate ranges all we can say is that the higher is $\frac{E}{K}$ the more rapid the rate of growth of property k, other things being equal. If earning power were equally distributed among our citizens (with $E_1 = E_2$), then this factor would be an equalising one as between any two properties K_1 and K_2.

$$k_1 = S_1 \frac{E_1}{K_1} + S_1 V_1 \quad \text{and} \quad k_2 = S_2 \frac{E_2}{K_2} + S_2 V_2$$

If $S_1 = S_2$, $E_1 = E_2$, and $V_1 = V_2$, then $k_1 > k_2$ if $K_1 < K_2$.

(2) The factor V, on the other hand, is unquestionably disequalising – at least in the United Kingdom where there is strong evidence that the rate of return on property is much lower for small properties than for large properties.[13] This is so even if one does not take into account capital gains; but, of course, capital gains should be included in the return on capital. Since the wealthy in the United Kingdom at least invest on tax grounds for capital gains rather than for income, the inclusion of capital gains in V_2 and V_1 would make the excess of V_2 over V_1 even more marked; and this is clearly an influence which will raise k_2 above k_1.[14] It is probable that there will be little difference in the V which is relevant for all properties above a certain range. It is doubtful whether the multi-millionaire can get any higher yield than the millionaire on his property. But as between the really small properties and the large range of big properties, this influence is likely to be disequalising and to be a factor enabling the whole range of large properties to grow more rapidly than the small.

(3) Finally, what is the influence of S, the proportion of income saved, on

k for different sizes of K? Economists have done a great deal of theoretical and statistical work on the factors determining the proportions of income saved and spent. These investigations are of basic importance not only for theories of employment and of growth (i.e. for the determination of the 'multiplier' and of the relationships between the rate of profit, the rate of growth, and the capital-output ratio) but also for the determination of the distribution among individuals of the ownership of property.

Let us consider only the implications of two possible features of a probable type of savings function.[15] Let us assume (i) that the proportion of income saved rises with a rise in real income, though not of course, without limit, since less than 100 per cent of income will be saved however great is income, and (ii) that the proportion of income saved out of any given income falls the larger is the property owned. This second assumption means that a man with £1,000 a year all earned will save more than a man with £1,000 a year which represents the interest on a property of £10,000. For the ability to save will be the same, but the need to accumulate some property will be higher in the first than in the second case.

If the savings function is of this general form, then as between two unequal properties ($K_2 > K_1$) owned by two persons with the same earning power ($E_1 = E_2$), we cannot, without more precise information, say which will be growing the more rapidly. The fact that a larger total income will be enjoyed by the man with the larger property will tend to raise the proportion of income which he can save; but, on the other hand, the fact that he already has a larger property will tend to reduce the proportion of income which he will save, and, in addition, the fact that $\dfrac{E}{K}$ is low in his case will keep down the rate of growth of his property. (See p. 44.)

But with the sort of savings function which we are assuming there are two other kinds of comparison which one can make with more definite results. If one compares two citizens with equal incomes but unequal properties, the small property of the man with the high earning power will be growing the more rapidly; he has the same ability to save but a greater need to accumulate; his savings will be greater and his existing property smaller. If one compares two citizens with the same property, but different incomes, the property of the man with the high income (i.e. the high earning power) will be growing the more rapidly; he has a higher ability to save and the same need to accumulate; his savings will be greater and his existing property the same. The result is, of course, that with our assumed savings function there will be exceptionally strong forces at work associating high properties with high earning power. This combination of forces will exaggerate the inequality in the distribution of total personal incomes.[16]

Let us pass to the second stage of our examination of the factors determining the distribution of property, namely the demographic factors. Consider two citizens, man and wife, each with a property. The rate of growth of their properties is determined by the economic factors we have just considered – S, E, V, and K. They have children. These children grow up and start to earn and to save – they acquire E's and S's of their own. They start to accumulate properties of their own, at first at indefinitely high proportional rates of growth, since they start with no property. At some time both parents die and leave their properties to their children. The children at some time – it may be before or after their parents' deaths – choose spouses. And so two citizens and two properties join together in holy matrimony and restart the same process of marriage, birth, and death.

What we want to consider is whether the factors of marriage, birth, and death will lead to a greater or a lesser degree of concentration of property ownership than would have occurred through the processes of capital accumulation which we examined at stage one in the absence of marriage, births, and deaths. The answer depends upon two things: the degree of assortative mating and the degree of differential fertility.

Suppose that any man was equally likely to be married to any woman in our society. Suppose, that is to say, that there were no assortative mating. Then the cycle of birth, marriage, and death would introduce an important equalising factor into the system. Let us isolate for examination this basic demographic factor by assuming for the moment that every married couple reproduces itself by producing one son and one daughter and then leaves half the joint property of the parents to each child. Consider in this context the wealthiest family in the community, i.e. the family which has the highest joint property of husband and wife; they have a son and a daughter who, if they married each other, would perpetuate the same extreme concentration of wealth which they inherited from their parents; but brother and sister do not marry each other; the rich son must marry a wife with less inherited property than himself and the rich daughter a husband with less inherited property than herself; they in turn have children who are not so much enriched by inheritance as they themselves were. The general reshuffle generation by generation through marriage tends to equalise inherited fortunes. If there were no assortative mating, there would be a strong probability that a citizen whose inheritance was exceptionally high would marry someone with a smaller inheritance and that a citizen whose inheritance was exceptionally low would marry someone with a larger inheritance. But of course in fact marriage is strongly assortative. The rich are brought up in the same social milieu as the rich, and the poor in the same social milieu as the poor. The reshufflement of property ownership is very much less marked.

Differential fertility could clearly have an important influence on the distribution of property. If rich parents had fewer children than did poor parents, the large fortunes would become more and more concentrated in fewer and fewer hands. If the rich had more children than the poor, the large properties would fall in relative size as they become more and more widely dispersed and the smaller would grow in relative size as they become more and more concentrated on a smaller number of children. At first sight it might, therefore, appear as if differential fertility might work in either direction – equalising property ownership if the rich were exceptionally fertile and disequalising it if the rich were exceptionally infertile. And this would, of course, be so in the short run; and it would be so in the long run as well, if there were some forces at work which caused riches itself to lead to exceptionally high or exceptionally low fertility.

But consider another possible type of cause of differential fertility. Suppose (i) that every couple has at least one child, but (ii) that there is some genetic factor at work which makes some couples more fertile than others and (iii) that this genetic factor is in no way correlated positively or negatively with any other relevant genetic characteristic. We may happen to start with the infertile at the bottom end of the property scale; if so, the immediate effect will be to tend to equalise property ownership. But gradually as time passes the infertile will be found, through the process of concentrated inheritance, further and further up the property scale. In the end it will be the rich who are the infertile and the poor who are the fertile. The permanent influence of such a form of differential fertility will thus ultimately be disequalising in its effect upon property ownership.

But sons and daughters are endowed not only with inherited property but also with earning power. Here we are confronted with the great problem of nature *versus* nurture. Earning power undoubtedly depends largely upon environmental factors. We have already observed (pp. 36–7) the great importance of investment in education in raising earning power. In a society which (as we are assuming in this second stage of our enquiry) left everything including education to private market forces rich fathers could educate their sons much more readily than could poor fathers. The inheritance of a good education would be just like the inheritance of tangible wealth from rich parents.

But high earning power is not wholly due to education and other environmental factors; there can be no doubt that there are also some genetic factors at work in determining a person's ability to earn. In so far as this is the case, there may be a social mechanism at work analogous to, although not identical with, the mechanism which some scholars have suspected to be at work in the case of social class and intelligence.[17] Let us very briefly outline this mechanism in the case of social class and intelligence and then point the possible analogy with property and earning power.

Suppose that whatever quality it may be which is measured by an intelligence test is a quality which enables one to succeed in modern life, so that there is some tendency for the intelligent to move up, and the unintelligent to move down, the social scale. Then at any one time one would expect to find a positive correlation between intelligence and social class; the more intelligent citizens will tend to be found with greater frequency at the top of the social ladder. Suppose further that whatever is measured by an intelligence test is a quality which has at least *some* genetic element in its causation. One would in that case expect to find some positive correlation, but a less than perfect correlation, between the intelligence of parents and the intelligence of their children. The children of intelligent parents would tend to be intelligent but not as intelligent as their parents; the children of unintelligent parents would tend to be unintelligent but not as unintelligent as their parents. This 'regression towards the mean' is to be explained by the fact that an intelligent father, transmitting only one of each of his chromosome pairs to his son, will on the average transmit only one half of the genes which made him exceptionally intelligent. The son of such a father has a higher chance than the average of being exceptionally intelligent, but on the average is not likely to be as exceptionally intelligent as his father.[18]

As the figures in Table 2.4 show, this is the pattern which in fact one finds.[19]

Column 1 shows how intelligence is higher, the higher the citizen concerned stands on the social scale. Column 2 shows the 'regression towards the mean'. The most (least) intelligent parents have children with above-average (below-average) intelligence, but not so much above-average (below-average) as the parents. The genetic 'regression towards the mean' tends to equalise the distribution of intelligence between social classes; but social mobility upwards of those children whose intelligence happens by the luck of the genetic draw to be high relatively to the social class of their parents, and mobility downwards for those children whose intelligence happens to be low relatively to the social class of their parents, restores the original association between class and intelligence displayed in the parents' generation.

Such is the hypothesis. If we had the figures and could draw up a similar table for property ownership and earning ability, would we find the same

Table 2.4   Mean IQs of Parent and Child According to Class of Parents

	Parent	*Child*
Higher professional	139.7	120.8
Lower professional	130.6	114.7
Clerical	115.9	107.8
Skilled	108.2	104.6
Semi-skilled	97.8	98.9
Unskilled	84.9	92.6
Average	100.0	100.0

kind of relationship? It is possible that by the mechanism of accumulation already described (that is to say, because high earning power makes it easier to accumulate property) there is some positive correlation between large properties and high earning power. But if earning power is to some extent genetically determined, one would expect to find rich parents with high earning power having children with above-average earning power, but not so much above-average as themselves; and one would expect to find the poorest parents with the lowest earning power having children with below-average earning power but not so much below average as themselves. But the association between property ownership and earning power may nevertheless be restored in the next generation by the exceptionally rapid accumulation of property by those children who happen to be born with exceptionally high earning power relatively to their inherited property and by the exceptionally slow rate of accumulation by those children to happen to be born with exceptionally low earning power relatively to their inherited property.

All that one can say in the present unhappy state of almost complete ignorance about this important aspect of society is that in so far as earning power is a factor which leads to the accumulation of property, then any 'regression towards the mean' in the inheritance of earning power would in itself tend to equalise the distribution of the ownership of property.[20]

	Earning power of	
	Owners	*Children of owners*
Very large properties	?	?
Large properties	?	?
Medium properties	?	?
Small properties	?	?
Very small properties	?	?

We have so far considered some of the economic and biological factors which may systematically work towards the equalisation or the dis-equalisation of the ownership of property. But there are, of course, for any individual enormously important elements of pure environmental luck. Was a man lucky or unlucky in the actual school to which he went as a child and in the actual teachers which he there encountered? Was he lucky or unlucky in the actual locality in which he sought work or took his business initiatives? Was he lucky or unlucky in the choice of the subject matter of his education and training? In the choice of industries in which he invested his first savings or initial inheritance? In the bright ideas which he tried to exploit? A lucky combination of an able man with the right idea in the right place at the right time can – as in the case of men such as Ford – lead to an explosive growth of an individual property. We must regard society from the point of view of property ownership as subject to a series of random strokes of good and bad luck, upsetting continuously the existing pattern of ownership. But at the same time there are at work the systematic economic forces of accumulation and the systematic biological and demographic forces of inheritance which are some of them tending to equalise and some of them to disequalise ownership. The striking inequalities which we observe in the real world are the result of the balance of these systematic forces working in a society subject to the random strokes of luck. That is all we can say until this most important field for research and enquiry has been cultivated much more extensively than has been the case up to the present.

We turn then to stage three of our enquiry into the factors which affect the distribution of the ownership of property, namely governmental policy of various kinds. Let us start by considering the effects of various forms of tax.

We have already considered the possibility of using a progressive income tax as part of the machinery of the Welfare State to tax the rich in order to raise funds to subsidise the poor, and we have already noted the fact that progressive income tax of this kind may have adverse effects upon incentives to work, enterprise, and save. Such taxation will also have some effect as an equaliser of the distribution of the ownership of property. Since large properties are an important cause of high incomes, the subjection of high incomes to highly progressive taxation will reduce the ability to save of the owners of large properties more than it will reduce the ability to save of the owners of small properties. This will help the small properties to grow at a higher rate relatively to that of the large properties. This tendency will be still more marked in so far as the progressive income tax discriminates against unearned incomes and in favour of earned incomes. For a tax on incomes from property as contrasted with a tax on incomes from work is a more direct imposition on the owners of large properties as such.

But different properties may earn different incomes according to the form in which they are invested – cash earns nothing; short-dated gilt-edged securities a very small yield; and so on until one comes to the high average yields from risky and enterprising ventures. An annual tax of a progressive character which is based not on the level of total income nor even on the level of unearned income, but upon the value of the total property owned by the taxpayer is the tax which would most directly militate against large properties with the least adverse effects upon incentives to take risks and enterprise with one's capital. This tax like all progressive direct taxes is bound to reduce the level of private savings; it reduces the ability to accumulate capital by the richest citizens who are the most able to save.

Indeed, the essential argument in favour of these taxes which we are at present examining is that they will reduce the net savings and so the net capital accumulation of the largest property owners. If, because savings tend to fall below the optimum level (see pp. 30–1), it is desired to maintain the level of total savings and at the same time to discourage the accumulation of the largest properties, it is essential to combine these progressive tax measures with other measures which will stimulate the savings of the small property owners and/or which will raise the public savings (the budget surplus) of the government itself. We will return to these alternative sources of savings in due course.

But while all forms of progressive taxation are likely to reduce private savings, we may legitimately ask which of these various measures of progressive tax will achieve a given reduction in the rate of growth of the largest properties with the minimum adverse effects on other economic incentives – namely the incentives to work and to take risks. All these forms of progressive taxation may well have some adverse effects upon incentives to work and risk as well as upon the level of savings. For one of the motives to work and risk is to achieve the large income which enables one to accumulate a large property for one's own enjoyment and to bequeath to one's children; and tax arrangements which beyond a point make it very difficult to accumulate property may blunt incentives to make the additional effort to earn the means for further accumulation. But it is probable that a progressive tax on unearned incomes will have less effect in reducing the incentive to earn than will a similar tax on earned incomes; and it is probable that an annual tax assessed on capital wealth (whether it be invested in secure or risky forms) will have less adverse effect upon enterprise than one based on unearned income (which is the fruit of risky rather than of secure investments). The case for an annual tax on capital wealth is thus a strong one. Its disadvantage is the serious extra administrative task of assessing persons' capital wealth as well as their annual incomes; but, as we shall see below, there are other desirable policies which may depend upon the assessment of individuals' capital wealth.

There is a second type of fiscal attack on the maldistribution of property – namely death duties. Can one find a system of tax which reduces very little the ability or incentive of the large property owner to work, enterprise, and accumulate during his life time, but which gives him a high incentive to distribute his property widely among those with small properties at his death?

If death duties are to be used seriously as an instrument for the equalisation of properties, it is essential that gifts *inter vivos* should be taxed in the same way as bequests at death. Otherwise, as in the United Kingdom at present, the whole operation becomes farcical. Any rich property owner, in the absence of a similar tax on gifts *inter vivos*, can avoid any death-duty obstacle to the concentration of his own wealth into the possession of a single wealthy heir by transferring the greater part of his property as a gift during his life time. Treating gifts *inter vivos* in the same way as bequests at death raises administrative problems which it is essential to face if a serious effort is to be made by fiscal means to redistribute properties.

Let us consider four possible principles upon which death duties and taxes on gifts *inter vivos* might be assessed.

(i) First, there is the principle of the United Kingdom Estate duty according to which a duty is assessed at a progressive rate which rises according to the size of the total estate. In the United Kingdom at present the rate of duty starts at 1 per cent on estates of £5,000 and rises by gradual increments to 80 per cent on estates of over £1,000,000. A progressive estate duty of this kind (provided that it is accompanied by similar taxation of gifts *inter vivos*) must, of course, exercise a strong equalising tendency on the distribution of property as it taxes at progressively higher rates the large properties as they pass at death. But it does nothing to induce the rich property owner to distribute his property on his death more widely among a number of beneficiaries.

(ii) The second possible principle would be to tax estates passing at death and gifts *inter vivos* according to the size of the individual bequest. Thus an estate of £1,000,000 bequeathed to a single heir might be taxed at 80 per cent; but if it were left in 100 bequests of £10,000 each, each bequest might be taxed only at 6 per cent.[21] This principle would certainly improve the incentive to split up large properties at death. But it would not encourage the large property owners in choosing his numerous beneficiaries to give preference to those who were not already the owners of large properties. If a large number of rich men split up their estates among a large number of rich children, little is gained as compared with the situation in which each rich man leaves the whole of his estate to one rich child.

(iii) A third principle would be to tax each individual gift or bequest not solely according to the size of the individual gift or bequest but also according to the existing wealth of the beneficiary. Thus a higher rate of duty would be paid according to the total property which the beneficiary would possess when the gift or legacy was added to his existing wealth.[22] This principle would give a strong incentive to large property owners not only to split their properties into many parts, but also to bequeath these parts to persons who were already the owners of only small properties.

This principle (iii) has an added advantage over the previous principle (ii). If principle (ii) is adopted, it is possible to avoid duty by making successive gifts to the same person, unless special provisions are introduced to remove this possibility. Thus under principle (ii) if A wishes to pass £1,000,000 on to B, he will pay, say, 80 per cent in tax if he passes his fortune in one single lump. But if he passes on by gift one £500,000 to B this year and the other £500,000 to B some years later, he will pay only the reduced rate of duty appropriate to the smaller gift on each of the two halves of his fortune. This possibility is very much reduced by the application of principle (iii). If the beneficiary B has had his fortune increased in one year by £500,000, the rate of tax payable on the second £500,000 will be greatly increased.

Principle (iii) does, however, require that the value of the existing capital wealth of any beneficiary should be assessed, as well as the value of the gift or bequest itself, in order that the tax liability should be assessed. If an annual tax on capital wealth were itself introduced, this would itself provide an assessment of individual's capital wealth which would be available for the assessment of the duty payable on gifts and bequests under principle (iii).

(iv) With the fourth principle every gift or legacy received by any one individual would be recorded in a register against his name for tax purposes. He would then be taxed when he received any gift or bequest neither according to the size of that gift or bequest nor according to the size of his total property at the time of the receipt of that gift or bequest, but according to the size of the total amount which he had received over the whole of his life by way of gift or inheritance. The rate of tax would be on a progressive scale according to the total of gifts or bequests recorded against his name in the tax register.

The rich property owner would now have every incentive to pass on his property in small parcels to persons who had up to date received little by way of gift or inheritance. This system should serve to diffuse property ownership with the minimum adverse effects upon incentives to earn, enterprise, save, and accumulate property. The testator or donor could avoid tax on handing on his property by leaving a moderate amount to each of a number of persons who had not yet received much by way of gift and inheritance. And, unlike principle (iii), no prospective heir would be discouraged from accumulating a property of his own by his own efforts: the duty which he would have to pay on the receipt of any subsequent gift or bequest would not be higher because he had already enriched himself by his own efforts. It would only be higher if he had already been enriched by the receipt of property from someone else.

Principle (iv) would thus probably be superior to principle (iii) in its effects on incentives to work, risk, and accumulate. Moreover, with principle (iv) unlike principle (iii) there would be no incentive at all to hand over one's property in small successive doses to any one heir, because the tax payable would be progressive according to the total amount received by gift or inheritance regardless of the timing and size of each individual gift or bequest. On the other hand principle (iii) would have a more equalising effect than principle (iv), since it would discourage the passing on of property to rich men whether the source of their riches was their own effort or not.

From the administrative point of view principle (iv) is probably basically simpler than principle (iii). Both principles require the assessment of the value of each gift or bequest when it is made; but principle (iv), unlike principle (iii), does not require the assessment of the beneficiary's existing wealth as well. All that it requires is the assessment and recording of the receipt of each separate gift or bequest. If, however, all individuals' properties were already being regularly assessed for the purpose of an annual tax on capital wealth, principle (iii) might well be the simpler from an administrative point of view; for the assessment of a beneficiary's existing property would already be available for the tax on capital wealth and no record of previous gifts or bequests would be needed.

Principles (ii), (iii), and (iv) all raise a problem in the case of discretionary trusts. For if property is left in such a way that the trustees are able to exercise a discretion at some time in the future as to who should be the actual beneficiary from the property, it is not possible to assess the size of the individual bequests enjoyed by particular beneficiaries at the time of the passing of the property from its previous owner. There are three possible lines of attack on this problem. The first would be to legislate in such a way as to restrict considerably the possibilities of setting up such trusts. The second would be to ensure that such properties were not taxed at the time of the setting up of the trust, but were taxed as and when the funds were in fact used to enrich individual beneficiaries. The third would be to name some rather high, but arbitrary fixed rate of duty which the tax authorities could levy on such trust funds at the time when they were set up and which would exempt such funds from further tax when they were actually used to the benefits of particular individuals.[23]

So much for the progressive taxation of income or wealth. Such fiscal measures are not, however, the only policy measures which may substantially affect the distribution of the ownership of property. Arrangements which encourage the accumulation of property by those with little property are certainly as important as those which discourage further accumulation or encourage dispersal of their fortunes by large property owners. Such arrangements might include: the encouragement of financial intermediaries in which small savings can be pooled for investment in high-earning risk-bearing securities; measures to promote employee share schemes whereby workers can gain a property interest in business firms; and measures whereby municipally built houses can be bought on the instalment principle by their occupants.

We have already noted (pp. 36–7) the extreme importance of education as a form of investment which affects earning power. Future developments of educational policy could have a profound effect upon the distribution of earning power and so indirectly, through the power to accumulate, upon the distribution of property. We have already explained how in the past the spread of public elementary education in the developed countries has almost certainly been an important equalising factor. It has in essence been an investment of capital with a high return, financed out of general taxation for the benefit of every citizen; indeed in countries like the United Kingdom where the rich, in addition to contributing through taxation to the general system of public education, have invested their own funds in their own childrens' education in private schools, public education financed from general taxation has represented an educational investment in the children of the poor.

There is undoubtedly great scope for educational developments which will have further equalising effects of the same kind. We are becoming aware[24] how greatly within the State system of education itself environmental factors of one kind or another enable the children of the relatively rich to gain more than the children of the poor from such education. It may be that steps can be taken to counteract these forces. Moreover many educational developments, such as the raising of the minimum school-leaving age or the improvement (through the reduction in the size of classes) of the education which is common to all, will expand the equalising forces which have been so prominent in the past.

But the picture is less certain when one considers possible educational developments in higher education at universities and similar institutions. There is, of course, one extremely important way in which the expansion of higher education is likely to exercise an equalising influence. Highly trained persons command a higher wage than do the untrained and the unskilled; the transformation of the relatively untrained into the highly trained through an expanded programme of higher education will decrease the supply of the former and increase the supply of the latter type of worker; the low wages of the unskilled should thus be raised relatively to the high wages of the trained as there are fewer untrained and more trained persons seeking employment in the labour market.

But, on the other hand, there are two reasons for believing that future developments of higher education may be less equalising than were the earlier educational developments. Indeed they might conceivably in the end turn out to be positively disequalising in their effects upon ability to earn and to accumulate property.

The first of the marked differences between elementary and higher education is in the division of the costs of such education between the State and the students or their families. None of the cost of elementary education takes the form of earnings foregone; the young boys and girls would not nowadays be in the factories if they were not in the schools. But for higher education earnings foregone make up a very large part, indeed the greater part,[25] of the cost. Though the State provides free of charge the actual educational services and even if it pays in addition some modest maintenance allowances to students, there is a very substantial cost borne by the student or his family in earnings foregone. Such a cost can be more easily met by the rich than by the poor parent. Higher education still involves the investment of private property in the student; and the children of poor parents may be discouraged from it by the desire to start earning at an early date.

But the second difference between elementary and higher education is probably much more important. Even though there is a great expansion in the numbers who receive higher education, it will remain selective; and the basis of selection will be more and more the able boy or girl rather than the son or daughter of wealthy parents. This means increased equality of opportunity. But equality of opportunity is not the same thing as equality of outcome. Indeed, greater equality of opportunity could in the long run mean less, and not greater, equality of wealth. Of course, as between two boys of equal ability, if the son of the poor man is given the same opportunity as the son of the rich man, their ultimate earnings will be equalised. Equality of opportunity does lead to equality of result between those with equal ability. But not all have the same ability and the whole object of selection for higher education will be to select those who are innately able to enjoy the advantages of higher education.

When all have the same access to higher education, it will be the innately able who will succeed. Innate ability will receive the high earnings, accumulate property, and rise in the property scale. This rise of the meritocracy[26] will cause there to be a closer association between ability, earning power, and property at the top of the scale and between lack of ability, low earning power, and small property at the bottom of the scale. The ultimate inequalities in the ownership of property could be greater than before.

The outcome will depend very much upon the educational principle which is adopted. Here there is a possibility of a conflict between 'efficiency' and 'distributional' considerations in educational policy which is not always fully appreciated. Let us suppose that there is a certain additional amount of money which is going to be spent on education. How should it be spent? On reducing the size of classes in the primary schools? On raising the school-leaving age for all children? On increasing the period at the university for the ablest students? On enabling a number of less able students to go to the university?

Now there are many ends to be attained through education other than economic ends. I do not wish to depreciate these ends and in the ultimate choice they will no doubt play an important role in the formation of educational policy. But I do not intend to discuss them on this occasion simply because I want to concentrate attention on the economic effects of educational expenditures. One economic principle for the use of resources in education would be to devote them to those uses which would increase most the productivity and future earning power of the students concerned. I will call this the 'efficiency' principle. Another economic principle would be to use the available resources in education in such a way as to equalise the future earning power of different students. I will call this the 'distributional' principle. Taken to its logical extreme the 'distributional' principle would mean concentrating educational effort and training facilities on the dullards to the neglect of the bright students until the educational advantages of the former just made up for the greater inborn abilities of the latter in the future competition for jobs.

258 *Liberty, Equality and Efficiency*

But what would the 'efficiency' principle involve? It is very probable that in the past there was little or no conflict between the 'efficiency' and the 'distributional' principle – universal elementary education was needed on both tickets. But now that this stage in education is virtually complete, will such harmony reign in the future? I do not know; but it would be of great importance if it could be discovered whether, given the present stage of educational development, further expenditure on simple improvements in the basic education of all (for example, smaller classes in primary schools, a higher minimum school-leaving age), or a concentration of expenditure on a few able men and women (for example, more expensive laboratory facilities in the universities and longer periods of postgraduate work for the ablest technicians) would in fact increase the national product most. It is possible that automation itself may mean that production would be most effectively promoted by the most profound training of a few technicians rather than by the general training of the many. There is a crying need for yet more research into these matters. It may be that the most efficient educational developments will also tend to equalise earning ability and so indirectly property ownership. But one would be betraying one's calling to hold this view without enquiry simply because it is a comfortable view to hold.

I come now to the controversial subject of public policies which might be adopted to influence differential fertility among different sections of society. There is an old standing conflict of view here. The radical left-winger in politics lays great stress on the importance of environment in determining a citizen's achievement in social life. The conservative right-winger lays great stress on the importance of inherited genetical ability in determining performance. It is fashionable today among students of society who wish to improve affairs to lay all the emphasis on improvements of one kind or another in environmental conditions in sharp contrast to the excesses of the early conservative Social Darwinists who saw the amelioration of society largely in terms of promoting the breeding of the successful rich and of discouraging the breeding of the unsuccessful poor.

I regard this dichotomy as unfortunate and unnecessary. As a radical in politics, but a believer in Eugenics, I would like to explain briefly my views on this matter because it is very relevant to the problem of the distribution of the ownership of property which we are discussing. I am as impressed as any environmentalist by the importance of social reform to enable all citizens to develop in the best way their innate capacities both of intelligence and of character. But the greater is the success of radical environmental policies of this kind, the greater probably are both the need for and the possibility of a eugenic policy. For there is likely to be some truth in the old eugenic view that as society makes it easier for all – whatever may be the innate characteristics – to survive and to flourish, so there is a greater need for a conscious humane policy, other than the cruelties of the *laissez-faire* competitive struggle, to restrain the reproduction of those who are innately ill-fitted to make their way in society.

But eugenic policies will at the same time be becoming not only more necessary but also more possible. For consider what will be happening as we environmentalist radicals (for I insist on having it both ways and numbering myself among them) increase the real opportunities for achievement in education, reduce the inequalities in endowment in inherited wealth and opportunity to earn, and so reorganise society that both the private and public demands for goods and services increasingly represent the real needs of private consumers and the desirable public ends of society. We shall be moving to a state of affairs in which there are ever increasing positive correlations (i) between wealth and innate ability to earn and (ii) between ability to earn and ability to serve the real needs of society. Measures which encourage some differential fertility in favour of those whose earnings are high will become increasingly eugenic in their effect and will be less and less open to criticism on other grounds.

What form might such measures take?

An undesirably high rate of population growth is nowadays almost universal throughout the world and is certainly once again a real threat in the United Kingdom. It is essential that any change in differential fertility should be based upon a substantial reduction in fertility at the lower end of the scale rather than in a rise in fertility at the top end.

For the lower end of the scale I would advocate extensive positive and open measures by the public health and welfare services to bring the full choice of means for contraception within everyone's reach and understanding – and particularly within the reach and understanding of the 'problem families'. It is still true in the United Kingdom that the rich, successful, and intelligent have readier access to contraceptive methods than the poor, unsuccessful, and unintelligent.

For the top end of the scale I would suggest that in due course tax arrangements might be recast so as to make it taxwise more advantageous for those with high earned incomes to have children. This can be done just as well by increasing the tax burden on the childless rich as it can by decreasing the tax burden on the high earners who have the larger families. I am not advocating anything which reduces the taxation of the rich relatively to the poor, but something which reduces the taxation of the high earners with children as contrasted with the childless rich. There is no reason why at the higher end of the scale of incomes, the tax on earned incomes should not differentiate more than it does at present in favour of the larger families. Another suitable measure would be the removal of the means test for the public maintenance of children in higher education so that the bringing up of a family was a smaller cost than it is at present to the richer parents.

Let me remove certain possible misconceptions. In the moderate eugenic policy which I have advocated there is no where any element of compulsion. Any parents would be free to have whatever sized family they choose. There is also no suggestion that the ability to earn is the only desirable quality, but merely that, particularly in a society which had been reformed environmentally, ability to earn is one of the desirable sets of qualities which should be encouraged. Even within the set of qualities which gave ability to earn there is, of course, an enormous variety: musical ability, mathematical ability, general intelligence, qualities of leadership, physical abilities of various kinds, and so on and so on. Above all versatility and variety would be encouraged. This is a quite different matter from the encouragement of one very specialised and particular set of characteristics.

Finally let me remind you of the relevance of all this to the main theme of these lectures. I would be the last person to advocate policy measures to discourage the fertility of the poor or to promote the fertility of the rich simply in order to equalise the ownership of property – by splitting the large fortunes among many children and the small fortunes among few. But if such policy measures are desirable on other grounds – and I believe that as we reform society environmentally they will become increasingly desirable on eugenic grounds – they should be doubly welcome because they could incidentally make a substantial contribution to our problem of redistributing property ownership more equally.

VI   A SOCIALIST STATE

Let us turn now to the Social Ownership of Property as an alternative means for combining an efficient level of the real wage rate with an equitable distribution of income. Suppose that by the wave of some alternative magic wand – and we will later examine the nature of this wand – the ownership of all property were transferred from private individuals to the State. The real wage rate is set at the level which enables it to be used exclusively as an 'efficiency' guide for the use of labour. If this 'efficiency' level is a low one, then a large part of the national income accrues as profits on capital of all kinds. But these profits now go to the State, which could use them to pay out an equal social dividend to every citizen. In one basic respect this system is the same as a system in which property is privately owned but is owned in equal amounts by every citizen. In both cases income from property is equally divided between all citizens.

In one important respect the social ownership of property has an important advantage over the equal distribution of private ownership. In the both cases, in the interests of preventing total savings from falling below the optimum level (see p. 31), private savings may need to be supplemented by public savings, particularly since with a more equal distribution of income from property there will remain no very large private incomes from property out of which high personal savings might have been made. In both cases the promotion of public savings through a budget surplus may be necessary. In the case in which property is in private ownership the achievement of the budget surplus will require increased tax revenue; and the rise in rates of taxation may have unfortunate effects on economic incentives. In the case of the social ownership of property, on the other hand, all income from property accrues to the State. The State can, therefore, generate a given level of public savings through the budget with a lower level of tax rates and therefore with less adverse effects on efficiency in the case of State ownership of property, than in the case of equalised private ownership of property.

At first sight it might appear that if all property were owned by the State, then all industrial activities would have to be managed in socialised concerns, so that the price mechanism would no longer be working in a free-enterprise competitive economy. This would not essentially alter our present argument. In a modern centrally planned and fully socialised economy it is increasingly difficult (because of the increasing complexity of relationships between different industries) to conduct affairs efficiently without using the mechanism of prices of various inputs and outputs as measures of their relative scarcities. Thus in a centrally planned and fully socialised economy with an automated technique of production the level of the real wage rate which will act as the efficient guide for the use of labour may be very low. In this case the profits of state enterprises will be high. But these profits will be available to the State to use in any way which the State decides to be equitable.

But in fact there is no one-to-one relationship between the amount of real property which is directly managed by the State (as in the case of a socialised industry) and the amount of the economy's total real wealth which is in the unencumbered possession of the State. The two things may differ because of the existence of a national debt. There are in fact two quite distinct measures of the degree of socialist ownership of property, which we may express as

$$\frac{K_s}{K} \quad \text{and} \quad \frac{K_s - D}{K}$$

where K is the value of the total real property of the community (the value of all the land, buildings, plant, machinery, and stocks of goods in the community), K_s is the part of this total which is directly managed by the State (the land, buildings, plant, machinery, and stocks of goods used in the provision of public services or in socialised industries), and D is the value of the national debt owed by the State and other public authorities to the private sector of the economy. In the United Kingdom at the present time K is some £50,000 million, K_s £21,000 million and D £28,000 million[27] so that

$$\frac{K_s}{K} = 42\% \quad \text{and} \quad \frac{K_s - D}{K} = -14\%.$$

While some 42 per cent of the real property of the community is in the management-ownership of the State or other public authorities, the value of the total amount of property owned privately is actually greater than the value of the total real property of the community, because the national debt is greater than the real property owned by the State or other public authorities.[28]

For our present purpose we are interested in the measure $\frac{K_s - D}{K}$. We are interested, that is to say, in the ultimate destination of income from property and not in the immediate control over real property. In the United Kingdom at present $\frac{K_s - D}{K}$ is a negative quantity; we are dealing with a society in which, far from the State receiving a net income from property for use as it seems equitable, private property owners own more property than the total real property of the community and the State is a net debtor to the private sector. As far as the management of real property is concerned we live in a semi-Socialist State; but as far as the net ownership of property is concerned we live, not in a semi-Socialist State, but in an anti-Socialist State.

Suppose, however, that, by a wave of our present magic wand, this position could be reversed and a large part of private property became public property so that $\frac{K_s - D}{K}$ was transformed from a negative figure to a large positive fraction. It is, of course, merely a question of degree how far this should go. But the larger is $\dfrac{K_s - D}{K}$, the larger will be the State's income from productive capital (K_s) or the smaller will be the State's current expenditure on interest on the national debt (D). What advantages or disadvantages would this change have?[29] The Socialisation of the ownership of property will give the State a larger net income from property and in consequence rates of taxation can be reduced or larger social-security payments can be made to the poorer members of society without any reduction in other forms of State expenditure. The *gross* incomes of the private sector are lower because less interest is paid on the national debt or less profit is received on property now transferred to the State; but *net* incomes of the private sector are unchanged because taxation is lower or social-security benefits are higher. There is an improvement in economic incentives and/or in the distribution of income because of the lower rates of tax and/or the equitable social benefits. At the same time, since private net incomes are the same, but private properties are smaller, there is likely to be an improvement in the incentives for private savings.

Is there then nothing to be said in favour of private property? If the foregoing argument contained the whole of the truth, then the greater the ratio $\dfrac{K_s - D}{K}$ the better for society. Best of all would be the absence of all private property; the state would be able to go to the utmost in the reduction of tax and/or in the increase of social benefits and thus achieve the maximum improvements in incentives and/or in the equitable distribution of income. But, alas, as is so often the case in this wicked world there is much to be said on both sides of the question. Private property does have advantages. A man with the same net income of £1,000 without any property (situation I) and with £10,000 of property (situation II) is better off in situation II than in situation I. The property itself gives him security and independence. If this were the whole of the story, the State could always improve matters by printing and handing out to every citizen another £1,000,000 of national debt and raising each citizen's taxes to the extent necessary to cover the interest on £1,000,000 of debt. Each citizen would have the same net income as before and each would be a millionaire into the bargain. Where is the snag? Simply that the rate of tax of 19s 11 $\frac{3}{4}$d. in the £[30] (or whatever would be necessary to meet the gigantic bill for interest on the debt) would kill all economic incentives. We would all sit back and do nothing intending to live on our ample capital, and economic life would grind to a standstill.

Thus if we started from a position with no private property, as the amount of private property rose (i.e. as $\dfrac{K_s - D}{K}$ fell) (i) tax incentives would worsen but (ii) the security and independence gained from property ownership would rise. As we proceeded the extra loss from (i) would become more and more acute and the extra gain from (ii) less and less important. Somewhere there is an optimum point though I am afraid that I cannot tell you where it is. Indeed, I am not sure that I can even define it rigorously. But I have a hunch that it would be better if the index $\dfrac{K_s - D}{K}$ (now so low that it is highly negative) were substantially raised in the United Kingdom, particularly if the property which did remain in private ownership could simultaneously be much more equally distributed. In my view what we need is a combination of measures for some socialisation of net property ownership and for a more equal distribution of the property which is privately owned.

But what is the nature of our socialist magic wand? How can some socialisation of the net ownership of property be achieved? It would be possible to devise a once-for-all capital levy which transferred some slice of property from each private property owner to the State. This direct method is, I fear, open to serious objection. It would in any case be administratively difficult. But apart from that we are faced with the following dilemma. For it to be a success it must be accepted as a once-for-all measure which will not be repeated; otherwise the fear of a repetition would kill all future incentives to accumulate capital. But for it to be both successful and accepted as being unlikely to be repeated, it must be on a very large scale; it must be believed that it will not be repeated simply because enough transfer to the State has already been achieved. But if it is on a very large scale, the administrative and political, to say nothing of the economic and financial, difficulties of the operation will be very great indeed.

Much more practicable is to devise a suitable budgetary policy which will result in a continuing substantial annual budget surplus which, year by year, can be used for the redemption of the national debt (so that D falls) or for investment in State-controlled income-earning assets (so that K_s rises). For this purpose one needs to find a form of tax by which considerable additional revenue may be raised with the minimum adverse effects upon the incentives to work and enterprise. But it does not matter for our present purpose if the tax does discourage private savings. Our whole purpose is to use the tax to increase public savings through the budget; even if it does this wholly at the expense of private savings, total savings would not thereby be reduced. If the tax is paid only partially out of private savings, but is used wholly to add to public savings, there will be some net increase in total savings. As we have already argued (p. 51), a progressive annual tax assessed on the capital value of individual properties would probably have minimal adverse effects upon incentives to work and enterprise, though it would discourage the accumulation of the largest private properties. It would seem, therefore, to be a suitable additional tax for the increased socialisation of net property ownership.

In advocating in this way the old-fashioned policy of generating a budget surplus in order to redeem national debt, I am not forgetting the overriding importance of using financial policy for the maintenance of full employment and the promotion of economic growth. When the economy is threatened with stagnation because effective demand is not growing sufficiently to maintain a full pressure upon the available real resources of the community, expenditure on goods and services both for consumption and for investment should be stimulated by a monetary policy (which eases the terms on which funds can be borrowed for expenditure) and by a tax policy (which increases the funds available for, and the incentive for, expenditures on goods and services.) What is needed is short-run flexibility of monetary and tax policies to preserve the desired level of effective demand in the interests of full employment and economic expansion. Over the long-run average of years this flexible short-run monetary and budgetary policy, while it is successful in controlling total demand so as to maintain the full employment of resources, may fail in either of two other ways. (i) It may fail to maintain the 'optimum level of savings' which in the ultimate analysis means a failure to ensure that a sufficiently large part of the desired total expenditure takes the form of expenditure on new capital goods for investment for the benefit of future consumers, too large a part being devoted to expenditure on current consumption. (ii) It may, secondly, fail to maintain a sufficiently high surplus of tax revenue over current budgetary expenditure to ensure that there is the desired rate of gradual socialisation of property ownership.

To remedy failures (i) or (ii) it is not desirable to abandon the short-run flexibilities of monetary and budgetary policies designed to maintain full employment, but to alter the structure of financial policies so that the outcome of these flexible monetary and budgetary policies over the average of the years does not display either of these two undesirable weaknesses. Thus to remedy failure (i), measures to promote expenditure on investment (e.g. an easier monetary policy or special tax remissions on investment expenditures) may be combined with measures to restrict consumption expenditures (e.g. higher rates of tax on spendable incomes.) Or to remedy failure (ii) measures may be taken to increase the total of tax revenue without any adverse restriction of total private expenditure on goods and services; for example, rates of tax might be raised in the case of duties which are likely to be paid out of past savings rather than out of current expenditures on consumption or capital goods (such as death duties or an annual tax on wealth) and any minor adverse effects of these tax increases in reducing expenditures might be offset by much smaller tax reductions in the case of duties which are likely to have been paid mainly out of reduced expenditures (such as taxes on spendable incomes).

In fact the State has many different financial weapons: monetary policy which can affect total expenditure and in particular expenditure on new capital goods without any direct effect upon the budgetary surplus; some taxes which will discourage above all expenditure on consumption; other taxes which discourage above all investment expenditures on capital goods; yet other taxes which raise revenue primarily from property already accumulated and discourage neither consumption nor investment very substantially; and many forms of subsidy and tax remission which will affect either consumption or investment expenditures. Short-run changes in monetary and budgetary policies should continuously be made to maintain full employment. But structural changes in the balance between monetary policy and various forms of tax and subsidy can also be made. By such structural changes short-run adjustments of monetary and tax policies for the maintenance of full employment can be made compatible with long-run averages over the years of an optimum level of total savings and of an optimum budget surplus by means of which there is the desired gradual socialisation of property ownership.

VII   CONCLUSION

The problem discussed in the preceding sections has been presented in its most acute form in terms of the future of our economy if automation reduces markedly the importance in productive processes of men relative to that of machines. We have argued that to combine efficiency in the use of resources with equity in the distribution of income would in that case cry out for measures to equalise the distribution of the ownership of private property and to increase the net amount of property which was in social ownership. But the problem is not simply a hypothetical one of the future. Private property is at present greatly inflated by the national debt, and is very unequally distributed. With a real wage rate that acted as an 'efficient' price, property income (without any further automation) is already a very important element of total income. The combination of efficiency-in-use with equity-in-distribution already calls in the United Kingdom for measures for the equalisation and the socialisation of property ownership. These measures are needed, for the most part, to supplement rather than to replace the existing Welfare-State policies.

The sort of measures which might be appropriate for these purposes are:

(1) a radical reform of the death duties which turned them into a progressive tax dependent upon the total amount which each beneficiary had received up to date by way of gift or inheritance;

(2) the extension of the reformed death duties to cover gifts *inter vivos*;

(3) the generation of a substantial budget surplus for the redemption of the national debt or for investment in other appropriate forms of public property by means of a progressive annual tax assessed on capital wealth;

(4) the encouragement of institutional forms (such as profit-sharing schemes, the instalment purchase of municipal houses by their tenants, and the development of suitable investment trusts) which would make easier and more profitable the accumulation of small properties;

(5) the development of educational policies which would equalise the chances of promotion in life for boys and girls of equal innate ability; and

(6) the reduction of the relative fertility of those with low earning capacity (i) by giving easy and equal opportunity to all citizens for acquiring and using contraceptives and (ii) by increasing the tax burden of the childless relatively to those with children within the high earned-income brackets.

The adoption of this six-point programme could greatly change the social structure of the United Kingdom. But there remains one major difficulty in its implementation which has not so far been mentioned. The world is made up of a number of separate national states with ever increasing communication and movement between those which practice a free and liberal way of life. It might be difficult for one such nation alone to implement as fully as it would otherwise desire the sort of programme outlined above. No one perhaps can tell in advance for any one country how great would be the incentives for the able and enterprising to move from a country in which measures had been deliberately taken to damp down the accumulation of the biggest private properties to countries in which no or few such measures were in operation. Undoubtedly in some cases at least some moderation in the rate of reform would be necessary on these grounds.

The main moral is a simple one. In this, as in so much of their economic and social policies, it is not necessary that all the liberal countries should adopt precisely the same policies. But it is desirable that they should keep very broadly in step in their general philosophy and practice of reform. Otherwise the only alternative might be the growth of illiberal national controls over international movements. The problem of the ownership of property is, in my view, one of great importance and of common concern throughout the free world.

APPENDIX I   THE DISTRIBUTION OF PERSONAL INCOMES. THE UNITED KINGDOM, 1959[31]

The figures given in Table 2.2 of the main text (p. 35) are to be regarded as rough indications of the order of magnitude of the problems involved in the United Kingdom rather than an exact representation of the actual situation. At that point of the argument in the main text we were neglecting the effects of State action and in particular the effects of taxation, of social security benefits, of the State ownership of property, and of State indebtedness to the private sector (the national debt). In the absence of the State the distribution of the cost of the national product (i.e. of the net national income) between wages and salaries on the one hand and interest, profits, and rents on the other hand would coincide with the distribution of personal incomes between earned incomes and incomes from property. But the existence of the State breaks this one-to-one correspondence in many ways. For example, part of interest, profit, and rent (e.g. the profits of nationalised industries and the profits tax levied on companies' profits) will accrue directly as budgetary revenue to the State and will not appear in the figures of personal incomes. On the other hand, interest payable on the national debt is part of personal incomes, but is not part of the interest cost of the national product. Other transfer payments (e.g. social security benefits) are also part of personal incomes but not part of the factor cost of the national product. In the case of wages, employers' compulsory insurance contributions are part of the labour cost of the national product but will not appear in the statistics of personal wage earnings.

In the United Kingdom there is a special reason why the figures of personal incomes derived from the Income Tax returns will seriously underestimate personal incomes from property. They exclude capital gains. But the increase in the value of companies' shares which is due to the accumulation of undistributed profits represents in effect a personal income of the shareholders which has been saved for them by the companies themselves. Similarly, the interest and dividends received by the life funds of insurance companies enhances the capital value of the life assurance policies, though it does not appear in the statistics of the personal incomes of the owners of the life policies.

The figures in Table 2.5 give for 1959 the distribution of personal incomes declared for tax in the United Kingdom. The figures for the p's and l's given in the two last columns of Table 2.5 are those used for the p's and l's in Table 2.2 of the main text. But the Inland Revenue figures in Table 2.5 show personal incomes from property (£1,184 m.) as only 7.1 per cent of total personal incomes (£15,391 m.). This value for the ratio $(1 - q)$ is certainly a gross underestimate.

In the net national income as a whole for 1959 interest, profits, and rents made up 19.1 per cent of the total. In the gross national product for 1959 earned incomes are estimated as £15,966 m. and the remainder of the gross national product at £5,192 m. But to obtain the relevant figures for the net national product we must deduct a depreciation allowance of £1,904 m., £400 m. in respect of earned incomes and £1,504 m. in respect of other income. This gives property income after depreciation (£3,688 m.) as 19.1 per cent of total net national income after depreciation (£19,254 m.). This 19.1 per cent would, as we have seen, be the relevant value of our ratio $(1 - q)$ in the absence of the State.

Table 2.5   Personal Incomes (before deduction of tax) in the
United Kingdom, 1959

Percentage of total population with largest personal incomes from all sources	Percentage of total personal incomes from all sources (i)	Percentage of personal incomes from property (p)	Percentage of personal incomes from earnings (l)
1	9	47	6
5	21	66	17
10	31	73	27
Total income £ million	15,391	1,184	14,207

The figures for personal property incomes and earned incomes in Table 2.5 give £1,184 m. and £14,207 m. respectively. The figures for net property incomes and for wage incomes included in the net national product give £3,688 m. and £15,566 m. respectively. A rough reconciliation of these two sets of estimates is given in Table 2.6. From that table it would seem that personal incomes from property in Table 2.5 may be underestimated by as much as £1,500 m. (£200 m. for certain deductions allowed by the Inland Revenue £800 m. for underestimated profits net of depreciation, £200 m. for the incomes of life assurance funds, £300 m. for owner-occupied houses). If we add this figure to personal incomes from property and to total personal incomes in Table 2.5 we obtain a value of about 16 per cent for $(1 - q)$.

Table 2.2 of the main text does no more than apply values for $(1 - q)$ of 5, 15, and 25 per cent to the values for the p's and l's of Table 2.5.

Table 2.6   Personal Incomes and the Net National Income Compared

		Property Incomes	£m.
Personal Property Incomes as given in Table 2.5			1,184
Add	(i)	Certain Deductions from Income allowed by the Inland Revenue	207
	(ii)	Gross Undistributed Profits	2,321
	(iii)	Direct Taxation paid by Companies (home and abroad)	1,169
	(iv)	Additions to Life Assurance and Superannuation Funds	236
	(v)	Imputed Income from Owner-Occupied Houses	301
	(vi)	Government Income from Property ..	618
Deduct	(i)	National Debt Interest	− 915
	(ii)	Depreciation on above Incomes	−1,504
			3,617

Earned Incomes

Personal Earned Income as given in Table 2.5		.. ..	14,207
Add	(i)	Certain Deductions from Income allowed by the Inland Revenue	509
	(ii)	Employers' National Insurance Contributions	990
	(iii)	Income Received in Kind	179
	(iv)	Capital Allowances for Self-Employed ..	98
	(v)	Farmers' Incomes	534
Deduct	(i)	Family Allowances and Pensions	− 639
	(ii)	Depreciation on above Incomes	− 400
			15,478

APPENDIX II   THE ACCUMULATION OF PERSONAL PROPERTY

This Appendix provides greater precision for one or two of the relationships discussed on pp. 43–5 of the main text. Its main purpose, however, is to stress how much still remains to be done in this field and to stimulate others, better equipped than the author, to do it.

Assume that the amount which an individual saves and invests in new property (I) depends upon the size of his income (Y) and upon the size of his property (K). Since his savings are equal to what he adds to his property, we have

$$\frac{dK}{dt} \equiv I = I\,(Y, K) \tag{1}$$

We suppose that his earned income (E) is equal to WL, where L is the amount of work which he chooses to do and W is the wage rate which he can earn per unit of work done. His total income is composed of his earnings (E) and of his income from property (VK) where V is the rate of interest or profit which he can command on his property. It follows that

$$Y = E + VK = WL + VK \tag{2}$$

We may further assume that our individual's ability to earn and the rate of return on his property both depend partly upon the passage of time and partly upon the size of his property. In the case of the wage rate the labour market may be improving because of technical progress and capital accumulation in the economy as a whole, so that the wage he could earn would be rising even if his property were not growing. But in addition a larger property might give him a greater opportunity to earn, so that

$$W = W\,(K, t) \tag{3}$$

where t represents time. Similarly, the rate of profit on capital generally may be rising or falling over time in the economy as a whole so that the return on his property will depend partly on the passage of time and partly on the size of his own property if at any one time large properties are able to earn higher returns than small properties. In this case,

$$V = V\,(K, t) \tag{4}$$

In the absence of birth or death or ageing and of governmental interventions (i.e. in stage one of our enquiring in the text on pp. 43–5) equations (1) to (4) give us a differential equation in K and t, which would show the growth pattern for our individual's property. By comparing the growth patterns of K' and K'' for two different individuals with different innate earnings abilities and different initial properties we could examine the movement of $\frac{K'}{K''}$ over time. To do this we would have to have full information about the functions I, W, and V in equations (1), (3), and (4).

A more limited exercise is to ask whether, at the particular point of property accumulation reached by any one individual, the proportional rate of growth of his property $\left(k \equiv \dfrac{1}{K} \dfrac{dK}{dt} \right)$ is likely to be rising or falling. This may give us a clue as to which types of property will in fact be growing the more quickly. We can express equation 1 as $kK = I(Y, K)$; and by differentiation of this expression and of equations (2), (3), and (4) and on the assumption that L is constant we obtain:

$$\frac{K}{k} \frac{dk}{dK} = -1 - E_{SK} + E_{SY} \left\{ Q \left(E_{WK} + \frac{w}{k} \right) + (1 - Q) \left(1 + E_{VK} + \frac{v}{k} \right) \right\} \qquad (5)$$

where $E_{SK} = -\dfrac{K}{I} \dfrac{\partial I}{\partial K}$, $E_{SY} = \dfrac{Y}{I} \dfrac{\partial I}{\partial Y}$, $E_{WK} = \dfrac{K}{W} \dfrac{\partial W}{\partial K}$, $E_{VK} = \dfrac{K}{V} \dfrac{\partial V}{\partial K}$, $w = \dfrac{1}{W} \dfrac{dW}{dt}$,

$v = \dfrac{1}{V} \dfrac{dV}{dt}$, and $Q = \dfrac{WL}{Y}$, the proportion of earnings to total income. E_{SK} is an elasticity measure of the effect of an *increase* in property in *discouraging* savings. E_{SY} is an elasticity measure of the influence of a rise in income in encouraging savings. E_{WK} and E_{VK} are elasticity measures of the influence of increased property in increasing the ability to earn and the chance of getting a better return on property. w and v are the proportionate rates at which the wage rate and the rate of profit at which our citizen could sell his labour or invest his property would be changing in the market if his property were constant in size.

Whether at any particular point the growth rate of property (k) will be rising or falling as property (K) is being accumulated will depend upon whether

$$\frac{1 + E_{SK}}{E_{SY}} \lessgtr Q \left(E_{WK} + \frac{w}{k} \right) + (1 - Q) \left(1 + E_{VK} + \frac{v}{k} \right) \qquad (6)$$

The growth rates w and v are external market phenomena. In a state of steady growth with a constant population, with a constant proportion of the national income going to wages, and with no relative shifts in the demand for different types of labour, w would be equal to the rate of growth of the total national income. In a state of steady growth v would be zero. But the importance of the parameter w in the inequality (6) would depend for any one individual very greatly upon the value of Q for him, i.e. upon the extent to which at that particular point of time in his accumulation process earnings were or were not of great importance in his total income. For a man with little property relatively to his earnings a high rate of increase of demand for labour in the market (w) would be an important factor raising the rate of accumulation of his property.

If we make some greatly simplified assumptions about the form of equations (1), (3), and (4) we can see how property would be accumulated over time. Let us assume that equation (1) is of the form

$$\frac{dK}{dt} = S(Y - \bar{Y}) - \theta K \qquad (7)$$

where S, Y, and θ are constants. This would imply that if a man's property were zero, he would save a constant proportion (S) of the excess of his income over some basic subsistence level ($\overline{Y}$). His marginal propensity to save (S) would remain constant but his average propensity to save $\left(S - \dfrac{S\overline{Y}}{Y} \right)$ would rise and approach his marginal propensity to save (S) as his income (Y) increased. But we add the assumption that as his property grows this amount of savings is reduced by an amount θK, because the higher his property the less he needs to save.

Let us assume that in equations (3) and (4) both W and V are independent of K, that W grows through time at a constant proportional rate w, and that V remains constant, so that in place of equations (3) and (4) we have

$$W = W_0 e^{wt} \tag{8}$$
$$\text{and } V = \text{constant} \tag{9}$$

From equations (2), (7), (8), and (9) we derive the differential equation

$$\frac{dK}{dt} = SW_0 L e^{wt} + (SV - \theta) K - S\overline{Y} \tag{10}$$

The solution of this equation gives

$$K = \frac{S\overline{Y}}{SV - \theta} + \frac{SW_0 L}{w + \theta - SV} e^{wt}$$
$$+ \frac{1}{V} \left(Y_0 - \overline{Y} - \frac{wW_0 L}{w + \theta - SV} \right) e^{(SV - \theta)t} \tag{11}$$

where $Y_0 = W_0 L + V K_0$.

The nature of the outcome of this process of accumulation will depend upon which of the two roots in (11) is the larger, w or $SV - \theta$. In our constant-population growing economy we can perhaps make a first approach to the relationship between w and $SV - \theta$ on the following lines. Consider a production function for the economy as a whole

$$Y^* = Y^* (K^*, t)$$

where the starred terms represent the aggregate sum of all the corresponding items for all the individual citizens. We have

$$\frac{1}{Y^*} \frac{dY^*}{dt} = \frac{\partial Y^*}{\partial K^*} \frac{\dfrac{dK^*}{dt}}{Y^*} + \frac{1}{Y^*} \frac{\partial Y^*}{\partial t}$$

We can write this as

$$y^* = S^* V + r \tag{12}$$

where y^* is the rate of growth of the total real national income, $V = \dfrac{\partial Y^*}{\partial K^*}$ is the rate of profit, S^* is the proportion of the total national income saved and invested, and

$r \equiv \dfrac{1}{Y*}\dfrac{\partial Y*}{\partial t}$ is the rate of technical progress. If every individual has the same savings function as given in equation (7), then

$$S* = \frac{SY* - S\overline{Y}* - \theta K*}{Y*} \tag{13}$$

where $\overline{Y}* = \overline{Y}$ multiplied by the number of individual savers. It follows that

$$S - S* = \frac{S\overline{Y}* + \theta K*}{Y*} \tag{14}$$

Since $SV - \theta = S*V + (S - S*)V - \theta,$
we have from (12) and (14)

$$SV - \theta = y* - r - \theta Q* + SV\frac{\overline{Y}*}{Y*} \tag{15}$$

where $1 - Q* = \dfrac{VK*}{Y*}$ is the proportion of the national income paid in profits.

It follows from (15) that

$$w \gtreqqless SV - \theta$$

according as

$$w - y* + r + \theta Q* \gtreqqless SV\frac{\overline{Y}*}{Y*}$$

If the process of economic growth is such as to keep the proportion of the national income going to wages ($Q*$) fairly constant, then w will be approximately equal to $y*$. In this case

$$w > SV - \theta, \text{ if } r + \theta Q* > SV\frac{\overline{Y}*}{Y*}$$

which is very likely to be the case.[32]

We are not, of course, yet building a reliable bridge between the theory of economic growth and the theory of the distribution of the ownership of property. For in the equations which refer to individuals, such as equation (11), we are simply assuming that w and V are constant. But the total amount saved by the community as a whole depends upon the aggregate of individual savings arising as each individual, starting from whatever situation he happens to be in, saves according to equation (10). But we have no right to assume w and V constant unless the aggregate savings which do so arise happen to provide such a level of total savings as do in fact (given the rate and form of technical progress) cause w and V to remain constant. We still need to incorporate into the general model of economic growth the savings which will result from our aggregate of individuals' behaviour and then see whether and, if so, along what path – starting from any arbitrarily given distribution of the ownership of property – the economy will approach a state of steady growth in which w and V will be constant and there will be a corresponding steady-state pattern for the distribution of the ownership of property. But until such a general model has been built we must content ourselves with the partial model of equation (11). If w and V were given and constant, then our individual's capital stock would behave as in equation (11).

If in equation (11) $w > SV - \theta$, then,

$$\frac{1-Q}{Q} \equiv \frac{KV}{WL} \to \frac{SV}{w + \theta - SV} \text{ as } t \to \infty.$$

The ratio of each individual's unearned to his earned income will approach this value. Another way of putting this is to say that in each individual's case the value of his property (K) will approach a given ratio $\left(\dfrac{S}{w + \theta - SV}\right)$ of his earnings. It follows that if there were two citizens 1 and 2 starting with different properties $(K'_0$ and $K''_0)$ and different earning powers $(W'_0 L'$ and $W''_0 L'')$ but with the same savings function $(S, \theta,$ and $\overline{Y}$ the same for both) and the same market opportunities $(w$ and V the same for both) they would end up with properties proportional to their earning powers, so that

$$\frac{K'}{K''} \to \frac{W'_0 L'}{W''_0 L''} \text{ as } t \to = \infty.$$

If in equation (11), $w < SV - \theta$, then $\dfrac{1-Q}{Q} \equiv \dfrac{KV}{WL}$ grows without limit. Income from property becomes an ever greater proportion of total income. But if we take again two individuals with different initial endowments of property and earning power but with the same savings functions and market opportunities, we find that

$$\frac{K'}{K''} \to \frac{W'_0 L' \dfrac{SV - \theta}{SV - \theta - w} + VK'_0 - \overline{Y}}{W''_0 L'' \dfrac{SV - \theta}{SV - \theta - w} + VK''_0 - \overline{Y}} \text{ as } t \to \infty.$$

If $w = 0$, this means that the ratio between their properties will ultimately equal the ratio between the excesses of their initial incomes from work and property $(W_0 L + VK_0)$ over the basic subsistence level from which no saving is made ($\overline{Y}$). But if $SV - \theta > w > 0$, then it is still the initial excess of earned and unearned income over the subsistence level which will determine the outcome but with the initial earned income raised by the factor

$$\frac{SV - \theta}{SV - \theta - w}.$$

APPENDIX III   A PROPOSED SCALE FOR A NEW LEGACY AND GIFT DUTY

If, as is discussed in the main text (pp. 53–5), it were desired to make a new legacy and gift duty dependent upon the total wealth of the beneficiary, it would be necessary to devise a scale of progression for the duty which made the rate of duty dependent both upon the size of the beneficiary's existing property and also upon the size of the legacy or gift. It is suggested that the basic formula for the rate of tax (T) on the legacy or gift might be of the form $\frac{B+K}{B+C}$, where B is the value of the bequest, K is the value of the beneficiary's existing property before the receipt of the legacy or gift, and C is a constant. If $K \geqslant C$, the above formula for T would give a rate of duty $\geqslant 100$ per cent. Clearly one could not envisage a rate of duty above 100 per cent, so that one would have to set an upper limit to T. If one set this upper limit at 100 per cent, then C would represent the upper limit to which the value of an individual property could be raised by a legacy or gift. It is, however, proposed in this Appendix that an upper limit for T be set at 90 per cent, so that the rate of tax be $\frac{B+K}{B+C}$ or 90 per cent, whichever was the lower. It is also proposed in this Appendix that C be set at £100,000.

In order to avoid the administrative problems of taxing many small legacies and gifts, it is proposed that the first £1,000 of duty under the tax formula be remitted in all cases. The tax payable would thus be $TB - 1,000$ or nil, whichever were the greater.

Table 2.7 on page 78 shows the effect which this formula would have for various combinations of values of B and K. The figures against the lines D show the total duty payable under this formula, and those against the lines P show the total value of the property of the beneficiary after the receipt of the legacy or gift. The figures to the north-west of the heavy line are all cases in which no tax would be charged; those to the south-east of the heavy broken line are all cases in which the fixed maximum rate of duty of 90 per cent would be payable. In the cases in between these lines an accurate valuation of existing properties as well as of legacies or gifts would be needed for the administration of the scheme.

Table 2.7 A Proposed Scale for Revised Duty on Gifts and Legacies (£000s)

B, i.e. Gross Legacy or Gift

		K, i.e. Property before Legacy or Gift									
		0	1	2	5	10	50	100	200	500	1000
1	D	0	0	0	0	0	0	0	0	0	0
	P	1	2	3	6	11	51	101	201	501	1001
2	D	0	0	0	0	0	0·02	0·8	0·8	0·8	0·8
	P	2	3	4	7	12	51·98	100·2	200·2	500·2	1000·2
5	D	0	0	0	0	0	1·6	3·5	3·5	3·5	3·5
	P	5	6	7	10	15	53·4	101·5	201·5	501·5	1001·5
10	D	0	0	0·1	0·36	0·82	4·5	8	8	8	8
	P	10	11	11·9	14·64	19·18	55·5	102	202	502	1002
50	D	15·7	16·0	16·3	17·3	19·0	32·3	44	44	44	44
	P	34·3	35·0	35·7	37·7	41·0	67·7	106	206	506	1006
100	D	49·0	49·5	50·0	51·5	54·0	74·0	89	89	89	89
	P	51	51·5	52·0	53·5	56·0	76·0	111	211	511	1011
200	D	132·3	133·0	133·7	135·7	139·0	165·7	179	179	179	179
	P	67·7	68·0	68·3	69·3	71·0	84·3	121	221	521	1021
500	D	415·7	416·5	417·3	419·8	424·0	449	449	449	449	449
	P	84·3	84·5	84·7	85·2	86·0	101	151	251	551	1051
1000	D	899	899	899	899	899	899	899	899	899	899
	P	101	102	104	106	111	151	201	301	601	1101

D shows the total Duty paid

P shows the value of the Property after receipt of legacy or gift and after payment of duty.

Notes

1. The paper was written for the United Nations Conference on Trade and Development. It is reproduced in *Lloyds Bank Review*, July 1964.
2. 'Mauritius: A Case Study in Malthusian Economics', *Economic Journal*, September 1961. The following paragraphs are based on this article.
3. The fact that in many underdeveloped countries the wage rate is higher than it would be in full-employment competitive equilibrium may be one of the main reasons which explains the paradox that capital appears to be attracted for investment into developed countries such as the United States, the United Kingdom and Germany, where the ratio of capital to labour is already high, rather than into underdeveloped countries where the supply of capital is low relatively to that of labour. The return on capital in such underdeveloped countries would be much higher if the wage rate were reduced to correspond to the marginal product of labour in conditions of full employment.
4. I am indebted to Mr J. R. S. Revell of the Department of Applied Economics of the University of Cambridge for these figures.
5. The figures for the concentration of property ownership and those for the concentration of income from property are not strictly comparable, since in the former the population relates to all individuals over 25 in England and Wales while in the latter it refers to the total number of income-tax units in the United Kingdom.
6. For the source of these figures see Appendix I (pp. 69–71). It is to be noted that the figures in the last column of Table 2.1 (p. 34) differ from those for (p) in Table 2.2 because the former show the percentages of income from property accruing to the persons who have the largest incomes *from property* whereas the latter show the percentages of income from property accruing to persons who have the largest incomes *from all sources*. Thus in Table 2.2 the richest citizens include some who have very high earnings but not such high incomes from property. Income from property is necessarily more concentrated in Table 2.1 than in Table 2.2. The figures in Table 2.2 show the distribution of incomes before equalisation through taxation.
7. These figures are taken from Theodore W. Schultz, *The Economic Value of Education*.
8. Even if one confined one's attention to the capital sunk in the education of the labour force, this percentage would still be 30 per cent.
9. Theodore W. Schultz, *op. cit.*, mentions rates of return of 35 per cent per annum on elementary education, 10 per cent per annum on high school education, and 11 per cent per annum on college education for the United States of America in 1959.
10. Theodore W. Schultz, *op. cit.*, gives an estimate of a rise in the number of years of schooling completed per person from 4.14 in 1900 to 10.45 in 1957 in the United States of America. Since the later years of schooling are so much more expensive than the early years of elementary school, the cost of capital sunk in education per person has gone up even more markedly between 1900 and 1957 from $2,236 to $7,555 (dollars of constant 1956 purchasing power).
11. In the 'Rate of Profit and Income Distribution in Relation to the Rate of Economic Growth' (*Review of Economic Studies*, volume XXIX, no. 4) Dr

Pasinetti assumes two classes of persons: workers who save a low proportion of their income and capitalists who do no work but save a high proportion of their income. Since workers save, they also accumulate property; and Dr Pasinetti is concerned with the distribution of property between workers and capitalists which will result from this dual process of capital accumulation as time passes. His object is to consider the ultimate steady-state ratio between savings and profits in order to use this relationship for the theory of economic growth. In an article by myself on 'The Rate of Profit in a Growing Economy' (*Economic Journal*, December 1963) I criticised some of Dr Pasinetti's assumptions but suggested that the Pasinetti process, with certain modifications of assumptions about the distribution of earning power and about propensities to save, might serve as a powerful instrument in analysing the forces affecting the distribution of the ownership of property. It is this application of the Pasinetti process which is the subject of the present section of this chapter.

12. *Absolute* inequality (i.e. K_2-K_1) might, of course, be increasing; but it is, I think, *relative* inequality which should concern us most. That one property should be £10,000 greater than another may be of great importance where K_1 is £1,000 and K_2 is £11,000 and of very little importance if K_1 is £100,000 and K_2 £110,000.

13. See Table 2.1 (p. 34). It will be remembered that at this stage we are dealing with incomes before tax is deducted.

14. The influence of capital gains could be even more marked than is implied in the text. Suppose that property owners regard as their income only the income paid out on their property and save a fraction of this, but in addition automatically accumulate 100 per cent of any capital gain not paid out in dividend or rent or interest. Then the formula for k becomes $k = S\dfrac{E}{K} + SV + V'$ where V is the paid-out rate of return on capital and V' is the rate of return from capital gains. An excess of V'_2 over V'_1 will have an even more marked effect than an equal excess of V_2 over V_1 in raising k_2 above k_1.

15. Strong evidence for the importance of these factors in the savings function is given in Richard Stone, 'Private Saving in Britain: Past, Present and Future' The Manchester School, May 1964.

16. These processes of accumulation and their effects upon the distribution of property are examined more technically in Appendix II (pp. 72–6).

17. See Michael Young and John Gibson, 'In Search of an Explanation of Social Mobility', *British Journal of Statistical Psychology*, XVI, 27–36.

18. See C. O. Carter, *Human Heredity*.

19. These figures are quoted from Sir Cyril Burt, 'Intelligence and Social Mobility' (*British Journal of Statistical Psychology*, XIV, 3–25) by Michael Young and John Gibson *op. cit.*, p.29. [*Note added in 1992*. The reliability of Sir Cyril Burt's table has been severely criticised for the slipshod and unprofessional way in which the figures were collected and presented. See Leon J Kamin, 'The Science and Politics of I.Q.', 1974. However, in so far as there is an inherited factor in whatever is measured by general intelligence tests there will almost certainly be a marked regression to the mean since the inherited factor is unlikely to be determined by only a small number of genes.]

20.   The preceding paragraphs suggest that (i) low fertility and (ii) high ability to earn may both be factors which tend to raise people upon the social scale and the property ladder. These factors probably both have some genetic elements in their determination. Moreover, it is a well-known fact that men and women are likely to marry within their own class. Thus there may be a continuous process tending to mate the genes for ability with those for infertility and the genes for inability with those for fertility. The dysgenic aspect of such a social arrangement is obvious (cf. Professor R. A. Fisher, *The Social Selection of Human Fertility*).

21.   This is the present [1964] rate of United Kingdom duty on estates of £10,000.

22.   An actual scale of duty which might be used is expounded in Appendix III (pp. 77–8).

23.   Some other and perhaps lower fixed rate of duty might be set for all charitable gifts and bequests.

24.   See, for example, Brian Jackson and Dennis Marsden, *Education and the Working Class*, and J. W. B. Douglas, *The Home and the School*.

25.   See Theodore W. Schultz, *op. cit.*

26.   See Michael Young, *The Rise of the Meritocracy*.

27.   I am indebted to Mr J. R. S. Revell of the Department of Applied Economics in the University of Cambridge for these figures.

28.   At the other extreme it is possible to conceive of a state of affairs in which $\frac{K_s}{K}$ is practically zero but $\frac{K_s - D}{K}$ is practically $+ 100\%$. This would be the case if practically no real property were in the management-ownership of the State ($K_s = 0$), if private entrepreneurs managed and ran for competitive profit practically all the real property of the community, and if these private businesses were directly or indirectly financed to a very large extent by loans from the State (D is a large negative figure). The State would ultimately own most property; but this would take the form of the opposite of a national debt, namely a large indebtedness of private persons to the State. The State's loans might be made to individuals, to business companies, or to investment trusts which held shares in business. Business would be managed on a competitive free enterprise basis, but ultimate ownership of much property would be in the hands of the State.

29.   For a fuller discussion of this point see J. E. Meade, 'Is the National Debt a Burden?' and 'Is the National Debt a Burden? A Correction', *Oxford Economic Papers*, June 1958 and February 1959.

30.   For the sake of the uninstructed may I explain that this is a British way of saying 99.9 per cent.

31.   I am indebted to Mr J. R. S. Revell and Mr A. Armstrong of the Department of Applied Economics of the University of Cambridge for the figures on which this Appendix is based.

32.   Suppose $S = \frac{1}{2}$, $V = 10$ per cent per annum, and $\frac{\bar{Y}*}{Y*} = \frac{1}{5}$, then if the rate of technical progress were more than 1 per cent per annum, w would be $> SV - \theta$ even if $\theta = 0$.

Part II

3 Can We Learn a 'Third Way' from the Agathotopians?*

The inhabitants of the Island of Agathotopia (A Good Place to Live In) claim to have built an economy which combines the best features of Socialism with the best features of Capitalism. What can we learn from them?

Wherever competition is possible a free price-mechanism market is a better method than a centrally designed and controlled plan for obtaining an efficient system of production in a free society.

But private competition does not necessarily involve a Capitalist Company, in which the owners of the capital funds hire workers at an agreed wage rate with or without some element of profit sharing and run the concern directly or through the appointment of managers. An alternative institutional set-up is the Labour-Managed Labour-Owned Cooperative where the workers hire the capital and run the concern. For their part the Agathotopians have developed an institutional arrangement, the Labour-Capital Partnership, whereby the workers and those who provide risk capital jointly manage the concern as partners. The capitalists own Capital Shares in the business, which are comparable to Ordinary Shares in a Capitalist Company. The worker partners own Labour Shares in the partnership; these Labour Shares are entitled to the same rate of dividend as the Capital Shares, but they are attached to each individual worker partner and are cancelled when he or she leaves the partnership. If any part of the partnership's income is not distributed in dividends but is used to develop the business, new Capital Shares, equal in value to their sacrificed dividends, are issued to all existing holders of Labour as well as of Capital Shares. These partnership arrangements greatly reduce the areas of conflict

---

* First published in the *Royal Bank of Scotland Review*, September 1990, and subsequently presented at an International Economic Association Conference on 'The Economics of Partnership' in September 1991, the proceedings of which were published in 1993 as *Alternatives to Capitalism*, edited by Anthony B. Atkinson (Macmillan).

of interest between workers and capitalists, since any decision which will improve the situation of one group by raising the rate of dividend on its shares will automatically raise the rate of dividend on the shares of the other group.

I

This participatory private enterprise competitive structure raises three quite basic issues concerning:

—   the bearing of risks,
—   the distribution of income, and
—   the maintenance of a high and stable level of employment (full employment)

These are considered in turn.

The Bearing of Risks

In Labour-Managed Cooperatives, in Labour-Capital Partnerships and in Capitalist Companies with profit-sharing arrangements the workers must bear the risks of the enterprise in whole or in part. Moreover, if workers are to participate in decision-making they will inevitably have to participate in the results of those decisions and, in one or other of these institutional forms, to share in the risks that the decision may not be a successful one. In the Agathotopian Labour-Capital Partnership, for example, they share with the capitalists the risks of variations in the rate of dividend which can be paid on their shares.

There is, however, one very simple reason why capitalists who can spread their shareholdings and thus their risks over a large number of concerns should be better able to face risks than workers who will earn all their income from one single concern in which their risk is concentrated. A fall in the demand for the product of a Labour-Capital Partnership, of a Labour-Owned Cooperative or of a Profit-Sharing Company will cause a reduction of a worker's income, whereas in a fixed-wage Capitalist Company it would lead to a reduction of employment. Thus while the risk of a reduction in a worker's income is greater, the risk of his or her employment is less. Nevertheless the question remains whether workers will be willing, and indeed whether they should be urged, to accept a variable dividend rather than a fixed wage for the work which they undertake, unless their variable income from work can be combined with some other source of secure fixed income.

The Distribution of Income

The problem of the distribution of income between the workers and the owners of capital arises in any system of production which rests on free competition in a free market. There are certain basic features of the market which will determine in any free competitive system how much of the product will go to the workers and how much to the owners of capital. These are:

— the extent to which consumers spend their money on products which require a high or on products which require a low proportion of labour to capital in their production;
— the extent to which technological advances are primarily labour-saving or capital-saving; and
— the extent to which there is a high or a low proportion of labour to capital seeking productive employment.

If consumers demand products which require much capital equipment and little labour in their production; if technical methods of production save labour rather than capital; and if there is much labour seeking employment against a restricted supply of available capital, earnings on work are likely to be low and profits on the use of capital are likely to be high. This is true of Labour-Managed Cooperatives and of Labour-Capital Partnerships as well as of Capitalist Companies in free market competitive conditions. In Labour-Capital Partnerships, for example, the amount of Capital Shares which would be needed to attract a part of the restricted supply of capital into any one of the many competing capital-intensive uses would have to be great relatively to the amount of Labour Shares which would need to be offered to attract many otherwise unemployed workers into the restricted openings for labour. Labour-Capital Partnerships or Labour-Managed Co-operatives or Profit-Sharing Schemes enable workers to enjoy a part of exceptionally high profits made in exceptionally successful enterprises, but the underlying basic distribution will depend upon the underlying supply–demand conditions for labour and capital. In present conditions, with heavy unemployment and much technical innovation designed to replace labour with capital equipment, full employment in competitive conditions may imply an increase in the proportion of income which accrues to profits.

The Maintenance of Full Employment

The problem of full employment is thus essentially the mirror image of the problem of distribution. The maintenance of a high real wage rate or other form of earnings on work may prevent a shift from earnings on work to profits on capital, but it will discourage the employment of labour and will thus imply a reduction in output and employment below the potential full employment level.

II

Necessary Changes in Economic Institutions

Agathotopian experience suggests that a successful attack on this joint problem of distribution and full employment requires two simultaneous changes in economic institutions. First, there must be some change in institutions and policies which concern the fixing of money prices and of rates of pay and other earnings in order to make them more flexible, particularly in a downward direction, to promote employment. Second, there must be some arrangements outside the individual enterprises to ensure that all workers receive a supplementary reliable income outside their work place. This is needed both to offset a lower rate of earnings from work and also to provide security if their earnings from work take a risky and uncertain form.

The Need for Wage and Price Flexibility

In Agathotopia there is a widespread structure of Labour-Capital Partnerships. But there remain cases in which such partnerships are not suitable and in which fixed-wage private or public corporations exist. For all forms of activity the Agathotopians have a very extensive set of rules and institutions to prevent monopolistic arrangements, to promote competition, and, where monopolistic action is unavoidable as in many public utility services, to control prices and other charges. They apply these principles to the labour market as well as to other economic activities. Thus they have set strict limitations on the use of monopolistic powers by trade unions and similar worker organisations.

In the case of fixed-wage private companies or public corporations they have instituted a system of compulsory arbitration to settle disputes about rates of pay, the arbitrators being required to set the wage at a level which will promote employment. They have also introduced a scheme for the taxation of any rise in a company's average rate of pay which exceeds a given moderate growth-rate norm.

In the case of their Labour-Capital Partnerships they recognise that workers' participation in decision-making exacerbates the problem of attaining and maintaining full employment. In such Partnerships and in Labour Cooperatives, the objective of the existing working partners will naturally be to raise the income per existing partner to the highest possible level. In a fixed-wage Capitalist Company the objective of the owners is to maximise their total income, which will be achieved by taking on more workers at the agreed wage rate so long as this adds to the total profit of the concern. In an enterprise in which working partners share the profit, the working partners will wish to restrict the taking on of more workers as soon as this threatens, not the *total profit* of the enterprise but, the *profit per head* of the enterprise. Restricting the number of heads will be as important to them as increasing the total profit. Expansion of employment in a profitable Labour Co-operative or Labour-Capital Partnership will tend to be more restricted than in a profitable fixed-wage Capitalist Company.

To offset this restrictive tendency the Agathotopians have laid much stress on running Labour-Capital Partnerships on the principle that in a successful partnership the extra profit being enjoyed by the existing partners need not be shared by any additional partners who are added to the enterprise. This rule avoids the restrictive effects. New partners are taken on with an issue of additional shares which is sufficient to attract them but which is not necessarily as great as the number of shares held by existing working partners. This means that in any exceptionally successful partnership the bonus enjoyed by existing partners in the form of the high dividends being earned on their shares is not diluted by issuing an equally large number of shares to the newcomers. In one way or another this involves the discontinuation of the old rule of 'equal pay for equal work' for old and newly employed workers. With these arrangements in any given partnership the principle of discrimination thus leads to a high level of employment; and the principle of variable dividends on labour shares leads to a more stable level of employment, because the immediate impact effect of a fall in the demand for the products of the enterprise is a fall in the dividend incomes of the working partners rather than the dismissal of fixed-wage workers.

The Agathotopians have thus succeeded in preserving full employment without inflation in their competitive market economy by means of a combination of two factors.

First, they have instituted a very effective set of financial policies (both monetary and fiscal) to ensure that the total of money expenditure on the Island's production of goods and services grows at a steady but moderate rate and is not subject to inflationary or deflationary surges.

Second, against the background of this steadily rising demand for the products of labour they leave it to their anti-monopoly policies, to their price controls, to their arbitration procedures, to their anti-inflation tax, and above all to the discriminatory principle in their partnerships to ensure that increased demand wherever possible leads to increased output and employment rather than to inflated money prices and rates of pay.

The system works in the following way. Suppose there to be a situation in which employment is low, output is restricted and the price level is inflated because of the scarcity of products for sale. With the discriminatory principle every partnership would take on more worker partners so long as unemployed workers were willing to join the partnership at a rate of pay which did not exceed the value to the partnership of the additional output produced by the additional worker partner. With the individual competing partnerships expanding in this way output would be increased and prices would be deflated.

The Need for an Assured Basic Income

The Agathotopians regard the successful introduction of institutions for achieving the necessary flexibility of rates of wages and of other forms of earnings as by far the most difficult economic problem which they have had to face. They are quite clear that their introduction would have been impossible if they had not been accompanied by effective measures to ensure that workers had, in addition to their earnings from work, a secure fixed income from some other source. They realised that such an alternative source of income would have an obvious equalising effect on the distribution of income. It would greatly reduce the problem of risk-bearing by worker partners since it would constitute a completely risk-free component of income. Finally, by reducing the concentrated reliance of workers on their earnings for the finance of their needs it would be a necessary condition for the political acceptance of that flexibility in rates of pay which was necessary for the attainment and maintenance of full employment.

The Agathotopians recognise that the payment of a secure fixed income from some source other than pay for work done may in some cases lead to a citizen choosing not to work but to live solely on this unearned income. They have accepted the danger of this result for four reasons.

(i)   They have restricted the payment of this secure income to a basic level low enough to ensure that not many are tempted to idleness of this kind.

(ii)   The payment of this secure income was introduced only as and when the measures for the downward flexibility of rates of pay took effect to increase the demand for labour. They set the resulting reduction of previous involuntary unemployment against any rise in voluntary idleness.

(iii) The payment of the secure income, unlike the previous payment of unemployment benefit, was not cancelled when a citizen found work, so that with the new system there would always be some incentive for a citizen to add to his or her income by accepting work however low the rate at which it was paid.

(iv)   Finally the Agathotopians are immune from the unbridled urge for unlimited growth and unnecessary consumerism. They were prepared if necessary to accept some reduction in total national output as a price for an improvement in its distribution.

III

The Necessary Fiscal Measures

There are in fact three main ways in which there can be assured to every citizen an income which is divorced from the level of, and the risks attached to, earned income.

—   A first method is to design measures to attain and maintain a widespread ownership of capital wealth, so that every citizen has the benefit of some income from rent, interest, or dividends with the opportunity of reducing the risk of such incomes by spreading his or her ownership of property over a large number of independent sources. At the extreme if the ownership of wealth were distributed among citizens in the same widespread manner as the ability to earn income, a shift of national income from pay for work to profits on capital would have no adverse distributive effects. What the citizen lost on the swings of pay he or she would gain on the roundabouts of profit.

—   A second method is to replace existing social benefits which are paid to various categories of people (e.g., unemployment benefit, sickness benefit, etc.) by a single Basic Income payable to every citizen and financed simply out of the general tax revenues of the State.

—   A third method is to arrange that, by one means or another, the State itself becomes the beneficial owner of a large part of the country's capital wealth so that it can use the rents, profits, or dividends received on that wealth for distribution in the form of an equal Social Dividend for each citizen.

The Agathotopians have made use of all of these three methods.

The Ownership of Capital

They have taken steps to attain and then to maintain a more widespread and less unequal distribution of the ownership of capital in a way which is compatible with the greatest possible freedom of enterprise. They have exempted all savings from income tax and have combined this with a moderate annual rate of tax on large holdings of wealth and with heavy taxation on the transfers of wealth above a certain limit by gift *inter vivos* or by bequest at death. This enables citizens with little wealth to accumulate savings without any tax and allows individual entrepreneurs to use their wealth and plough back their savings into their business with little adverse tax effects. But the heavy taxation of transfers of wealth means that heavy concentrations of wealth in single ownership cannot be passed on.

The Role of Taxation

The Agathotopians pay a Basic Income free of tax to all citizens. This payment has replaced expenditure on many other social benefits which are no longer needed. It has also been combined with the elimination of all personal allowances under their saving-exempt income tax, all sources of income other than the Basic Income being subject to tax. For example, they include in the tax base an imputed rent on all owner-occupied homes or other real property. In Agathotopia tax evasion is considered a very serious crime and they devote substantial resources to ensuring that such evasion is kept to a minimum. But the payment of a Basic Income on an adequate level they found to be a hideously expensive affair even after allowance was made for all these offsets. An intolerably high marginal rate of tax on savings-exempt income would have occurred if they had not had recourse to other sources.

The strain on the Agathotopian budget has recently been much relieved by improved political relations with their neighbours in the surrounding Topian Islands. This has enabled them to make substantial reductions in their expenditure on defence. This so-called peace dividend has been helpful to finance the raising of their Basic Income to a more adequate level.

Also recently their tax revenue has been transformed by their concern to reduce the pollution of the environment which has resulted from modern methods of production. They set up a special Commission to survey the problem and to specify the cases in which the social environmental costs of certain activities were not being reflected in the private costs and prices at which such activities were being marketed. Such activities were the pollution of the atmosphere through the burning of fossil fuel; the congestion of road space through its free use for traffic and for the parking of vehicles; the disposal of wastes in rivers; the use of fertilisers which indirectly affected water supplies; and so on. The Agathotopians have consistently tackled these problems wherever possible by charging the polluter for the previously free use of the atmosphere or natural resources.

This they have done by the application of three rules: (i) to reduce the pollution by a tax or other charge rather than by direct regulation which raises no revenue; (ii) to tax the polluter rather than subsidise the non-polluting alternative (e.g., to tax the private car rather than to subsidise the public bus as a means of reducing road congestion); and (iii) to raise revenue by auctioning the necessary pollution permits to the highest bidder rather than distributing the permits without charge on some other principle in those cases in which quantitative regulation is deemed to be necessary.

The yield of revenue raised in this way has been very good. Not all this gross yield represents a net gain, since the pollution taxation of some activities has led to the reduction of the yield of other taxes on those activities. Moreover, in order to avoid the most undesirable distributional effects the level of Basic Income has had to be raised to offset the rise in price of such amounts of the newly taxed goods and services as were necessary to maintain an adequate minimum standard of living. However, there remained a very substantial net revenue bonus even after allowing for these offsets. The reliance on a pollution tax (whose incentive effects are socially desirable) rather than on taxes, such as the income tax (whose disincentive effects on work and enterprise are undesirable), has enabled a given level of real Basic Income to be maintained at a markedly lower social cost.

The Agathotopians also raise a considerable revenue through the taxation of expensive commercial advertising. This measure is a matter of some controversy in the Island. Its proponents regard such advertising as wasteful and polluting: wasteful because A spends money to attract B's customers while B spends money to attract A's customers to little or no advantage to

either; polluting because it encourages the undesirable attitudes of consumers in throwing away the old for the new and in purchasing goods and
services which they do not really need, but which put a strain on the
community's resources.

Another form of tax employed by the Agathotopians to finance a really
adequate Basic Income is the imposition of a special surcharge on the first
slice of every citizen's income other than the Basic Income itself. This is a
form of levy which in effect withdraws part of the Basic Income as a
citizen's other income increases, a levy which is additional to the ordinary
current rate of tax on income. This turned the Agathotopian Basic Income
into something which is half way between a fully conditional social benefit
and a fully unconditional social benefit. With a fully conditional benefit a
citizen without other income is given a full-scale benefit, but this benefit is
reduced pound for pound as the citizen's other income increases. This is the
cheapest way to ensure that everyone has a minimum guaranteed income.
Benefit is paid only so far as it is needed to bring income up to the minimum
level. But it has the well-known effects of removing any incentive to earn
any additional income, so long as any such income will be matched by an
equivalent reduction in social benefit. On the other hand a completely
unconditional social benefit removes this disincentive effect, since the same
tax-free social benefit is received regardless of the level of other income.
But it is hideously expensive in that it hands out free of tax an adequate
social benefit to every citizen however rich or poor. The Agathotopian
Basic Income with a Surcharge on the first slice of other income falls
between these two extremes. Every citizen, rich or poor, receives the same
tax-free Basic Income but the Surcharge on the first slice of other income is
the equivalent of a withdrawal of part of the Basic Income, not pound for
pound but, say, one pound for every two pounds earned. The Surcharge may
weaken but will not eliminate the incentive to earn more income; it can
however, enormously reduce the cost of the Basic Income.

State Ownership of Capital: Topsy Turvy Nationalisation

Finally, there is a still more radical way in which the Agathotopians have
raised finance for a Basic Income. The Agathotopian State does not possess
a National Debt; it possesses instead a National Asset equal in value to
some 50 per cent of the total productive wealth of the country. The government does not manage the productive concerns which lie behind this wealth.
It simply invests its wealth on the competitive Stock Exchange in the form
of holdings in private competitive investment trusts and similar financial

institutions. Thus the State's wealth is mingled with the savings of the private sector of the economy for investment in productive enterprises which are competitively managed as free-enterprise undertakings.

This arrangement corresponds to what has been called Topsy Turvy Nationalisation. With the Nationalisation schemes undertaken, for example, by the Labour government in the UK after the Second World War the State took over the ownership and the centralised management of steel, railways, electricity, coal, etc. But the State paid full compensation to the previous owners which meant that the State did not receive for its own free use the profits of such concerns, since this was offset by the payment of interest on the national debt issued to raise the compensation cost of the nationalisation schemes. Thus the State became the owner-manager but without the benefit of an increased income. With Agathotopian Topsy Turvy Nationalisation the State obtains the beneficial ownership of the income earned on certain capital assets without undertaking any responsibility for the management of the business concerns which is left to the private market.

The post-tax income so acquired by the Agathotopian State is used towards the finance of the Basic Income payable to all citizens. This source of revenue once it had been established has had no disadvantageous disincentive effects. The revenue accrues directly to the State and does not involve levying any rate of tax on anyone's earnings or expenditures; and since the transfer of capital assets to the beneficial ownership of the State has not been carried to excess, it is compatible with leaving the conduct of businesses to private competition. There are enough privately owned capital funds left for the operations of an effective free competitive capital market.

How did the Agathotopians ever reach this happy state of affairs in which the State came to own a National Asset in place of an existing National Debt?

There was one possibility which made a limited but nevertheless worthwhile contribution to the outcome. The State owned a number of business concerns which it managed itself and these enterprises were earning smaller profits than they would have made if they had been operated for maximum return by private competitive enterprise. Their privatisation was a help. They were sold to private entrepreneurs at the highest possible price which the State could achieve and the sale proceeds were used by the State to redeem National Debt on terms which led to a reduction in interest on the National Debt which exceeded the low profit previously being earned on these assets under State management. Of course such privatisation was a help only because the revenue received from the sale of such assets was used by the State to reduce debt. It would not have helped if it had been used to finance current expenditures. In any case its contribution to the problem was strictly limited and the Agathotopians sought a further measure for raising the funds necessary for the accumulation of a National Asset.

For this purpose they drew a distinction between capital taxes, (i.e., those which were likely to be paid largely out of the current savings or holdings of wealth of the taxpayer), and current taxes, (i.e., those which were likely to be paid largely at the expense of the taxpayer's current consumption). They realised that any such distinction was bound to be very rough and ready. But they made it by putting the yield of their Wealth Tax and Capital Transfer Tax into the capital tax category, leaving all other tax revenue in the current tax category.

They defined the current account surplus or deficit of the government's budget as excluding expenditures on capital assets and revenues from capital taxes; and they adopted the policy of ensuring that the government's budget should be managed in such a way as to show a surplus on current account to the extent to which, in the government's opinion, private savings needed supplementation in the national interest.

They instituted a National Asset Commission and arranged that any budgetary surplus on current account and the whole of the yield of their capital taxes were paid into the National Asset Commission. This commission used such funds to redeem the originally existing National Debt and to purchase National Assets investing these funds through investments trusts and similar bodies on the Stock Exchange. The current dividends or other current receipts on such assets were then paid as revenue into the government's current-account budget.

By these means their capital taxes were in fact treated as a continuous, moderate, and acceptable form of capital levy for the gradual building up of an endowment from which a social dividend might be earned to improve the level of Basic Income payable to all citizens. The process was continued until the National Asset Commission held some 50 per cent of the nation's productive wealth, at which point the rates of capital taxation were reduced to the level which was required simply to maintain the National Asset at this 50 per cent level of a growing total national wealth.

The process was a very prolonged one; but it proved to be a method of introducing a steady, reliable and continuous improvement in the level of their Basic Income.

IV

An International Perspective

So much for the question: 'Can we learn a "Third Way" from the Agathotopians?' But this leads to a second question: 'Who are we?' It is interesting to broaden one's horizon and to include among 'us' the countries of Eastern Europe which are in the process of reformulating their own basic structures of economic institutions and policies. What have they to learn from the Agathotopians?

In certain basic matters the Eastern European countries will have a much greater problem than the Western countries in copying the Agathotopians. The institution of free competitive price-mechanism markets to replace centrally designed and controlled plans for their main sectors of production will require a much more radical change than anything needed in Western Europe. It requires not only the development of free markets for products, for capital and for labour, but also the acquisition of the skills, the attitudes and the experiences needed to replace bureaucrats with entrepreneurial managers.

There is, however, one important feature of the Agathotopian society which the countries of Eastern Europe should find it easier to adopt. As already explained, in Agathotopia the State is the beneficial owner of a net National Asset equal in value to some 50 per cent of the island's real capital wealth. The real assets which lie behind this National Asset are operated and managed in private enterprises, the State merely receiving indirectly the dividends, profits, rent or interest paid on 50 per cent of the capital of these private businesses. The countries in Western Europe start with no net National Asset of this kind but for the most part with a National Debt, their holdings of real assets being outweighed by their debt to the private sector of the economy. The socialist economies of Eastern Europe on the other hand start with the State owning a very large proportion of the total real assets of the country.

Thus the Western European State faces the problem of transferring wealth from private to State beneficial ownership, while the Eastern Europe State faces the problem of transferring the beneficial ownership of wealth from the State to private owners. It is not too difficult to guess which of these two forms of transfer would prove the more acceptable proposition politically.

In a number of the socialist economies of Eastern Europe private individuals possess large sums of the country's currency which they have accumulated because of the difficulty of finding goods on which to spend the money: such private unspent liquid funds at present hang over the market. Their expenditure threatens to lead to a great inflation as price controls are removed in the process of setting up free competitive markets. Might not these unspent balances be mopped up by the sale of State-owned property to private citizens in the process of setting up free-enterprise markets? Private citizens could be allowed to use these funds for the purchase from the State of a citizen's house or other dwelling, farm land or of shares newly issued by private enterprises as they were organised to take over the management of existing centrally owned and controlled concerns. The timing of these developments would present difficulties. But might not a currency reform take the form of blocking an appropriate part of present private holdings of liquid funds, these blocked funds being released as State-owned properties of one form or another were put up for sale in privatisation schemes?

Another feature of Agathotopian society which may be of special interest to the Eastern European countries is the structure of the Agathotopian Labour-Capital Partnership. In such partnerships the capitalists do not hire labour at a fixed wage rate nor do the workers hire capital at a fixed rate of interest. Both parties form a partnership to control the enterprise jointly. In the typical Agathotopian partnership the worker partners and the capitalist partners each elect one half of the members of the enterprise's board of directors, who in turn appoint a suitable impartial outsider to act as independent chairman. The board then appoints a general manager together with the other senior managers who are left free to run the enterprise for the mutual benefit of the shareholders irrespective of whether they be holders of Labour or of Capital Shares. With this arrangement there is no exploitation of labour since no capitalist is hiring a worker at a fixed wage to do his bidding. The socialist distaste for the classic form of capitalist–worker relationship should not therefore apply to such partnerships.

V

Conclusion

A study of Agathotopian arrangements suggests a large variety of different institutional and policy possibilities concerning the structures of different forms of private enterprise, of social benefits, of capital taxes, of taxes on income, of taxes on consumption, of pollution charges, of ownership of wealth and of the management of the country's assets. It is unlikely that all

European countries would select exactly the same set of arrangements. This leaves open for future consideration a vast field of study. If one wishes to construct a Community of all European countries which are democratically governed and which operate a basic free competitive market mechanism, how far and by what international means can diversity of experiments in different national economic institutions and policies be made compatible with freedom of movement of goods, capital and people between the member States of the Community?

This is one of the most pressing and important, but sadly neglected, fields for careful thought and study.[1]

Note

1.   These problem are discussed in Chapter 5 of the present book.

4 Agathotopia: The Economics of Partnership*

A Tract for the Times Addressed to All Capitalists and Socialists who Seek to Make the Best of Both Worlds

FOREWORD

Economists have long debated whether or not a capitalist system is compatible with an acceptable distribution of income and with harmony of interests between workers and capitalists. At one extreme have been hard-line Marxists who have claimed that nothing short of state capital ownership will fulfil these aims, whereas, at the other extreme, 'Austrian' economists have maintained that a competitive capitalist system will achieve these objectives but only if it is free from government intervention. At a rough guess it could reasonably be claimed that most western economists of repute would maintain an intermediate position with the distribution of their views along the political spectrum somewhat biased towards support for a free market economy of capitalist profit-making enterprises but one in which the government had a significant part to play in influencing income distribution and in regulating conditions of work.

A few major economists have sought the solution to the problem of economic conflict in the breaking-up of the traditional mould of a hierarchical system of business organisation. 'The form of association . . . which if mankind continue to improve must be expected in the end to predominate is not that which can exist between capitalist as chief and work-people without a voice in the management, but the association of the labourers themselves on terms of equality, collectively owning the capital with which they carry on their operations and working under managers, elected and removable by themselves.' So wrote John Stuart Mill in 1871.

---

* This chapter is a revised version of Hume Paper No. 16, published by Aberdeen University Press for The David Hume Institute, 1989.

In recent years, a burgeoning literature in economic analysis have invest-
igated Mill's 'dream', much of it governed by the hope that labour-managed
enterprises could be demonstrated to be at least as efficient as capitalist
ones, but with the additional satisfaction to workers that they controlled
their own destiny. Very broadly speaking, the verdict of 'not proven' seems
to be the correct label to attach to these demonstrations. In particular, it has
been shown that if firms attempt to maximise the average earnings per
worker in the business, an economy of labour-managed enterprises with
an increasing working population might be characterised by growing unemployment; for it would not be in the interests of those already in employment to expand output by expanding employment. This undesired result
suggests that careful attention has to be paid to the precise rules which
should govern the operation of such enterprises.

The author of *Agathotopia*, Professor James Meade, is one of the outstanding economists of this century, and one of only four British economists
who have become Nobel Laureates in Economics. Throughout a long career
as an economic theorist, who has made major contributions to international
trade theory and macroeconomic theory and policy, he has repeatedly
returned to the question of the ideal organisation of economic life. As the
reader will soon discover, his pursuit of this question is not governed
merely by intellectual curiosity but by his profound concern for the welfare
of his fellow men.

Professor Meade relates that he has discovered the answer to the problem
of reconciling capitalism and socialism by a journey in search of Utopia –
the Perfect Place (strictly speaking 'no place') – but instead he found
Agathotopia – the Good Place which has essayed the modest task of producing good institutions for imperfect people. The Agathotopians, as explained
by their spokesman, Dr Semaj Edaem (whose name will somehow seem
familiar to the reader), have developed, not without difficulty, a novel form
of worker-capitalist partnership in which both workers and capitalists share
the risks, but special fiscal arrangements ensure that income and wealth do
not become intolerably unequal and the poor and unfortunate are cared for
without humiliating enquiry into their circumstances. The retailing of their
views by Professor Meade is compelling. Summarising them would not do
them justice and is in any case unnecessary, given his well-known powers
of exposition. One suspects, however, that the Agathotopians who appear to
be a thoughtful people, have not resisted the importation and adoption of
ideas originating with the scholarly works of a Professor formerly at, to use
the Agathotopian form, the University of Nodnol and latterly at the University of Egdir-Bmac.

The Agathotopian interest has extended to the elaboration of some of their major propositions in mathematical form. Professor Meade has performed the additional service of satisfying those readers who prefer this alternative mode of exposition.

I suspect that readers of Hume Papers may be sharply divided in their opinions of the acceptability of Agathotopian economic institutions, but united in their admiration of the skilful presentation of the Agathotopian case by the author. The Institute has no collective view on policy matters, but feels particularly privileged to act as Professor Meade's vehicle of publication. David Hume, to be sure, would have applauded his approach having himself sought to outline the political rather than the economic organisation which would form 'The Idea of a Perfect Commonwealth' – one of his superb essays. He wrote: 'all plans of government, which suppose great reformation in the manners of mankind are plainly imaginary', which is why he found Utopia wanting and preferred Harrington's Oceana. Like James Meade, he saw his task as that of designing 'good' institutions for imperfect beings. Only great minds are equal to such a task.

ALAN PEACOCK
Executive Director
The David Hume Institute

PREFACE

In March 1988, the Italian 'Lega Nazionale delle Cooperative e Mutue' (League of Cooperative Societies) held a two-day conference in Rome. They were concerned with the problem of introducing equity capital into their cooperative societies and for this purpose were considering the possibility of admitting capital-providing members as well as labour-providing members. This they wished to do without compromising their cooperative spirit and without losing their legal status as cooperatives which gave them certain tax privileges. The strict purpose of the conference was to consider this particular problem and the second day of the conference was devoted to its discussion.

But the conference had also a broader theme. The organisers and promoters of the conference were convinced of the merits of a competitive market economy but, like so many members of the moderate left in politics, were much concerned with the question whether and, if so, in which way principles of compassion, equality, antipoverty, and social responsibility could at the same time be incorporated in the system. In particular could the cooperative movement help to provide the answer? Dr Edwin Morley-Fletcher of the University of Rome, a principal adviser of Mr Turci, the President of Lega, was familiar with my ideas about Labour-Capital Partnerships and about the organisation of economies which paid attention to equality and participation as well as to incentives for efficiency. Accordingly I was invited to the conference and was given the opportunity on the first day to express my views at the morning session on the organisation of Labour-Capital Partnerships and at the afternoon session to open a panel discussion on the general characteristics of an economy in which such a partnership principle might flourish.

Sections II and III of the present chapter, on the Partnership Enterprise and the Partnership Economy respectively, cover the grounds of my talks at the morning and at the afternoon sessions of this conference.[1] The interest shown in these ideas has led to their publication in an Italian translation in the form of a book covering the present chapter together with an introduction by Dr Edwin Morley-Fletcher.[2]

The reader of the present chapter should bear in mind that its origin has greatly affected the range of subjects which it discusses. The Rome conference was about the possibility of organising individual enterprises on cooperative principles which accepted the providers of capital as full co-operators and about the background of fiscal and other arrangements which would mitigate any undesirable effects upon risk-bearing or upon the distribution of income and wealth. Thus there is a very wide range of economic features of a good society with which the present chapter does not treat. The control of pollution and other external economies and diseconomies, the case for and against central State planning of certain activities, and the economic and financial relations between different countries are outstanding examples. It should in particular be noted that the present chapter does not even touch upon the basic problem of the control of monopolistic practices. Competitive arrangements are advocated wherever possible, but no proposals are made about the treatment of various degrees of monopoly in those cases where inevitably monopolistic conditions prevail.[3]

I realised that I was being foolhardy in talking to a conference of the Italian cooperative movement in total ignorance of any of the distinctive features and problems of that movement. It was, therefore, totally inappropriate for me to deal with specific detailed arrangements. It was largely for this reason that I cast my remarks in the fanciful form of a visit to another community which had solved the basic problems – a country which had in fact devised 'the best of all possible arrangements' with due emphasis on the word 'possible'.[4]

I hope very much that this particular form of presentation will not hide the fact that it is serious possibilities which are at issue. I do not, of course, believe that one could introduce the whole structure discussed in this chapter without selection and modification and without the historical experience of much slow trial and error. But both the ideas underlying section II on the Partnership Enterprise and section III on the Partnership Economy are of great relevance in the present world, in which on one side of the Iron Curtain much thought is being given to the introduction of participatory market competitive enterprises into a command economy and on the other side many are searching for ways to introduce organised social responsibility for greater compassion and equality into a system of unbridled individual competitive money-making. The present time offers a golden opportunity for a constructive exchange of basic ideas.

In revising the text for this chapter I am much indebted to comments made by Dr Edwin Morley-Fletcher, Professor Mario Nuti, Dr Jeremy Edwards and Mr Martin Weale. I am grateful to Professor Sir Henry Phelps Brown for a powerful exposition of the obstacles which human relations between owners, managers and workers may well put in the way of the successful development of Labour-Capital Partnerships; but I have confined myself in this tract to a discussion of the institutional–structural arrangements which would give the best chance for their successful operation. The virtues of the macroeconomic arrangements discussed in section

III of this chapter remain relevant however limited may be the growth of participatory enterprises in the competitive sector of the economy.

J. E. Meade

Christ's College
Cambridge
February 1989

I   INTRODUCTION

I recently set sail to visit the island of Utopia which, I have been told, constitutes a Perfect Place to live in. But, alas, I could find the island Nowhere. However on my way home I chanced to visit the nearby island of Agathotopia. The inhabitants made no claim for perfection in their social arrangements, but they did claim the island to be a Good Place to live in. I studied their institutions closely, came to the conclusion that their social arrangements were indeed about as good as one could hope to achieve in this wicked world, and returned home to recommend Agathotopian arrangements for my own country.

I am making Agathotopian rather than Utopian recommendations simply because I could not find Utopia. But the reason why I could not find that island was something of a mystery. The Agathotopians seemed to have no basically hostile feelings towards their Utopian neighbours, but were very secretive about them and strangely unwilling to help me to find the island. I was very puzzled until some remarks by the rather decrepit Agathotopian economist Professor Dr Semaj Edaem inadvertently suggested to me the following explanation of their reserved attitude to the Utopians.

The Utopians have, I suspect, gone in for genetic engineering in a big way and have produced a race of perfect human beings. The Agathotopians are in many ways a conservative lot and have been either unable or, as I suspect, unwilling to follow Plato in taking the necessary measures to breed genetically a race of people with inborn perfect social behaviour. The Utopians, if I am right, have the task of producing perfect institutions for perfect human beings; the Agathotopians have tried only to produce good institutions for imperfect people.

If this is the explanation of the Agathotopian attitude towards the Utopians, my study of Agathotopia suggests a very important connection between institutions and behaviour. The Agathotopians have devised institutions which rely very largely on self-centred enterprising behaviour in a free competitive market but which, at the same time, put great stress upon cooperation between individuals in producing the best possible outcome and upon a compassionate attitude to those who would otherwise lose out. The typical Agathotopian has a more cooperative and compassionate attitude in his or her social behaviour than is the case at present in the United Kingdom, where we have, alas, been subject for so many years to such a regime of devil-take-the-hindmost and grab-as-much-money-as-quickly-as-possible. This suggests that there is some positive feedback between social institutions and social attitudes.

If this interpretation is true, it means that it will be difficult at first for us to enjoy the advantages of Agathotopian institutions until there has been time for the positive feedbacks between institutions and attitudes to operate effectively. But there is also the implication that it may not be a waste of time to make Agathotopian institutional changes which are somewhat out of harmony with present attitudes, but may well in time help to mould these attitudes in the desired direction.

II THE PARTNERSHIP ENTERPRISE

At the level of the individual competitive business enterprise the Agathotopians have encouraged the formation of what they call Discriminating Labour-Capital Partnerships.

A Pure Form of Labour-Capital Partnership

The easiest way to explain the basic idea of such a partnership between labour and capital is to imagine it to be suddenly applied to an existing firm in a completely undiluted form. Consider then a Capitalist Company of the familiar kind. Suppose that of its revenue 80 per cent is being paid to the employees and the remaining 20 per cent is accruing to the capitalists. Simple conversion of this into a pure Labour-Capital Partnership would consist of the issue of two kinds of Share Certificates, namely:

(1) Capital Share Certificates which would be distributed to all the persons who were in fact receiving directly, or indirectly through profit, interest, rent etc., the capitalists' 20 per cent share of the firm's revenue, this distribution to each beneficiary being *pro rata* to his or her existing income from the business; and

(2) Labour Share Certificates which would be distributed to all employees *pro rata* to their individual earnings of the remaining 80 per cent of the firm's revenue.

All share certificates, whether Capital or Labour, would carry an entitlement to the same rate of dividend.

The immediate result of this conversion would be that everyone concerned would receive an unchanged income, but in every case in the form of a dividend on a shareholding, which would replace all interest, rent, wages, etc.; but everyone concerned in the operation of the business would now have a share in the future success or failure of the enterprise.

There would, however, be one basic distinction between Capital Share Certificates and Labour Share Certificates. Capital Share Certificates would correspond more or less exactly to a Capitalist Company's existing Ordinary Shares. They could be freely traded on the Stock Exchange or elsewhere in the market and could be transferred from one owner to the other.

Labour Share Certificates on the other hand would be tied to the individual working partner and would in principle be surrendered and cancelled when he or she retired or voluntarily left the business.[5] They would not, however, be cancelled if the worker left the partnership involuntarily (e.g. because of redundancy), unless the dismissal was due to grave misconduct or illness which incapacitated the worker for the job. The worker would thus normally be guaranteed employment, or at least an appropriate share of income from employment until retirement. His or her claim on the firm would, however, be tied to availability to perform the work for which the dividend on Labour Share Certificates was the reward. There could, of course, as now be separate pension arrangements for those who had retired, together with separate arrangements for the support of worker partners in ill health.

In a similar manner an existing Labour-Managed Cooperative which had raised all its capital funds in the form of fixed interest debt and in which the working members of the cooperative shared the net revenue produced by the cooperative could be transformed into a Labour-Capital Partnership. The fixed interest debt would be transformed into holdings of Capital Share Certificates with an initial rate of dividend which provided the same income as before to those who had provided the capital funds; and the existing distribution of the cooperative's net revenue among the working cooperators would be transformed into individual holdings of Labour Share Certificates in such amounts that the initial rate of dividend would provide an unchanged income to each individual cooperator.

A Capitalist Company owned by persons providing risk-bearing capital can be changed into a Labour-Capital Partnership by admitting 'partners' who provide risk-bearing work. A Labour-Managed Cooperative can be changed into a Labour-Capital Partnership by admitting 'partners' who provide risk-bearing capital funds.

Modified Forms of Labour-Capital Partnerships

In Agathotopia there are not many cases in which the partnership principle has been applied in the undiluted form which has just been described. Thus a partnership may well need to be free to borrow some capital funds on fixed-interest contracts with the creditors (e.g. bank loans, debentures, etc.).

On the labour side the partnership may well desire to be free to hire some forms of labour – temporary or part-time workers or consultants, for example – on fixed-wage contracts. There are also some Labour-Capital Partnerships requiring all new workers to start on a fixed-wage basis and only later offering them the option of converting a part or the whole of their pay into dividends on Labour Share Certificates.

Even more importantly some existing workers prefer to remain on fixed-wage contracts and, indeed, in some cases all the workers desire, as an insured fall-back in the case of the firm's poor performance, to remain for part of their reward on fixed-wage contracts and only for the remaining part of their reward on participation in a share of the firm's net revenue.

All of these various mixes between fixed payments and share dividends in the case both of capitalists and workers, can be incorporated in the structure of a Labour-Capital Partnership. We may define a firm's 'distributable surplus' as the value of its net revenue on current account less expenditure on fixed interest, fixed rents, and fixed wages. Capital and Labour Share Certificates can then be issued and distributed to those who have a claim on the firm's distributable surplus. The rules and activities of the partnership can then proceed on the principles already discussed for a pure undiluted Labour-Capital Partnership. All share certificates, whether Capital or Labour, receive the same rate of dividend; and in effect those who have a claim on the distributable surplus, whether capitalists or workers, constitute the risk-bearing entrepreneurs.

The Management of Labour-Capital Partnerships

As will be argued later, a basic advantage which can be claimed for an Agathotopian Labour-Capital Partnership is the removal of a large range of potential conflicts of interest between labour and capital in the running of the enterprise. If the Labour-Capital Partnership principle removed literally all conflicts of interest between labour shareholders and capital shareholders the management of the enterprise would be a fairly straightforward problem. The simple answer would be to arrange that all share certificates, whether held by worker or by capitalist shareholders, carried an entitlement not only to the same rate of dividend but also to the same voting power at shareholders' meetings. But, as we shall see later, Agathotopian experience suggests that some areas of conflict will inevitably remain, and to resolve these it might be wise for a partnership to rule that certain decisions – or indeed that all decisions – would require the agreement of representatives of both types of partner or in the case of dispute would be referred to some form of agreed arbitration. In any case it is clear that

Labour-Capital Partnerships can work only in a general atmosphere of mutual trust in which the partners wish to make the partnership work and are prepared to accept some machinery for sensible compromise in any such cases of dispute.

The following arrangement has in many cases in Agathotopia provided a reasonably independent management together with a workable process for the resolution of any conflicts of interest between workers and capitalists. The capitalist shareholders and the labour shareholders each separately elect the same number of full-time members for a board of directors. These directors appoint by agreement an additional chairman with a casting vote who thus acts as an 'arbitrator' in the case of a conflict between the two sets of directors. The board appoints a general manager who is responsible for the day-to-day conduct of the business, the agreement of the board of directors being required only for major policy decisions.

Two Definitions of Distributable Surplus

We have defined a partnership's distributable surplus as its net revenue on current account less its expenditure on fixed interest, fixed rents and fixed wages. But there are two ways of defining a partnership's net revenue on current account; and, as we shall see in what follows, the choice between them can make a very great difference to the way in which the partnership should be operated.

A concern's net cash revenue measures the value of its cash receipts less the value of its cash payments; but to measure its net revenue on current account it is necessary to adjust its total receipts of cash (e.g. by deducting any receipts from the sale of its capital assets) and to adjust its cash payments by deducting any payments made for the purchase of new assets or adding a depreciation allowance for any of its capital assets which are still in use but whose value has deteriorated. One way of measuring net revenue on this year's current account would be to define it as that amount of money which could be paid out this year to the owners of the labour, land, and capital employed in the partnership without there being any change in the real value of the total capital assets owned by the partnership. This may be called the capital-maintenance principle.

But an alternative principle could be adopted which might be called the income-maintenance principle. In this case a concern's net revenue on current account this year would be defined as that amount of money which it was calculated could be paid out this year and in every succeeding year to the owners of the resources employed in the partnership without there being any further addition to or subtraction from the amounts of labour and/ or capital employed by the partnership. In this case a partnership's distributable surplus would be defined as that surplus which it could be hoped to sustain indefinitely given the present resources of the partnership. This may be called the income-maintenance principle.

In a stable unchanging situation, these two principles would coincide. But in a changing situation there would be an important distinction between them. Suppose, for example, that this year a partnership does very well because of some market change such as a rise in the selling price received for its product; with the capital-maintenance principle the whole of this year's increase in revenue will be added to its disposable surplus because no change in its capital resources has been needed to cause the change. But with the income maintenance principle, if the higher selling price were expected to last only for one year, the annual distributable surplus would be raised by slightly less than a year's interest on the increased revenue, since practically the whole of that increase would have to be added to the partnership's capital assets in order to finance an increase in distribution which could be sustained indefinitely in the future.

A partnership's distributable surplus can be divided into two parts, namely a cost element and a pure-profit element. The cost element is that amount which it would be necessary to offer to the owners of the labour, land, or capital resources concerned if they were being admitted to the partnership for the first time in the current market situation, i.e., broadly speaking, what they could earn in alternative uses. The pure-profit (or pure-loss) element in the distributable surplus is the excess of the total distributable surplus over (or its deficiency below) the cost element. Thus a substantial improvement in a partnership's net revenue on current account which is expected to be only temporary will lead to a substantial, but expectedly temporary, rise in the pure-profit element of the partners' incomes, if the capital-maintenance accounting is adopted; but it would lead to a small, but expectedly permanent, rise under the income-maintenance principle.

It may be noted that in Agathotopia the choice between the capital-maintenance and the income-maintenance accounting principles has no direct implications for the taxation of Labour-Capital Partnerships. As will be explained later, savings in Agathotopia are exempt from direct taxation. Whether a sum put to reserve in a Labour-Capital Partnership is counted as a saving or profit (under the capital-maintenance principle) or as a cost of production of sustainable current revenue (under the income-maintenance principle) would in itself have no effect on the tax liability of the partnership.

The Treatment of Undistributed Surplus

Whether it be measured on the capital-maintenance or on the income-maintenance principle there is, of course, no assurance that the whole of the year's distributable surplus should or would be distributed. Part of the surplus may be held back from distribution and used to finance additional capital investment in the partnership.

In these conditions an appropriate arrangement would be that there should be an issue of additional Capital Share Certificates equal at current valuations to the amount of distributable surplus which was not distributed in dividend, and that these additional Capital Share Certificates instead of being sold in the market should be distributed in lieu of dividend *pro rata* to all existing shareholders whether workers or capitalists. Thus workers as well as capitalists would acquire Capital Share Certificates (which they would be perfectly free to hold or to sell as they chose), to represent that part of the partnership's income which had been held back from distribution on their existing share certificates. Alternatively it would be possible to arrange for the dividend on Capital Share Certificates to be cut without cutting the dividend on Labour Share Certificates and to issue the additional Capital Share Certificates solely to the existing holders of such certificates so that it was only the capitalists who financed and who benefited from the ploughing back of revenue into an expansion of the capital resources of the business.

It is also appropriate that funds that are devoted by the partnership to major projects of research and development should not be treated as current costs of production, but as capital investments financed out of undistributed surplus. Holders of Labour Share Certificates, particularly those near the age of retirement, will be less interested than holders of Capital Share Certificates in the future prosperity of the partnership. Since the returns on major research and development expenditures are likely to show themselves in the future it is proper that such expenditures should be treated as capital investments.

It is of interest to consider the difference between the effects of the capital-maintenance and of the income-maintenance accounting principle with respect to undistributed surplus. Suppose, for example, that a partnership experienced a specially prosperous year which was not expected to be repeated and that it did in fact cautiously retain this exceptional revenue and invested the funds in additional capital assets. With the capital-maintenance principle new Capital Share Certificates would be issued to all share holders, so that holders of Labour Share Certificates would gain in the future dividends on additional Capital Share Certificates issued *pro rata* to their holdings of Labour Share Certificates. With the income-maintenance principle no extra share certificates would be issued in respect of the extra undistributed year's revenue which would be treated as a cost necessary to finance an addition to a sustainable rise in distributable surplus. Holders of Labour Share Certificates would gain in the future from the sustainable increase in distributable surplus on their existing Labour Share Certificates. Thus there would be no major difference in the rewards of worker partners so long as they remained in employment in the partnership. In both cases they would receive the same increase in income, in the former case in the form of dividends on new Capital Share Certificates and in the latter case in the form of increased dividends on their existing Labour Share Certificates. Whether or not there would be a difference on their retirement would depend upon the treatment of Labour Share Certificates at that time, which we discuss later on pp. 124–32.

The Treatment of Capital Gains

The implications of these two accounting principles for the treatment of capital gains may be noted. Suppose that as a result of a general inflation of all money costs and prices the monetary value of a partnership's net revenue on current account rose by, say, 10 per cent. In the absence of any assets or liabilities which were fixed in money terms there would have been a 10 per cent gain in the monetary value of the partnership's capital assets and of the partnership's sustainable distributable surplus. But with all prices and costs inflated by 10 per cent there would have been no change in the real value of the partnership's capital assets nor in the real value of its sustainable distributable surplus. Thus no special adjustment of holdings of Capital Share Certificates would be appropriate, regardless of whether the income-maintenance or the capital-maintenance principle were adopted for accounting purposes.

But the position would be different if the 10 per cent rise in the money value of the partnership's net revenue on current account had occurred as a result of an improvement in the particular productive or marketing activities of the partnership without any general inflation of the general level of money prices and costs. The partnership would have experienced a 10 per cent rise in the real value of its sustainable future distributable surplus and in the real value of its partners' holdings of Capital and Labour Share Certificates. Once again, if the income-maintenance principle were adopted, no special financial adjustment of shareholdings need be made. With no change in shareholdings both labour and capital continue to enjoy a 10 per cent rise in their real incomes. There has simply been an exogenous increase in real value of the distributional surplus and no further adjustment of capital assets is needed to sustain it.

But there has been an increase in the real value of the partnership's capital assets. When this occurs the capital-maintenance principle demands either that some special once-for-all extra dividend distribution should be made to eliminate the capital gain or else that additional Capital Share Certificates should be issued *pro rata* to holders of Capital and of Labour Share Certificates on a sufficient scale to eliminate any real capital gain on the pre-existing Capital Share Certificates. The appropriate action thus is to capitalise at the current rate of interest the whole of the exogenous increase in the partnership's sustainable money net revenue on current account and to distribute *pro rata* to existing shareholders (whether of Capital or of Labour Share Certificates) a number of additional share certificates equal in total money value to the total capitalised value of the existing increase in distributable surplus. By this means the real value of the pre-existing holdings of Capital Share Certificates will remain unchanged.

The only difference then between the outcome under the income-maintenance and the capital-maintenance principles will be the form in which worker partners receive their share of the improved fortunes of the partnership. With the income-maintenance principle worker and capitalist partners both gain by a 10 per cent rise in the dividend payable on their pre-existing Capital and Labour Share Certificates. With the capital-maintenance principle the dividend payable per share certificate remains unchanged; but the capital partners gain by a 10-per-cent increase in the number of Capital Share Certificates which they hold and the worker partners gain with no change in their pre-existing holdings of Labour Share Certificates but by an issue of new Capital Share Certificates equal to 10 per cent of their pre-existing holdings of Labour (or Capital) Share Certificates. The change in the incomes of the worker partners is the same under both principles so long as they remain in the partnership's employment. Whether or not it will later affect their treatment will depend upon the rules governing their treatment on leaving the employment of the partnership, which we discuss below (pp. 124–32).

Finally, it may be of interest to note that both these treatments of real capital gains in a Labour-Capital Partnership differ from their treatment in a Capitalist Company. The pay of the workers would not be increased automatically as a result of a rise in the net revenue on current account of a Capitalist Company. The whole of the value would benefit the capitalists either in the form of a rise in the dividend on what corresponds to Capital Share Certificates or by what corresponds to an issue of additional Capital

Share Certificates to the existing holders of such certificates. In a Labour-Capital Partnership under both accounting principles the gain is immediately shared between worker and capitalist partners, the unresolved question being only whether the worker partners continue to enjoy any part of this gain when they retire.

A Dividend Equalisation Fund

There is one further relevant complication which has to be introduced into the accounting procedure of a Labour-Capital Partnership. For worker partners who rely for a main part of their income on Labour Share Certificates it is necessary to pay such dividends at frequent intervals, possibly even weekly, and at rates which are reasonably stable and reliable. Any such distribution involves some administrative costs and accounting problems, even though dividends on Capital Share Certificates can continue to be paid yearly or half-yearly. But more importantly rates of dividend have to be announced some time in advance of payment so that worker partners have some knowledge of the incomes on which they can rely at least for a number of months in advance. This involves for accounting purposes some kind of dividend equalisation fund into which distributable surplus can be paid subject to inevitable variation between good and bad periods and from which more stable, reliable and frequent dividends could be paid.

In general the Agathotopians make every effort to apply the principle that in the case of undistributed net revenue new Capital Share Certificates should be issued to those, whether capitalist or worker partners, who have been deprived of the distribution. But they recognise the accounting difficulties in applying this principle and regard its applications as contributing one of the most important reasons for ensuring that every partnership has an agreed arrangement for seeking appropriate impartial arbitration in case of potential conflict of opinion on issues of his kind.

The Removal of Certain Conflicts of Interest Between Labour and Capital

In a Labour-Capital Partnership all partners receive the same dividend on their shareholdings, whether they are capitalist partners or worker partners. This arrangement removes many basic causes of conflict since a decision which raises the incomes of the existing holders of Capital Share Certificates will necessarily raise the incomes of the existing holders of Labour Share Certificates. For this reason there is much improvement in incentives and in cooperative relations between labour and capital since all stand to gain by using the existing resources of the partnership in such a way as to produce the maximum possible net revenue.

In a Capitalist Company increased profit due to efficient and well applied work by the employees accrues directly to the profits earned by the owners of the company's capital resources. Any loss due to slack work falls primarily on the capitalist entrepreneurs. In a Labour-Capital Partnership it falls directly on all recipients of dividends, that is to say on worker partners as well as on capitalist partners. This certainly will improve the general atmosphere in which work for the partnership is conducted. But the fact that any loss incurred through an individual's slackness in work will be spread over all other workers as well as the capitalists does not in itself eliminate the temptation for an individual worker to slack at other people's expense. It does, however, mean that his or her efficient and conscientious colleagues will all have a direct incentive to discourage slack and inefficient work since their pay depends upon the financial outcome of their joint efforts. To this extent the problems and supervision costs of ensuring good and effective work would be lower in a Labour-Capital Partnership than in a Capitalist Company.

There are, of course, certain forms of 'income in kind' which may be produced in a partnership with effect upon the ease and quality of work without directly affecting the capitalist partners. One obvious case of such a possible conflict of interest could be due to a decision to devote part of the firm's resources to the provision of social amenities or fringe benefits of a type (such as canteen facilities) which would be valued by the workers but which would not confer any direct benefits on the owners of the capital invested in the business. But Agathotopian experience suggests that in an otherwise harmonious partnership differences of interest of this kind do not cause serious difficulty.

In a Discriminating Labour-Capital Partnership it is not only decisions about the use of existing resources which can in the main be taken without conflict of interest; it is also true that major decisions about capital investment can be taken in such a way that any action would be to the advantage of all shareholders, whether capitalists or workers, since, if a high dividend is to result, it will result for all owners and all working partners. Thus the purchase of a new machine could be financed by issuing and selling on the market an issue of additional Capital Share Certificates sufficient to raise the necessary funds. All existing partners, whether capital or labour shareholders, would gain if the dividend payable on the new additional Capital Share Certificates was less than the addition which the new capital equipment would add to the firm's net revenue. In this way the answer to a question whether to carry out an investment plan would depend upon a judgement whether it was to the advantage or disadvantage of all persons, whether capitalists or workers, who were concerned with the firm's activities.

Discrimination Between Old and New Capital Partners in a Successful Partnership

It should be noted that the discussion of capital investment in the previous paragraph rested on the assumption that the terms offered to new capital shareholders were not as favourable as those enjoyed by existing capital shareholders. This is the normal procedure in an ordinary Capitalist Company. It has the advantage of encouraging capital development in successful businesses where capital development is in the social interest; and on these grounds it is applied in Agathotopian Labour-Capital Partnerships. A numerical example may help to explain the implications of the principle.

Consider a business in which the purchase of a new machine costs £100 in an economy in which the market rate of interest is 5 per cent. The machine is expected to produce a net profit for the business of £5 a year, i.e. a yield of 5 per cent per annum. A capitalist buys 100 newly issued Capital Share Certificates at £1 a certificate; the business uses the £100 so raised for the purchase of a machine which the business uses to pay a dividend of 5p on each of the 100 Capital Share Certificates. The capitalist earns his 5 per cent on his purchase of 100 share certificates, which is equal to the market rate of return which he could obtain elsewhere.

Suppose that this business does extremely well because the selling price of its product soars. The profit produced by the machine doubles to £10 a year; the rate of dividend per share certificate is raised from 5p to 10p. With a market rate of interest unchanged at 5 per cent, the market value of a share certificate rises from £1 to £2 per share certificate. In its present prosperous conditions the business by investing in a second machine costing £100 would be able to raise its net profit by, say, £8 which is not as great as the £10 being earned on the first machine but remains higher than the £5 which is the outside market yield on £100 of capital. The business decides to expand and put in a second machine costing £100 which will enable it to raise its net profit from £10 a year to £18 a year. It issues not 100 but only 50, extra share certificates which, selling as they do in the market at £2 instead of the original £1 a share certificate, raises the £100 needed to purchase the second machine.

The situation is then as follows. The business is operating two machines costing £200 and is making a net profit of £18 a year. It has issued 150 share certificates so that it can pay a dividend of £18 ÷ 150 = 12p per share certificate. Both the original set of capitalists (who bought 100 share certificates at £1 a share) and the second set of capitalists (who bought 50 share certificates at £2 a share) have put the same real resources, namely one machine costing £100, into the business; but the original set of capitalists are receiving £12 a year and the second set only £6 a year in dividends in payment on their investment. But everyone is better off as a result of the second investment. The income of the first set of capitalists has risen from £10 to £12 a year and that of the second set of capitalists to £6 from the £5 which they were offered elsewhere on their capital of £100.

This gives the original capitalists in the successful prosperous business an incentive to expand. If the business is earning a better rate than in the outside market, the existing owners will have an incentive to expand if they can hire extra capital at any rate below the high rate which it can earn in the prosperous business; and the outside capitalists will have an incentive to put more capital into the prosperous business if they are offered any rate of return above the low rate they are earning in the less prosperous businesses. At some intermediate rate both the prosperous business has an incentive to invest in the additional capital resources and the less prosperous outsiders have an incentive to supply the necessary funds. If the original capitalists in the prosperous business had been obliged to pay to the new capitalists the same amount of dividend on the same amount of machinery as they were paying to themselves, they would have had no incentive to expand.

It is precisely this same discriminatory principle which the Agathotopian Labour Capital Partnership applies to its investment decisions which were described in the previous section of this tract. Both the existing capitalist partners and the existing worker partners in a prosperous successful Labour-Capital Partnership stand to gain if they can hire additional outside capital by the issue of a number of Capital Share Certificates which provides to outside capitalists a rate of return on their capital which is higher than their existing low rate of market return but which absorbs only a part of the high extra revenue which the new capital resources will produce and which will then be available to raise the dividends paid to all existing holders of share certificates, that is to say, to existing holders of both Labour and Capital Share Certificates.

Discrimination Between Old and New Worker Partners in a Successful Partnership

This same principle of discrimination between the financiers of old and of new capital equipment in a successful partnership is applied in Agathotopia to the engagement of old and new worker partners for precisely similar reasons. It removes conflict between existing worker partners and capitalist partners in expanding employment in a successful partnership, where expansion of employment is desirable in the social interest.

The managers of the partnership would be free to decide to employ an additional worker partner by offering to him or her a new issue of Labour Share Certificates which was sufficient to attract the worker to the enterprise. If the expected dividend on these shares, while sufficient to attract the worker, was nevertheless lower than the additional revenue expected to result from the work of the new partner, all existing shareholders, whether capitalist or workers, would stand to gain by the decision, since the addition to the firm's revenue available to be paid out in increased dividends on all shares of both kinds would be greater than the additional dividend payable to the new worker on the newly issued Labour Share Certificates. Since the new worker would presumably be attracted only if there was some advantage in accepting the offer everyone would gain from such a decision.

Plans for expansion may often involve the simultaneous investment in new capital equipment and the employment of additional labour, and this may be so not only to expand current activities but also for the improvement of the quality of the product, for diversification into new products, for greater flexibility, for improvement of managerial control systems and so on. Moreover, much of the expenditures involved may not be on physical equipment but on the work of design and development engineers, market researchers, and other specialists. The general principle, however, remains the same. If the dividends payable on the extra Labour and Capital Share Certificates needed to attract the resources required for the firm's new plans are expected to be less than the additional net revenue which will result from the firm's new plans, the development will be to the advantage of all existing shareholders, whether workers or capitalists.

The End of Equal Pay for Equal Work

The application of this principle to the expansion of employment in a successful partnership would mean that newly engaged worker partners worked side by side with original worker partners at a somewhat lower rate of pay (i.e. in receipt of the same rate of dividend on a smaller number of Labour Share Certificates). This means the abandonment of the strict principle of Equal Pay for Equal Work. So important a change of principle deserves detailed consideration.

The necessity for the change arises in the following way. Consider the position of a Labour-Capital Partnership which by efficient organisation, by a wise choice of product, by the development of technical improvements, or by other means is operating successfully. The rate of dividend which it can pay on Labour Share Certificates provides worker partners with incomes markedly in excess of the incomes of similar workers who are unemployed or are occupied in less successful enterprises.

Suppose the inside earnings of these particular worker partners is 200 while the outside incomes of many comparable workers in the rest of the economy is only 100. It may well be that an additional worker would add more than 100 but less than 200 – let us say 180 – to the net revenue of the partnership. If the principle of equal pay for equal work were strictly applied in the sense that a newly admitted worker partner must be offered share certificates which would earn him or her the 200 income of existing worker partners, the admittance of the new worker partner would be to the disadvantage of all existing partners (whether workers or capitalists) since the new worker would add 180 to the revenue but would be paid 200.

On the other hand if the new working partner were offered an issue of new Labour Share Certificates which would produce an income somewhere inbetween 100 and 180 – let us say 150 – everyone would gain. All existing partners whether capitalist or labour would gain since the net revenue of the partnership would be raised by 180 at the cost of paying 150 to the new worker partner, and the new worker partner would gain by receiving 150 instead of an outsider's income of 100.

In the absence of any arrangement which insisted upon the observance of the principle of equal pay for equal work on a national basis, it would always be possible to set up a new partnership with a lower rate of workers' remuneration to compete with any successful and prosperous partnership whose worker partners enjoyed an exceptionally high rate of remuneration. Such competition from new units is a basic feature of any successful competitive market structure and will serve to inhibit exceptionally high rewards due to unnecessary monopolistic practices. It is in Agathotopia a familiar and effective method of preventing unnecessary inequalities in earnings. But it cannot be relied upon as the sole method of ensuring a sufficiently large and efficient expansion of employment. In many cases there will be increasing returns to scale in a small but exceptionally prosperous business, and this means that expansion of output and employment in that business will be more efficient than a corresponding increase in the number of small businesses. In any case the problems of organising the new capital, management and labour, the wastes involved in not expanding the old successful organisations of capital, management and labour, and the marketing difficulties encountered by newcomers in the invasion of old markets are too great to rely solely on the launch of new enterprises as the means of ensuring full employment.

As an alternative it has been suggested[6] that outsiders should somehow or other be given the right to demand entry to any existing partnership on the same terms as those enjoyed by the existing partners. Outsiders would presumably exercise this right and thus expand existing successful partnerships until the incomes enjoyed by the worker partners had been so reduced as to offer no further inducement for further entry. The Agathotopians have rejected this solution. It could have a disastrous effect on the incentive to invest capital in risky businesses if any successful enterprise could be expanded indefinitely by an inundation of unwanted labour. But in any case the arrangement is thought by the Agathotopians to be impracticable. It would raise too many problems of definition and judgement concerning the skills required from new entrants for particular types of job, of compatibility of old and new partners, of resentment by existing partners of the downward pressure on their dividends, and of motivation for the successful cooperative management of concerns with unwelcome newcomers.

The principle of equal pay for equal work can be formally maintained even though newly admitted worker partners receive less than the existing insiders if, as is the case in many professional partnerships, the new partner has to purchase the right to membership of the partnership. In the preceding numerical example a new worker partner had an outsider's income of 100 but could add 180 to the income of a partnership in which the existing partners were earning 200. It would be possible for the new working partner to be given the same number of Labour Share Certificates as the existing partners (equal pay for equal work) but to be charged for the right of membership a capital sum which would finance an annuity of somewhere between 20 and 100 for a period equal to the number of years during which the new partner's pay was expected to be 200 instead of the outside 100 and the partnership was expecting to receive 180 from the new partner's work. The partnership would gain so long as the annuity was more than 20 and the new partner would gain so long as it was less than 100; and in an extreme case such as this there would be a wide margin within which a bargain could be struck which allowed for much uncertainty about future prospects. If subsequently the new worker left the partnership before the agreed period was up, he or she would be repaid by the partnership a capital sum corresponding to the remaining period of the annuity.

The Agathotopians have in some cases adopted this device. They have found it practicable to do so only in those cases in which special arrangements have been made to lend the funds necessary to enable duly qualified workers to purchase membership in successful partnerships which wished to admit them on terms agreed between the worker and the partnership. Certain groups of partnerships have in fact financed a central fund out of which loans are made to individual workers for this purpose. Due repayment of these loans out of earnings in the new partnership has been strictly enforced so that the central fund has operated on a continuously revolving basis. Experiments in which particular successful partnerships have themselves lent the necessary money directly to newly admitted worker partners have not in general been successful, since the direct deduction of repayments from dividends on Labour Share Certificates has led to individual claims for relief which have soured relations within the partnership. But where the finance of the charge for membership has been provided by a totally different independent institution the arrangement has made possible some expansion of employment at 'equal pay for equal work' to the mutual benefit of all concerned.

Yet another way of preserving the principle of equal pay for equal work without suppressing the incentives for expansion by successful partnerships may be sought by capitalising all exceptional earnings by worker partners.[7] In terms of the above numerical example suppose that in a successful partnership the existing worker partners are each receiving 200 in dividends on their Labour Share Certificates whereas the suitable rate of pay which it would be appropriate to offer to newcomers is only 100. In this case one half of the Labour Share Certificates of the existing worker partners would be converted into Capital Share Certificates so that they would now each be receiving 100 in dividends on Capital Share Certificates and only 100 for their work in the form of Labour Share Certificates. If in this way all exceptional gains of income by existing worker partners in successful partnerships were converted into returns on Capital Share Certificates, the same 'rate for the job' in terms of a fixed money wage or of dividends on Labour Share Certificates could be paid to old hands and to newly admitted workers.

This solution of the problem must be ruled out in all cases in which there is any prospect that a partnership's exceptional success has proved to be only temporary. In a growing, technologically innovative and expanding economy this is likely to be a frequent occurrence. A particular enterprise may have a particularly bright idea in introducing a new product or new technique of production. It may thereby earn an exceptionally high income but only until other enterprises have learnt to compete with it. To continue the above numerical example, suppose that a partnership has been so successful as to be able to double its rate of dividend on all share certificates; each working partner is receiving 200 instead of a representative outsiders' income of 100. Suppose that the special earnings of the worker partners had not been capitalised. If then the special features leading to its special success disappeared, the dividend would have to be halved and the income of each working partner would revert to the outside representative market rate of 100, all earned on their Labour Share Certificates.

But if the special earnings of 100 had been converted into dividends on Capital Share Certificates, the income of each worker partner would revert to 100, but of this only 50 would be received in the form of dividends on Labour Share Certificates, the other 50 accruing in the form of dividends on Capital Share Certificates. It is a basic feature of Capital Share Certificates that such shareholdings are not tied to particular individual workers, that they can be held independently of holding a job in the partnership, and that they can be freely sold, given away, or bequeathed to the holder's heirs. In the case illustrated above worker partners with only 50 income in dividends on Labour Share Certificates would have every incentive to leave the partnership, take jobs at 100 in outside employment, and carry with them the income of 50 payable on their holding of Capital Share Certificates in the previous partnership – if they had not already disposed of them.

To retain or to replace their services their Labour Share Certificates would have to be doubled in order to restore their earned income to 100. The net result would be a dilution of the existing original capitalists' income by the issue of the additional Capital Share Certificates to capitalise the worker partners' share of what turned out to be temporary gains. The additional risks thereby imposed on those providing risk capital would be unacceptable.

It is clear from this analysis that the solution of capitalising the excess remuneration (i.e. the element of pure profit) received by worker partners in an exceptionally prosperous partnership would be acceptable only if the accounting principle of income-maintenance rather than that of capital-maintenance (as described on pp. 110–11) were adopted. The danger described above in capitalising excess remuneration disappears if that excess includes only the element of income which it is confidently expected to be able to sustain indefinitely in the future. The capitalisation of excess remunerations which turn out to be temporary would ruin those who have provided the necessary capital funds.

This solution of capitalising the pure profit element in the remuneration of worker partners has an obvious implication for the treatment of worker partners on retirement, since Capital Share Certificates are not at any point cancelled.

But whatever particular form it may take it remains clear that the introduction of some element of discrimination between the incomes of old-established and newly admitted partners in successful Labour-Capital Partnerships is essential if the system is to succeed. But Agathotopian experience also suggests that the system has some other equalising effects upon the incomes of workers. Successful Discriminating Labour-Capital Partnerships aggressively seek expansion by sucking in unemployed and low-paid workers at improved incomes and this reduces inequalities between those employed in successful concerns and those who would otherwise be unemployed or earning their living in low-paid unsuccessful concerns. Thus while the system introduces an element of disparity between individual earnings within a partnership it reduces disparities of earnings between different groups of workers.

The Treatment of Retired Worker Partners

The possible capitalisation of the pure-profit element in the earnings of worker partners is closely connected with the arrangements made for their retirement. In the Agathotopian Labour-Capital Partnerships there are usually arrangements under which the retiring member obtains a pension financed out of contributions previously paid into a pension fund by the individual worker partner and by the partnership.

These contributions are payable as a stated percentage of the annual earnings of the member and thus the pension does reflect both the cost element and the pure-profit element in the retiring member's past remuneration. The arrangement thus boils down to a system of financing a working partner's retirement out of compulsory savings by the member during his or her period of service with the partnership, the contributions in fact representing a part of the income which could have been paid to the member in the absence of a pension arrangement. These pension arrangements are in no essential way different from the pension arrangements normally found in a Capitalist Company.

What may be distinctive about the treatment of a retiring worker member of a Labour-Capital Partnership is the treatment of the Labour Share Certificates held by the member on his or her retirement. So far we have discussed the problem on the assumption that all Agathotopian Labour-Capital Partnerships operate on what they call the Rule of Cancellation, namely the rule that on retirement a worker partner surrenders for cancellation all his or her holding of Labour Share Certificates. But some partnerships have in fact experimented in the application of alternative arrangements.

A case is made out for drawing a distinction between the retiring working partner's cost and the retiring working partner's pure profit and for dividing his or her holding of Labour Share Certificates into two parts: (i) an amount of certificates the return on which is needed to pay for the worker's cost and (ii) any remaining excess of certificates the return on which will in fact be financing the worker's pure profit. These two parts are called the worker's cost certificates and pure-profit certificates respectively.

It is universally agreed that a retiring working partner's cost certificates should be surrendered and cancelled. This is necessary in order to offset the new issue of the same amount of certificates which will be needed to attract a new partner to replace the retiring worker partner. There is, however, a certain debate about what would be the appropriate treatment of the pure-profit certificates. One group supports a so-called *Rule of Retention*, namely that the retiring working partner's pure-profit certificates should be retained by the retiring member after being transformed into ordinary Capital Share Certificates; another group supports a so-called *Rule of Redistribution*, namely that the retiring working partner's pure-profit certificates should be redistributed in the form of Labour Share Certificates among all the remaining worker partners.

In brief in all cases a retiring working partner's cost certificates would be cancelled and thus make room for their reissue to a new partner to replace the retiring partner. The debate concerns only the treatment of pure-profit certificates which would also be cancelled under the rule of cancellation, retained by the retiring partner in the form of Capital Share Certificates under the rule of retention, and redistributed in the form of Labour Share Certificates among the remaining worker partners under the rule of redistribution.

The choice between these three modes of treating a retiring worker partner's pure-profit certificates can have important effects. Consider first the case of a partnership which is enjoying an element of pure profit. Initially when the partnership is first set up or when the pure profit is first experienced it is shared between labour and capital in the form of a high rate of dividend on Labour Share Certificates and Capital Share Certificates.

The Rule of Cancellation

The rule of cancellation operates in the following way. When a worker partner retires all his or her Labour Share Certificates are cancelled. When he or she is replaced by a newly engaged worker partner, sufficient new Labour Share Certificates must be issued to cover the cost of the newly engaged partner. As a result there is a net reduction in the total of Labour Share Certificates equal to the number needed to cover any pure profit over and above this cost which was enjoyed by the retiring and working partner. This enables the rate of dividend per share certificate to be raised as the partnership's distributable surplus is paid out on a smaller number of share certificates. This means that the pure profit enjoyed by the retiring member is in effect redistributed among all remaining partners whether holders of Labour or of Capital Share Certificates. As a consequence all existing worker partners, including any recent newcomers to the workforce, will enjoy their share of the surplus so long as the incomes of the 'old hands' who are retiring exceed the starting remuneration covering the cost of the 'new hands' who replace them. The 'new hands', as they gradually become 'old hands' will obtain their increasing share of pure profit.

But the existing capitalists will also receive their share of any pure profit released by the retirement of old hands; thus not the whole of the pure profit enjoyed by retiring worker partners will be transferred to other worker partners. As a result any permanent pure profit enjoyed by a successful partnership will bit by bit gradually seep away from the working partners to the holders of Capital Share Certificates. This process will in general be a prolonged one, though it will be more rapid in a capital-intensive concern in which the initial ratio of Capital to Labour Share Certificates is high. But in the long run the whole of any pure profit will be enjoyed by the owners of the capital which, unlike the labour input of the retiring worker partners, is not withdrawn from the partnership.

In this respect a Discriminating Labour-Capital Partnership operating on the rule of cancellation will in the long run come to resemble a Capitalist Company in which labour is paid its cost and all the pure profit reverts to the owners of the capital funds.

The Rule of Redistribution

It may be considered unjust that the whole of any pure profit should in the end accrue to the capitalist partners. May the prosperity of the concern not be due to the worker partners at least as much as to the capitalist partners? If the original creation of the prosperous conditions and their subsequent maintenance are considered to be the work of all partners, whether capitalists or workers, it might well be considered appropriate to substitute the rule of redistribution for the rule of cancellation, since under the new rule the body of working partners would maintain their due share of the fruits of prosperity just as long as that prosperity is maintained regardless of the fact that the particular individuals constituting the working force may change from time to time.

As we have already noted, the rule of redistribution unlike the rule of cancellation raises the problem of distinguishing between the cost element and the pure-profit element in the Labour Share Certificates held by the retiring partners so that the pure-profit element may be distributed in the form of Labour Share Certificates to be added to the holdings of the remaining worker partners. Such assessments about the size of the pure-profit element could be a real cause of conflict between the interests of the remaining worker and capitalist partners. With the rule of cancellation no deliberate assessment of the gain to existing partners from the substitution of new partners (at cost) for old partners (enjoying cost and pure profit) need be made. The future level of distributable surplus available to be paid in dividend on the future level of total share certificates will automatically reveal the gain. But with the rule of redistribution the gain to the remaining worker partners will take the form not of a rise in the rate of dividend on existing share certificates but of an increased issue of new share certificates equal to the pure-profit share certificates surrendered by the retiring worker partners. The fact that the gain to existing partners takes the form in the one case of a rise in the rate of dividend on existing share certificates and in the other case of an unchanged rate of dividend on an additional holding of share certificates is essentially immaterial. What is of material importance is that in the first case the gain which will accrue to all partners will arise automatically through the future development of the partnership, whereas in the latter case in order to restrict the gain to one set of partners a deliberate and perhaps controversial assessment must be made of the amount of gain which can reasonably be expected to be available for redistribution from the pure-profit element in the retiring members' Labour Share Certificates.

The rule of redistribution carries with it one further possible disadvantage which should be noted. The principle of discrimination is advocated in Agathotopia on the grounds that it will lead to an expansion in the number of working partners so long as an additional working partner would add more to the partnership's revenue than the cost to the partnership of the new working partner.

But consider the attitude of some young working partners who have recently been engaged in a highly profitable partnership, working under the rule of redistribution. They will expect a rise in their remuneration as older partners retire and their pure profit is redistributed. It will be to the advantage of the younger partners that the engagement of new partners should be restricted so that there should be a smaller number of potential beneficiaries in the future redistributions of pure profit – an advantage which will disappear only if the number of working partners is so restricted that the potential addition to the total revenue of the partnership due to an expansion of the number of working partners is so large as to offset the redistributive loss.

The possible gain from restriction of membership will be greater for the younger partners than for the older partners on the point of retirement who have little to gain from future redistribution. It will be increased (i) if the amount of pure profit enjoyed by the partnership is large, (ii) if the partnership is a labour-intensive one so that little of the pure profit is enjoyed by the owners of Capital Share Certificates and (iii) if the rate at which younger partners discount the value of future benefits is low.

If the partnership operates under the rule of cancellation, the prospective redistributive gains for the younger members will from the outset be weakened because the pure profit of retiring worker partners will have to be shared by the capitalist members; and this weakening of the motive for restriction will be greater, the more capital-intensive is the partnership. Moreover as the years go by the motive for restriction will become smaller and smaller as the labour pure profit seeps away to the capitalists until in the end there is no labour pure profit left to be redistributed and thus no motive for restriction.[8]

The Rule of Retention

The rule of retention like the rule of redistribution, but unlike the rule of cancellation, involves the tiresome task of distinguishing upon retirement between the cost element and the pure-profit element of a worker partner's holding of Labour Share Certificates. It differs from the rule of redistribution in that the pure-profit share certificates of each individual retiring partner are converted into Capital Share Certificates and are retained in the ownership of the individual retiring partner, whereas with the rule of redistribution these pure-profit share certificates retain the character of Labour Share Certificates and are redistributed among the remaining body of working partners *pro rata* to each member's existing holding of Labour Share Certificates. From the point of view of the justice of the arrangement the rule of retention may be considered as being the more appropriate rule if it is thought that the specifically prosperous nature of a successful business is the lasting and permanent legacy of an original set of workers who produced it and does not need any specially skilled or intense activity for its maintenance. In this case it may be considered more appropriate that those who are working when a permanent improvement in a sustainable distributable surplus is produced should on retirement retain the extra income generated rather than let it be redistributed among a new generation of workers.

Thus the rule of retention has much in common with the suggestion[9] that a worker should acquire a property right in his job and on retirement should be free to sell the job to someone to replace him or her. Presumably any new worker would be willing to pay for the job only what we have called the pure-profit element in the retiring worker's pay; he or she would not pay for a job anything other than the prospective excess of earnings over what could be earned free of charge in alternative positions. This direct form of property right is, however, probably unacceptable because the partnership as a whole must be able to select the replacement of the retiring member in order to ensure that the replacement is properly qualified and personally acceptable. If those whose task it is to judge the size of the pure-profit element in a retiring worker's earnings make a fair and accurate assessment, the retiring member under the rule of retention would, as it were, sell the value of his job at a fair market price through the agency of the partnership.

We have already noted that the rule of redistribution, and to a lesser degree the rule of cancellation, might damp the motives for expansion of employment in a prosperous partnership because the smaller the size of the existing workforce, the greater would be the gain of each individual member of that workforce from the redistribution of the pure profit enjoyed by the older workers as they retired. With the rule of retention there would be no expectation of any such gain from redistribution of the pure profit of retiring members and thus no such dampening of the motives for the expansion of the numbers in the workforce.

Thus the rule of retention has the great advantage of not weakening the expansionist force of the principle of discrimination. But if a partnership's enjoyment of a pure profit turns out to be only temporary the rule of retention carries with it the danger of another kind from which the rules of redistribution and of cancellation are immune. Consider a partnership (i) which starts with no pure profit with Capital Share Certificates and Labour Share Certificates issued in amounts which just cover the costs of capital and labour, (ii) which then passes through a lucky period with a high demand for its product and with worker and capitalist partners enjoying a pure profit *pro rata* on their shareholdings, and (iii) which after a considerable period loses its market advantage and reverts to its original position just covering its costs. With the rule of redistribution this presents no special problems; during the lucky period even with a complete turnover of the working partnership, the working partners will enjoy the pure profit while it lasts and will just cover their costs when the lucky period is over.

The mechanism is different with the rule of cancellation but the final result is the same. During the lucky period the high pure profit will all seep away to the capitalist members of the partnership, the remuneration of the worker partners reverting to the level of their costs as new working partners are engaged on the discriminating principle. As we have seen, this transfer of the pure profit will be brought about by a rise in the rate of dividend on a diminishing total of share certificates. When the pure profit disappears the consequential reduction of the rate of dividend will mean that the new set of working partners will no longer cover their costs. In order to retain their services the partnership will have to issue additional Labour Share Certificates to them. But when they have received a new issue of Labour Share Certificates equal to the amount of labour pure-profit certificates which had been cancelled as working partners retired during the high-profit period, the situation will once more revert to its original position with worker and capitalist partners both just covering their costs.

The situation is, however, basically different with the rule of retention. In this case during the period of high profit retiring worker partners' pure-profit certificates will gradually be transformed into Capital Share Certificates held by retired working partners or dispersed among their heirs or among other persons to whom these Capital Share Certificates have been sold. When the high profit disappears the costs of the existing worker partners will no longer be covered unless they receive an issue of additional Labour Share Certificates to make up for the loss of such certificates due to their transformation into the Capital Share Certificates issued to retired worker partners; the result is a net increase in the total of Capital Share Certificates with a restoration of the issue of Labour Share Certificates to its original position before the high-profit period. The increased issue of Capital Share Certificates will merely dilute the return to those who originally supplied the capital funds. There would be a strong disincentive against investing capital funds in a risky enterprise with the prospect of fluctuating fortunes. Those who subscribed such risk capital would be confronted with a situation in which they shared any profit with working partners but must face the whole of any subsequent loss of such profits in so far as the labour share of the profit had meanwhile been capitalised on the retirement of working partners.

This analysis suggests that the rule of retention can be safely adopted only if the accounting principle of income maintenance is applied so that no temporary upsurge in the sustainable distributable surplus is to be expected. The argument in this respect is exactly the same as that expressed above (pp. 122–3) in connection with the proposal that the principle of equal pay for equal work could be formally retained if all pure-profit elements in

Labour Share Certificates were simply transformed into Capital Share Certificates. The retention principle would then be applied immediately upon the earning of a pure profit and would not have to wait until the retirement of the worker partner. The retention rule on retirement would simply become irrelevant.

The application of the retention rule on retirement has one advantage over the immediate capitalisation of all pure profits as they are earned. Both arrangements are acceptable only if the accounting principle of income-maintenance is adopted. But such a principle is extremely difficult to apply, since it depends essentially upon uncertain forecasts of the future fortunes of the enterprise. If an over-optimistic assessment of sustainable distributional surplus has been made, no future correction of the undesirable erosion of capital funds is possible if the overestimated element of pure profit has been immediately capitalised. But if the capitalisation of estimated pure profit is postponed until the worker partner retires, the estimate can be corrected over the period of the working partner's employment.

The rule of retention will have some advantage over the rules of both cancellation and redistribution. A worker partner who knows that a due share of any pure profit which he or she may help to produce will remain his or her property indefinitely in the form of a capital holding will have a greater incentive to produce such a result than would a worker partner whose enjoyment of a pure profit would last only so long as he or she remains in the employment of the partnership. Such an improvement of incentives would apply much more strongly to elderly workers near retirement than to young workers with a number of years of employment before them.

The rule of redistribution causes no change in the distribution of total pure profit as between capital and labour. As the years go by the pure profit of any retiring worker partner is simply handed back to the remaining worker partners. But with the rules of cancellation and of retention as the years go by the pure profit enjoyed by worker partners is reduced and that enjoyed by capitalist partners is increased by the same amount until in the end in both cases the original worker's pure profit has all be transferred to the enjoyment of capitalists. But there are three important distinctions between the two cases.

First, the mechanisms of transfer are very different in the two cases. With the rule of cancellation the mechanism works simply through cancellation of retiring worker partners' pure-profit certificates which allows the rate of dividend on the remaining total of share certificates to rise, thus enriching the original providers of capital funds. With the rule of retention the mechanism works simply by transforming the pure-profit certificates of retiring worker partners into Capital Share Certificates without any change in the total number of certificates issued.

Second, the process of transfer is much more rapid with the rule of retention than with the rule of cancellation. With the former the whole of a retiring worker's pure profit is immediately transformed into a capitalist pure profit; with the rule of cancellation at each retirement only a fraction of the working partner's pure profit is transferred to the capitalists, a proportion which may be very low in a labour-intensive partnership.

Third, there is a difference in the distribution of pure-profit among the owners of Capital Share Certificates. With the rule of cancellation the original capitalists obtain the whole of the advantage: with the rule of retention a new class of capitalist obtains the whole of the advantage, leaving the original capitalists' pure profit unchanged. Thus the rule of retention by creating new owners of capital out of retiring worker partners will lead to a wider spread of the ownership of capital.

The Effect of Partnership upon Distribution of Income between Labour and Capital

We have shown how different principles and rules can lead to different structures of Labour-Capital Partnerships. In fact we have specified six types of partnership. Retirement from work can be based upon rules of cancellation, redistribution or retention and each of these three cases can be structured upon accounting principles of either capital-maintenance or income-maintenance. The choice of regime for the partnership may modify to some extent the distributions of income and wealth. We now wish to consider the main effects upon such distributions of structuring enterprises as Labour Capital Partnerships rather than as Capitalist Companies. It would be too tedious to make the comparison between the Capitalist Company and each of the six possible varieties of Labour-Capital Partnerships. In fact in this section on the distribution of income and in all the following sections in which we are making general comparisons between Capitalist Companies and Labour-Capital Partnerships we will confine ourselves to a comparison between a Capitalist Company and a Labour-Capital Partnership which is structured on the accounting principle of capital-maintenance and the retirement rule of cancellation which is in fact the commonest form adopted in Agathotopia. The reader must be left to him or herself to consider the changes of result which would occur in any of the other five possible Labour-Capital Partnership structures.

The basic division of income in any particular business between labour and capital will be the same for all competitive market structures, whether they be of a capitalist or partnership pattern. The rewards which will be offered for particular uses of capital and labour will depend upon market conditions and, in particular, upon (i) how far final consumers want to purchase goods and services which are labour-intensive or capital-intensive in their production; (ii) how far technological inventions tend to save capital or to save labour in the various lines of production; and (iii) the relative amounts of capital and labour which are available to be employed. In fact the main purpose of the introduction of Labour-Capital Partnerships must not be regarded as a method of achieving a revolutionary change in the distribution of income and wealth as between the rich and the poor in society but rather as that of achieving a productive and constructive co-operation in industry. The Agathotopians are clear about this and rely upon a wide range of other measures to achieve a better distribution of income and wealth.

Nevertheless, the introduction of the partnership structures can have some appreciable redistributive effects of two main kinds.

As we have already argued, in the Discriminating Labour-Capital Partnership under the rule of cancellation it will in the long run pay all existing partners, both workers and capitalists, to engage an additional working partner so long as his or her marginal revenue product is greater than his or her cost. As a result of this the cost of a worker may be lower for the Discriminating Labour-Capital Partnership than for the Capitalist Company and thus the expansionary forces may be greater in the former than in the latter system. In a Capitalist Company existing workers (the insiders) wish through trade-union action or by other means to protect their rate of pay against the possibility of new workers (the outsiders) offering their services at a lower rate. In a Discriminating Partnership the lower the remuneration of new partners, the greater the gain to the existing members who are already inside the partnership; and thus the insiders will encourage the outsiders to offer their services at the lowest rate of remuneration which is attractive to them rather than impeding them from so doing. The result would be in principle the same as that which would be achieved by a set of similar Capitalist Companies on the assumption that their fixed wage rates were set at a low enough level to give an incentive to the capitalist employers to employ all workers who sought employment at those rates. There could be some important advantages in the partnership economy due to the greater productivity resulting from improvements in incentives and the reduction of conflicts between labour and capital in the running of businesses. But in principle in the final steady state the distribution of income between labour and capital in the Discriminating Labour-Capital Partnerships would be the same as in a set of similar Capitalist Companies on the assumption that the latter's fixed wage rates were held down to the level necessary to achieve full employment.

On the other hand, the disadvantage is, of course, the possible adverse effects upon the real remuneration of the working partners and on the distribution of income between the owners of Capital Share Certificates and of Labour Share Certificates. Full employment in a free market economy, whether it be composed of Capitalist Companies or of Labour-Capital Partnerships, may imply a relatively low rate of real remuneration for the work done and thus a substantial rise in the share going to the owners of capital, a phenomenon which could become particularly marked if modern technological developments proved to be basically labour-saving. For this reason the Agathotopians have always insisted that their system of Discriminating Labour-Capital Partnerships at the enterprise level should be combined with the very extensive fiscal and other measures for the redistribution of income and wealth which are described later in section III of this chapter.

The second main way in which the institution of a Labour-Capital Partnership may have distributive effects is in the division of a pure profit between Labour and Capital. All forms of competitive market enterprises must in the end cover their costs, that is to say, what the factors of production could earn in other employments. But they may earn something in addition to these costs, which we call a pure profit. In realistic conditions of imperfect competition all enterprises could simultaneously be earning some element of pure profit. The most familiar example of a pure profit is the monopoly profit that can be made by a business which for some reason is protected from the entry of any competing businesses in a particular market; it can restrict output and thus raise selling price above its costs of production. Although its selling price is above its average cost of production, it has no incentive to put more on the market because of the damage which that would do to its selling price. It may be protected from greater competition in its market because of the costs involved in setting up a new business, or because of the fact that low costs depend upon a large scale of operations and there would not be room in the market for more than one business of an efficient size or because of the cost of transport of competing goods from more distant markets or of its customers to more distant sources of supply or because of the special renown of its own brand name.

In fact all businesses simultaneously may have greater or smaller monopolistic elements of this kind. Each business may on average be setting a selling price which somewhat exceeds it average costs, i.e. which is somewhat greater than what other businesses would pay for the use of its labour and capital for the marginal expansion of their own somewhat monopolistic enterprises. They would all be enjoying a revenue from their sales which exceeded in various degrees the marginal value to other businesses of the labour and capital which they were employing.

In a structure of Capitalist Companies such elements of pure profit or goodwill or monopoly profit – call it what you will – would all tend to accrue to the capitalist entrepreneurs or owners of the equity shares in the company. As we have already argued, in a structure of Discriminating Labour-Capital Partnerships conducted under the rule of cancellation all such pure profit in static conditions would also eventually accrue to the owners of capital. But new pure profits as they emerged would be shared between labour and capital and would continue to be so shared for a prolonged period as they very gradually seeped away to the capitalists.

When a Labour-Capital Partnership was first set up the issue of Capital Share Certificates and of Labour Share Certificates would have to be such as to cover the capital costs and the labour costs; but bargaining strengths would determine the original distribution of Labour and Capital Share Certificates issued on a scale needed to account for any expected pure profit. Thereafter the development of the distribution of dividends between labour and capital would take place in the ways we have already described, subject to the original distribution of share certificates between the two categories.

The Renegotiation of Shareholdings

The main negotiation of the distribution of shareholdings between capitalist and worker partners must take place on the inauguration of the partnership. But some subsequent occasions will occur when a renegotiation of share certificates issued to existing worker partners or capitalist partners is needed. Individual promotions are, of course, a proper and desirable phenomenon – indeed, a necessary one if able persons are to be retained in the firm's service. In such cases promotions involving the raising of a worker's pay by a rise in his or her fixed-wage payment or by the issue to him or her of additional Labour Share Certificates are, of course, of ultimate benefit to all shareholders.

But the problem becomes much more serious if one considers the possibility of group claims for 'promotion', i.e. for renegotiation of the number of Labour Share Certificates issued to a whole class of workers. Suppose there were a threat of a strike by all the worker partners in a particular enterprise unless the ratio of Labour Share Certificates to Capital Share Certificates were radically altered. Or suppose that a particular small group of worker partners who were in a key position to hold up operations threatened to strike unless their claim to an increased issue of Labour Share Certificates was satisfied.

Such a claim, might of course, be justified if outside developments had so increased their value that they would be tempted to move elsewhere unless their claim was met. The Agathotopians have found that in every partnership there must be some agreed arrangement whereby claims for 'promotion' can be made by individuals or groups of partners on the grounds that new improved terms of payment which they are claiming are (i) necessary to offset the attraction of employment in other outside concerns and (ii) do not exceed the loss of net revenue to the partnership which would occur if they withdrew their services. It is an essential part of the agreed machinery of a Labour-Capital Partnership that such claims are submitted to some appropriate organ of the partnership for decision and that this implies the end of partnership membership for those who do not accept the award.

The Effect of Losses

Up to this point we have discussed what happens to prosperous and success-ful enterprises. To a large extent if demand falls instead of rising and a partnership's revenue decreases rather than increases, the analysis is simply unchanged except for the change of sign.

With rising demand in a Discriminating Labour-Capital Partnership the dividends on Labour and on Capital Share Certificates rise and the in-creased pure profit is thus shared between the two parties. With falling demand, dividends fall and the reduction in pure profit (or, after a time, any increase in pure loss) is similarly shared.

In so far as a rising demand for the partnership's product raises the marginal value product of the worker partner, new worker partners will be engaged; and similarly, if the marginal value product of the capital equip-ment increases new funds will be raised at market cost for the installation of additional capital equipment. Any additional employment of labour at cost to perform work which has now risen in value above cost will increase the pure profit of the partnership and will thus raise the dividends of all existing partners. Thus the expansion of labour and capital will raise pure profit to the advantage of all the existing partners.

If as a result of falling demand the marginal value products of labour and of machinery fall, there will be a corresponding reduction at the margin of worker partners and of the employment of machines. But these negative effects are not in all respects symmetrical with the positive effects of a rising level of demand.

Workers at the margin whose incomes fall below what they could get elsewhere will resign and leave the partnership. In so far as they can do so, these worker partners will gain by the move in the sense that they will raise their earnings once more back to their cost level and avoid the loss of dividends in their former partnership from causing them to bear any pure loss. The whole of the avoidance of pure loss will accrue to the individual migrating workers and not to the rest of the partnership.

In the case of a fall in the marginal value product of a machine, the machine when it wears out will not be replaced and the depreciation fund which would have been used for its replacement will be free to be invested outside the partnership at the going market-cost rate of return, to this extent avoiding the loss on the marginal machine. But this avoidance of loss will not accrue to any individual capitalist but will enable dividends to be cut less than would otherwise be the case for all members of the partnership.

This difference sets the balance against the interests of individual capitalists. In the case of a prosperous business, expansion will raise pure profit to be shared among all members. In the case of a declining business, contraction of employment will avoid loss for individual workers who change jobs but contraction of capital resources will avoid loss not for any individual capitalists and indeed not just for the capitalists as a class, but for all members of the partnership.

In a Discriminatory Labour-Capital Partnership based on the accounting principle of capital maintenance and the retirement rule of cancellation, there will be some favourable balance for the capitalists as a class in that pure profit will seep gradually away from Labour on to Capital Share Certificates. But there will be some unfavourable balance in that the avoidance of loss in a contraction will be easier for worker than for capitalist partners.[10]

The Effect of Security of Tenure for Worker Partners

In a Discriminating Labour-Capital Partnership a worker partner who became redundant would retain his or her income from Labour Share Certificates until the age of retirement so long as he or she was available for work in the partnership. In a Capitalist Company the worker would have no such security of tenure. The question arises whether this arrangement unduly shifts the distribution of income against the capitalist partners since redundant worker partners retain an income which in the case of a Capitalist Company would revert to the owners of the capital.

There is a very important offsetting advantage for the capitalist partners. If there is a reduction in the demand for the partnership's product which leads to a reduction in the enterprise's distributable surplus, the dividends on Labour Share Certificates will be reduced *pari passu* with the dividends on Capital Share Certificates. The reduction in the incomes of the capitalist partners is in large part offset by the reduction in the incomes of the worker partners. What in a Capitalist Company employing workers at a fixed rate of pay would lead to redundancy will lead to a reduction in labour costs in a Labour-Capital Partnership. In general those who provide risk capital to a Labour-Capital Partnership are likely to gain more by being able to retain worker partners who share the loss with them than they will lose by the risk of having to support them if they become redundant.

But there are certain other kinds of event which may lead to redundancies for which the security of tenure in a Labour-Capital Partnership does impose a burden on the return to be earned on risk-bearing capital which would be avoided in a Capitalist Company. This could arise in the case of what would otherwise be a profitable introduction of certain new technologies. The replacement of existing workers by a machine or by workers of a different skill would be profitable in a Capitalist Company if the wages payable to the existing workers were greater than the current costs of the new machine or of the new team of workers; such a replacement could be held up in a partnership in which the dismissal of an existing worker would, up to retirement age, save only the fixed-wage element but not the share-dividend element in the worker partner's remuneration. Any such delay would be mitigated in three ways: first it would operate only in so far as it would otherwise be desirable to introduce the new technology more rapidly than could be covered by the normal ageing and retirement of the workforce; second, the extra cost of replacement of an existing worker would refer only to that part of his or her pay which took the form of a dividend on Labour Share Certificates; and, third, it would be wholly avoided by any few firm which was set up to exploit the new technology. Moreover, the net loss arising from any such impediments to the introduction of new technologies should not be exaggerated. There are already in normal Capitalist Companies some serious impediments on account of trade-union and similar pressure to preserve existing jobs and demarcations of work and on account of statutory or other obligations to make redundancy payments to redundant workers.

The cost to a partnership involved in the support of redundant worker partners is also limited by the principle stated above that the claim of a worker partner on the partnership would be tied to his or her availability to perform the work for which the dividend on Labour Share Certificates was the reward. An 'availability' test might be applied by ruling that a partnership which made a worker partner redundant could at any time ask the worker to return to the partnership on the terms which he or she previously enjoyed with it. If the worker concerned declined the invitation, then his or her Labour Share Certificates would be cancelled. The existence of this rule would ensure that redundant workers who did subsequently find an alternative post which held out more attractive prospects of future work could be effectively asked once and for all to surrender their existing Labour Share Certificates.

The application of this simple 'availability' test does, however, raise an important and far-reaching problem. In the case of a worker partner the whole of whose pay consisted of dividends on Labour Share Certificates, there would be no problem in defining 'the terms which he or she had previously enjoyed' with the partnership. The worker would be offered a post with the retention of an unchanged number of Labour Share Certificates. But in the case of workers who had received a fixed-wage element in their previous pay in the partnership, the problem would arise as to what level of fixed pay they should be offered on reinstatement. The same money rate of pay might well be unfair if, for example, inflationary developments during the period of absence from the partnership had substantially eroded the value of money. Since the partnership is founded on the principle that fixed-money wages are not intended to represent the whole of, or indeed any specific proportion of, the real pay of any individual worker, there would be no obvious 'rate for the job' on which to base the new offer. It would be necessary to rely on some rather general definition such as 'the rate which the worker could reasonably be expected to be receiving if he or she had continued an unbroken membership of the partnership', backed by some form of arbitration or review by an independent tribunal in the case of disagreement.

There is one further source of trouble which may arise in the treatment of redundancy. It is proposed that worker partners who leave the enterprise voluntarily to seek better-paid jobs should surrender their Labour Share Certificates, whereas a worker partner who is made redundant should at least for the time being retain them. It would thus be to the interest of workers who wished to move elsewhere to be judged redundant rather than themselves to resign their membership of the partnership. For this purpose they might make themselves as useless as possible to the management without stepping over the borderline which would justify dismissal for misconduct with consequential surrender of their Labour Share Certificates. The conflict of interest in this case would be between the delinquent worker partners on the one hand and all other partners, whether worker or capitalist, on the other hand; but there is clearly here the possibility of tiresome disputes requiring judgement by some form of impartial tribunal. This particular problem would, however, be greatly eased if the test of availability proposed above were adopted, since a worker who obtained a more attractive job and who retained the Labour Share Certificates issued by the partnership in which he or she previously worked could always be induced to surrender them by being invited to rejoin the partnership on the original but now unattractive terms of service.

The Implication for Risk-Bearing

There is a very good reason why the owners of the equity capital rather than the workers should bear the risks of fluctuations in the profitability of any enterprise. Owners of capital can spread their risks by investing their capital in relatively small amounts in a large number of independent enterprises. If one enterprise fares very badly, they will not have all their eggs in one basket. It is impossible for a worker to split up his or her working hours into small periods of an hour a week and thus work one hour each week for, say, 40 different firms. Work eggs unlike capital eggs must all be held in one basket, or at the most in one or two baskets.

But any form of partnership enterprise in which the incomes of the worker partners depend in whole or part upon the fortunes of the enterprise necessarily implies that the workers face risks which they would not otherwise confront. In this way they share with the capitalists risks which would otherwise have been borne wholly by the capitalists. If the concern does well the capitalists share the gain with the workers; if it does badly the workers share the loss by receiving a lower rate of reward. In this way the capitalists face smaller risks and the workers greater risks of variation in their incomes.

There is thus a basic dilemma between the objective of concentrating risk-bearing on those who provide the capital funds and the objective of treating workers as full partners in a business enterprise. Certain forms of partnership enterprise accentuate this dilemma by requiring or at least encouraging workers to own capital shares in the enterprise in which they work and thus to become directly concerned with its profitability. But this increases the concentration of risks borne by the workers since it ensures that not only their work eggs but also a part at least of their capital eggs are in one and the same basket.

Agathotopian Discriminating Labour-Capital Partnerships avoid this anomaly. Measures are taken in Agathotopia (as described later in section

III of this chapter) to encourage a widespread ownership of capital funds so that the representative worker partner does own capital funds to invest in the Capital Share Certificates of Labour-Capital Partnerships. But there is no call on a worker partner to invest in the Capital Share Certificates of the particular partnership in which he or she works. On the contrary like good capitalists worker partners are encouraged to spread their capital risks over a wide range of other partnerships.

But even if this form of unnecessary concentration of capital risks is avoided, the basic dilemma regarding the risks to which earned incomes are subject in Labour-Capital Partnerships remains unsolved and gives rise to the following questions.

(1) Should partnership enterprises be encouraged in order to promote better incentives and better relations between labour and capital and, in their discriminating form, to promote full employment? Or should they be discouraged in order to enable risks to be concentrated on the owners of capital?

(2) Whatever answer be given to the first question, a second question arises. Can workers be persuaded to become risk-bearing partners rather than employees at fixed rates of pay or must Labour-Capital Partnerships be dismissed as an unacceptable pipe dream?

(3) If Labour-Capital Partnerships are in fact constructed with the worker partners playing an effective role in their management, will there not be a dangerous bias introduced against risky business, a bias which could seriously impede economic innovation and progress?

These considerations suggest that to enable a successful and acceptable structure of Labour-Capital Partnerships to be developed it will be necessary to introduce some measures to mitigate the risk problem for the worker partners. Such measures are discussed later in section III of this chapter.

This problem of risk-bearing should not, however be exaggerated. There are certain aspects of partnership enterprises which reduce the risks of workers. In particular a worker partner faces a smaller risk of unemployment than does an employee engaged at a fixed rate of pay. Thus while the worker partner stands to gain in income if the enterprise does well, he or she has less fear of his or her income falling to the level of unemployment benefit if the enterprise does badly. It is the capitalist and those workers who are most likely to become unemployed who face less risk in a Labour-Capital Partnership. It is the workers whose jobs are secure who face the greater risks in the fluctuations of their dividend income. Can workers then be free to choose between employment at a fixed wage rate and partnership with a variable dividend?

In a Labour-Capital Partnership the existing capitalist and worker partners would have an incentive to make a fellow worker partner redundant only if they judged that what he or she contributed to the firm's net revenue had fallen below the amount of the fixed-wage element in his or her pay, since any dividends payable on Labour Share Certificates would remain a charge on the partnership's income, whether the worker partner was made redundant or not. Thus a worker by choosing any given mix between a fixed-wage payment and a dividend on Labour Share Certificates would thereby in effect have chosen to distribute risks in a corresponding mix between unemployment and fluctuations in the inclusive rate of remuneration. The higher the fixed-wage element, the greater the risk of unemployment but the lower the risk of a drop – or indeed of a rise – in his or her inclusive rate of remuneration.

In many businesses the existing workers may have a pretty shrewd idea as to which of them are regarded as least productive by the management and are, therefore, the most likely to be made redundant if a reduction in the labour force becomes necessary. Thus a known minority of workers may face an important risk of unemployment which does not threaten the majority. In such a case if the mix between a fixed wage and a share dividend had to apply equally to all workers, the choice of the majority would be for a fixed wage. If, however, it were possible for individual workers to make their own choice, those most liable to redundancy might well choose a variable dividend. Such a choice would give them relative security of employment; the next layer of relatively unproductive workers would now be those who risked redundancy and would thus become more favourable to the variable dividend, and so on by a domino effect the total mix would contain a larger and larger proportion of variable dividend.

In a number of Agathotopian partnerships workers have been allowed freely to choose (on terms laid down by the management of the partnership) between fixed-wage payments and receipts of dividends on Labour Share Certificates, but their experience has suggested that while the resulting domino effect does something to help it cannot be relied upon alone to persuade the representative worker to accept a very substantial proportion of pay in the form of a variable dividend.

In addition to the lower risks of unemployment in a Labour-Capital Partnership there is a second factor which mitigates the risk to workers. In a Labour-Capital Partnership worker partners remain free to move to other occupations. To the extent to which this factor is operative, the worker is presented with a heads-I-win-tails-you-lose situation. If the enterprise does well the worker partner shares the gain with the capitalist partner; if the enterprise does badly the worker partner avoids the loss by moving else-where, leaving the capitalist partner to bear the risk in the same way as he would have done in a Capitalist Company. In reality the worker partner will normally not be able to avoid all risk in this way. If the bad fortune of the partnership is part of the phenomenon of a general depression, there will not be any attractive alternative occupations to move to. Even if the bad fortune is peculiar to the partnership, the availability of alternative occupations will depend upon the particular conditions of the region and the occupation in which the trouble has arisen; and in any case the search for and shift to the alternative occupation will be costly and will take time. But there may be cases in which the possibility of voluntary movement to alternative jobs significantly shifts risks back again from the worker on to the capitalist.

There are many other factors which affect the degree of risk borne by worker partners and by capitalist partners in a Labour-Capital Partnership. The preceding discussion has been confined to a comparison between a Capitalist Company and a Labour-Capital Partnership. If however, the relevant transformation had been that of a Labour-Managed Cooperative into a Labour-Capital Partnership, the changes to risk bearing would have been totally different. Moreover, the nature and degree of change will depend upon many other factors: whether the enterprise is in a capital-intensive or a labour-intensive activity; whether the risk to be borne is on the supply side (e.g. a risk concerning future techniques of production) or, as has been assumed throughout the above analysis, on the demand side; whether the change is expected to be permanent or temporary; whether it is expected to occur soon or only in the distant future; whether the change is general to a whole region or industry or occupation or whether it is confined to a single particular partnership; and so on.

It is impossible to cover all these possibilities. But Agathotopian experience suggests that it can be safely concluded that for the successful introduction of Discriminating Labour-Capital Partnerships as a major, if not the predominant, form for competitive private enterprise, it will be necessary to take some special measures to mitigate the risks borne by worker partners.

Conclusions

From the above discussion of the nature of partnership enterprises the following conclusions may be reached:

(i)   that they could lead to a great encouragement of cooperative action between labour and capital in running a competitive concern in the most efficient and productive manner; and

(ii) that they could lead to an expansion of an enterprise's workforce and thus to a reduction in unemployment, if the obstacle presented by a strict application of the principle of equal pay for equal work were overcome; but

(iii) that they cannot be expected in themselves to lead to any basic improvement in the distribution of income between labour and capital and

(iv) that their acceptance by workers may be seriously impeded by their implications as regards the bearing of risks.

In the following section III on The Partnership Economy an attempt is made to see how far Agathotopian experience suggests that general economic and financial institutions and policies may be moulded so as to reduce the obstacles to the widespread acceptance of partnership at the enterprise level.

III   THE PARTNERSHIP ECONOMY

The conclusions reached at the end of section II suggest that a successful and acceptable development of partnership enterprises depends upon three conditions: (i) the erosion of the principle of equal pay for equal work, (ii) the design of other measures for the improvement of the distribution of income and wealth, and (iii) the alleviation of the risks to be borne by worker partners. Thus the structure of a system of partnership enterprise needs to be undertaken against the background of a partnership economy in which general economic policies and institutions are designed to meet these three requirements. The present section III of this chapter is accordingly devoted to an analysis of the special features which in these respects distinguish the Agathotopian economy from that with which we are familiar in the United Kingdom.

The Distribution of Income and Wealth

As has been argued in section II, Labour-Capital Partnerships must not be relied upon as an instrument for achieving any desired change in the distribution of the product of industry as between the incomes of worker and of owners of capital. But what is really important is not the distribution of the national income between labour as a whole and capital as a whole, but the distribution of income between individuals. It is no doubt true that the common contrast between very rich capitalists on the one hand and very poor workers on the other has rather more reality than a contrived contrast between very poor capitalists (the proverbial widows and orphans) on the one hand and very rich workers (the great operatic singer or the computer expert) on the other. But the way to cope with the problem is to devise ways of influencing the distribution of income between rich and poor persons rather than to upset efficient working of the competitive market economy by direct control of the division between the return on capital and the earnings of labour.

What then are the general policies which might be adopted in a partnership economy to deal with this problem of distribution? Such measures can be summarised under four broad headings.

First, there are measures designed to encourage a more equal distribution of the ownership of property. If the representative citizen were both a representative worker and a representative capitalist providing the national average amount of work per head and owning the national average amount of capital per head, a market change which caused a larger proportion of the national product to go to capital and less to labour would have no effect on his or her individual income. What the citizen lost in payment for labour he or she would gain in payment on wealth. A widespread ownership of property is a most desirable feature of a partnership economy. Not only would it help to deal with the basic problem of the distribution of income between individuals. It would also at the partnership enterprise level help to promote the atmosphere of cooperative partnership if every worker owner of Labour Share Certificates also owned an appreciable amount of Capital Share Certificates, even if those were invested in other partnerships.

A second method for equalising the income accruing from the ownership of property is for the State itself to become the beneficial owner of a part of the country's income-generating capital resources and to use the income earned on this capital wealth to finance the payment of a Social Dividend to all citizens. This method involves the State in acquiring through its fiscal policy a Net National Asset to replace the customary present Net National Debt. Both methods have the effect of distributing to the private citizens the income earned on capital wealth on a more equal basis. These methods become the more significant, the greater is the proportion of the national product which in a free market economy would accrue to capital rather than the labour. It may well be true that in a competitive market economy the achievement and maintenance of full employment in the UK demands some reduction in the real cost of the worker's remuneration and thus some shift to profit, a development which would become even more important if future technological changes turned out to be markedly labour-saving in the sense that they markedly increased the importance of capital equipment relative to manpower in the process of production.

Third, there is the possibility of the State providing on the same equal basis for all citizens certain social services such as those for education and health.

Fourth, there is the possibility of direct redistribution of money incomes between rich and poor through the payment of direct monetary social benefits in support of the poor financed by some form of progressive taxation of the rich.

In Agathotopia, as will be explained later, special measures have been devised to encourage a more widespread ownership of property and to exert a direct equalising effect upon the distribution of income.

Risk-Bearing

In section II the question was raised whether the development of Labour-Capital Partnerships might be impeded by the unwillingness of workers to bear the risks of a form of pay which varied with the fortunes of the business in which they were employed.

The more equal distribution of the ownership of property which is one of the features of the Agathotopian economy has helped to deal with this problem. The greater the proportion of income which a worker receives from property which can be invested in other undertakings, the more ready he or she will be to face possible fluctuations in his or her remuneration for work.

A second feature of the same kind is the payment by the State to every citizen (dependent solely upon the age and family position of that citizen) of a given income, called a Social Dividend. This income is tax-free and is paid unconditionally to every citizen whether he or she is employed or unemployed, healthy or sick, active or idle, and – at the appropriate rates – young or old. The representative citizen then has four sources of income.

(i)   a certain and reliable tax free Social Dividend,
(ii) the return on his or her capital wealth which he or she can lend at fixed interest or at a probably higher yield in equity capital, the risks of which can be spread over a large number of enterprises,

(iii) any part of his or her remuneration for work which continues to take the form of a fixed wage payment, and

(iv) the whole or the part of the remuneration for his or her work which takes the form of a share in the fluctuating revenue of the partnership in which the work is done.

Items (i), (ii) and (iii) mitigate the risks involved in (iv).

Full Employment and the Flexibility of Pay for Work

Full employment implies a level of employment which is both stable and high. It is the flexibility of rates of pay in Discriminating Labour-Capital Partnerships which in Agathotopia leads to a satisfactory employment situation. A stable level is achieved in so far as remuneration for work takes the form of a variable dividend on Labour Share Certificates instead of a fixed wage rate. If demand for the products of the enterprise falls off, the rate of dividend on both Capital and Labour Share Certificates is reduced; production costs and prices are lowered; employment and output are maintained at lower money costs and prices rather than being reduced in volume at unchanged money prices. But a high level of employment is achieved not through the variability of the pay of existing workers but through the principle of discrimination which gives an incentive to existing partners to mop up any pockets of involuntarily unemployed persons at rates of remuneration which are attractive to the unemployed (the outsiders) but which do not threaten the incomes of existing worker or capitalist partners (the insiders).

It is, therefore, a basic feature of Agathotopian policy to encourage such discriminatory arrangements as well as to encourage the acceptance of risks of variation in rates of remuneration. The measures already discussed in connection with the distribution of income and the alleviation of risk-bearing are also helpful to ease the acceptance of discrimination in rates of remuneration. Measures such as a widespread ownership of capital and thus of income from capital and the payment of a tax-free fixed Social Dividend all serve to reduce the importance of earned relative to other income. These measures can thus help to promote a desirable shift of emphasis away from institutional arrangements for setting high levels of remuneration for work on to fiscal and similar measures as the main instruments for the maintenance of standards of living and for the distribution of income. The more this happens the easier it is for work and the reward for work to be regarded with less rigid commitment. Part-time work becomes more frequent and differences in the remunerations offered to different workers joining an enterprise at different times and in different conditions can become more acceptable.

The Budgetary Implications

The Agathotopians have had to face the hideous expense involved in solving these two problems of the redistribution of income and wealth and of risk-bearing. All the measures mentioned above involve in one way or another fiscal measures of taxation or levies to promote redistribution in the ownership of wealth, to finance social services, or to redistribute income between individuals. It is all too easy to build up a rosy picture of these three forms of redistributive measures without due attention to the financial cost. It is not difficult to produce an attractive redistributive programme the finance of which would involve a 90 per cent rate of tax on the total income of the community. There is a very real trade-off between efficiency and equality in the community. If one paid every citizen a Social Dividend equal to the national average product of industry per head whether the citizen worked or not, one would need a tax of 100 per cent on all production to finance it. No citizen would have any incentive to earn any extra income by going out to work. The national product and thus the Social Dividend would fall to zero. There would be complete equality at zero income per head. There is a similar trade-off between efficiency and the alleviation of risk-bearing. The payment of a tax-free Social Dividend sounds a very attractive way of mitigating the burden of risk-bearing; but even if it is paid only at a moderate rate it is an alarmingly expensive form of remedy.

This raises two issues which the Agathotopians have had to face: first, the moral-political problem of deciding how much efficiency one should be prepared to sacrifice for how much equality and for how much promotion of partnership; and, second, the economic-political problem of the choice of means for a given promotion of equality and of partnership which will avoid or minimise any adverse effects upon efficiency. A major feature of the Agathotopian reaction to this second issue has been to seek a new source of revenue through the State enjoying the beneficial ownership (without incurring the day-to-day management) of a substantial proportion of the island's capital wealth.

The rest of this section III is devoted to a more detailed description of the distinctive features of Agathotopian institutions and policies which have been designed to promote a true partnership economy with an acceptable balance between the conflicting considerations outlined above.

The Institutions of Agathotopia

(1) Discriminating Labour-Capital Partnerships and the Stabilisation of the Money GDP as a means of Maintaining Full Employment without Inflation

The competitive sector of the Agathotopian economy is marked by a widespread structure of Discriminating Labour-Capital Partnerships at the individual enterprise level. They do not cover the whole of Agathotopian economic activity. Many branches of the public service including, for example, defence, police, and administration of other services cannot be run by individual competitive private partnerships, even though a considerable range of relevant activities are contracted out by the public authorities to such private partnerships. Moreover there are activities which must be run on so great a monopolistic scale or which carry such external advantages or disadvantages to society that it is thought best to operate them as public nationalised monopolies.

There is no compulsion on private enterprise to take the form of Discriminating Labour-Capital Partnerships, and in fact there are many instances of familiar Capitalist Companies and Labour-Managed Co-operatives in the Agathotopian economy. But the Agathotopians have succeeded in transforming a very large part of the private sector of their economy into Discriminating Labour-Capital Partnerships by offering important tax advantages to such enterprises. These fiscal privileges are, however, strictly restricted to those partnerships whose constitution effectively introduces the principle of discrimination in their arrangements for the pay of working members.

In the absence of such discrimination Labour-Capital Partnerships could be very restrictive and lead to heavy unemployment and rapid cost inflation. The existing partners in any such enterprise, both workers and owners would have an incentive to restrict output, to limit the number of working partners, and to raise selling prices so long as they could thereby raise the dividend per share certificate. With all such enterprises acting in this way there would be grave danger of a cumulative inflation of prices combined with heavy unemployment throughout the economy. This outcome would be reversed if the principle of discrimination were effectively applied in an economy in which the total of money expenditures on the products of industry was also being effectively controlled. Suppose that in such conditions the existing worker partners had managed to inflate prices by restricting the size of the working partnership to that number which would serve to maximise labour pure profit per working partner. They would then find that they had an incentive to take on more working partners, to expand output and to reduce selling prices just so long as new working partners were willing to join the partnership for a rate of reward which was less than what the product of their work would add to the net revenue of the enterprise. The existing shareholders would thus all stand to gain so long as there were available any unemployed citizens who would welcome work at a rate of reward which was less than what their work would add to the net revenue of existing Labour-Capital Partnerships.

In combination with a widespread structure of Discriminating Partnerships the Agathotopians have accordingly adopted the stabilisation of their money GDP on a steady 5-per-cent-per-annum growth path as one of the major objectives of their monetary and fiscal policies. (Other objectives of their financial policies are discussed below.) Against this steady but restrained rise in the total money expenditure on the products of labour the expansionary forces of successful Discriminating Partnerships prevent the growth of any excessive unemployment without any undue inflationary developments.

(2) Savings-Exempt Income Tax Combined with Taxes on the Transfer of Wealth as a Means for Promoting the Widespread Ownership of Capital Wealth

In Agathotopia there is a much more equal spread in the ownership of private wealth than there is with us. Their problem was to devise means by which any such wide spread of ownership might be attained and indeed maintained when once it was attained. For there are very powerful influences in a free competitive society for the restoration of inequalities. By luck or special ability and enterprise some individuals may earn more than others by their work or invest their wealth more productively; others by bad luck or less than average ability may do worse. But those who happen to do well will be in a much better position to save more and thus to do still better, while those who do badly may actually have to live on what wealth they do possess. There are thus forces which make the wealthy more wealthy and the poor still poorer. If there is freedom of inheritance these differences are handed on; and those citizens who inherit much are in an easy position to accumulate still more wealth. Thus arrangements were sought not only to achieve a more equal distribution of the ownership of property but also to maintain the situation once it had been achieved.

They considered the merits of a system which exempted from tax all the savings of the poor and financed this tax exemption of the savings of the poor by a progressive tax on all personal holdings of wealth above a certain limit. For the poor the accumulation of wealth would be made easy; for the wealthy it would be more difficult to add yet more to their wealth. One way to do this would be to replace any existing income tax by a tax on expenditure on consumption. The procedure would be to assess as before each taxpayer's income, to add to that sum the proceeds of any sales of the taxpayer's property, and to subtract from that sum the cost of the acquisition of any new items of capital wealth. The result would be to levy tax on the net inflow of purchasing power which had been used to spend on consumption. All net saving would be exempt from tax.

If with such an arrangement which relieved all net savings from tax there were combined a tax on all holdings of wealth which exceeded a certain limit, it would be easier for everyone to accumulate wealth up to that limit and more difficult for everyone to accumulate wealth beyond that limit.

The Agathotopians did arrange for all net savings to be exempt from income tax, but they considered that there would be serious disadvantages in a heavy wealth tax. It would make it more difficult for a successful enterpriser, whether or not he or she was sharing that success with other partners, to find the funds to expand an existing adventurous business. In the environment of successful business enterprises which it was an important objective of the competitive market partnership economy to promote, such a stop to the accumulation of private wealth would have serious disadvantages.

For this reason it was thought preferable not to rely on an annual wealth tax on large holdings of wealth or at least to restrict such a levy to very moderate rates of tax. In its place they preferred to rely on duties levied on the passing of the ownership of large holdings of wealth from one owner to another on the occasion of death or of a gift *inter vivos*.

They combined this taxation of gifts and bequests with a low rate of tax levied annually on all personal holdings of wealth above a low exemption level. For the assessment of the annual wealth tax they accept each citizen's personal valuation of his or her various assets. But there is an added provision that the State can purchase any such asset at a price 10 per cent above its declared valuation, thus setting a strict limit to undervaluation. This low rate of annual wealth tax raises a significant revenue. (Thus a tax of 5 per mille on the capital value of an asset which produces a 5-per-cent-per-annum yield represents a tax of 10 per cent on that annual income.) But the tax has a most important secondary purpose in providing an inexpensive but reliable valuation of capital assets for the administration of the savings-exempt income tax and the taxation of gifts and bequests.[11]

The Agathotopians argued that such an arrangement would not interfere unduly with the accumulation of capital by an adventurous and successful entrepreneur over his or her lifetime; but the concentration of wealth through inheritance would be reduced, and the State would receive a revenue which would at least be sufficient to set against the loss of tax on the net savings of other citizens.

(3) The Payment of a Tax-Free Social Dividend for the Promotion of Equality, the Alleviation of Risk-Bearing, the Improvement of Incentives for Low Earnings, and the Simplification of the Welfare State

In Agathotopia a tax-free Social Dividend is paid to every citizen according to the citizen's age and family status but without any other conditions. Two of the basic reasons for this institution have already been noted; namely, (i) the equalising effect of providing everyone with the same basic income; and (ii) the reduction of risk when some part of income is unaffected by variations in a worker's remuneration for work.

Social Benefits which are conditional upon the recipient being unemployed or being in need because of inadequate alternative income imply serious disincentives for accepting low earnings. The Conditional Benefit may be one which like unemployment benefit will be entirely removed if the recipient finds work or may be one which will be reduced pound for pound as the recipient increases his or her income from additional outside earnings. A Social Dividend may be regarded as an Unconditional Social Benefit which is not removed or reduced because of increased earnings.

The payment of a substantial Social Dividend will diminish disincentives against acceptance of earned pay even if the Dividend is in itself inadequate and has to be supplemented by a Conditional Social Benefit. Thus, for example, a recipient of a Social Dividend of 80 supplemented by a Conditional Benefit of 20 will have an incentive to take outside earnings so long as those earnings after deduction of Income Tax are greater than 20; but if he or she had relied for the whole 100 on a Conditional Benefit, there would be no incentive to accept any outside earnings less than 100.

The Agathotopians have, however, in the end been able to pay Social Dividends on a sufficient scale to replace a very great range of the social benefits that would otherwise be needed to support the unemployed, the sick, the children and the old who were without adequate maintenance. The great obstacle to this happy institution of paying unconditional tax-free Social Dividends on what may be called an 'adequate' scale was, of course, the hideous expense involved and the consequent problem of raising the revenue needed for their payment. Indeed the payment of a fully adequate Social Dividend was ultimately achieved only at the cost of the most heroic and controversial fiscal measures. It is of interest, therefore, to note the

Agathotopian history of the development of this institution of 'adequate' Social Dividends.[12]

The first stage in this development took the form of a gradual elimination of all Conditional Benefits (such as unemployment or sickness benefit or State payments in respect of old age and retirement pensions) which were conditional on anything other than the lack of adequate sources of other income. These Benefits were all replaced by a single Conditional Benefit, set at a level 'adequate' for a very simple style of life. This Benefit was withdrawn pound for pound according as the beneficiary received any post-tax income from any other source. This reform was expensive in that it ensured that no citizen could fall through the social security net; everyone was assured of the moderate 'adequate' standard of living. On the other hand it saved much expense in that the unemployed, sick, or old who had other adequate means received no cash support from the State. The trans-formation simplified very considerably the administrative problem in that it removed the whole apparatus of bureaucratic control needed to ensure that beneficiaries were genuinely unemployed or sick. It increased the respons-ibility of the Income Tax authorities who already needed in principle to assess all personal incomes but whose responsibility at the lower end of the income scale became so much the more important. The great problem which this first stage of development left totally unsolved was the complete disincentive for citizens at the lower end of the income scale to make any effort to earn or acquire additional income unless it took them beyond the adequate standard level and thus took them out of the poverty trap.

The second stage was to abolish all personal allowances under the Income Tax and to replace them by a tax-free Social Dividend of equal values. Thus with a personal allowance of, say, 40 a week with a rate of Income Tax of 25 per cent, any person whose income was above 40 already received the equivalent of a tax-free Social Dividend of 10 (i.e. remission of tax of 25 per cent on 40) offset by paying a rate of tax of 25 per cent on the whole of his or her income. The first-stage arrangement was accordingly modified by replacing the former wholly Conditional Benefit by a Social Dividend of 10 topped up by a wholly Conditional Benefit which was 10 less than before. This purely administrative change in fact made no dif-ference to anyone's income, the Social Dividend replacing Conditional Benefit in some cases and replacing the loss of personal tax allowances in other cases. The great problem of the poverty trap remained unchanged. But the change set the background for a third stage.

The third stage was an attempt to raise the Social Dividend or, as it may the called, the Unconditional Benefit at the expense of the Conditional

Benefit. A substitution of Unconditional for Conditional Benefit reduces the poverty trap because a citizen has only to earn enough to replace the Conditional Benefit in order to enjoy the post-tax receipt of any extra earnings. If the Unconditional Benefit is raised enough to replace entirely the Conditional Benefit, the poverty trap disappears entirely; everyone can enjoy the whole of their earnings after payment of Income Tax at the ruling rate. This operation is however extremely expensive in that the increased Unconditional Benefit is payable to all citizens, rich or poor. Its finance would need a very great increase in the rates of a progressive Income Tax.

As they proceeded on this path the Agathotopians experienced, as they had expected, a further equalisation of incomes. They also experienced a further alleviation of risk-bearing on a scale which they had not expected because they had overlooked the fact that risk-bearing is alleviated not only by the receipt of a larger constant assured element of income but also by the higher marginal rates of tax on all other incomes which are needed to raise the revenue to finance the higher rate of Social Dividend.

In fact the higher the rate of tax, the less does an earner gain by earning more (since a higher proportion of his or her extra earnings is paid to the State in tax) and the less does he or she lose by earning less (since a higher proportion of the loss is offset by a reduction of tax payment). The development of the Social Dividend regime was thus found to alleviate risk both by making a larger proportion of post-tax income take the form of a tax-free constant income and also by reducing the effect of variations in the remaining element of income by linking variations in earnings with higher offsetting variations in tax liabilities.

Alas, however, the Agathotopians had to call a halt to this general development long before the Social Dividends had entirely replaced the Conditional Benefit, because the marginal rates of tax on increased earnings and profits combined with the assurance of the substantial unconditional income represented by the Social Dividend introduced an unacceptably large general disincentive for enterprising work and investment. This was only very partially offset by the tax on the earnings of those who were no longer deterred from working by the poverty trap.

In the fourth stage the Agathotopians raised additional revenue by imposing a substantial tax surcharge on the first slice of every taxpayer's income. This meant that, after receipt of the tax-free Social Dividend, the taxpayer not merely lost tax exemption from the first slice of earnings or other income (which he or she had previously enjoyed in the form of personal tax allowances) but actually paid an exceptionally high rate of tax on this first slice of such income.

It may at first sight seem very anomalous that the Agathotopians should have instituted such a surcharge which involves levying a higher rate of tax on low incomes than on the higher incomes. But the justification of the system becomes apparent if one compares the three systems of (1) a pure Social Dividend System, (2) a pure Conditional Benefit System, and (3) a Social Dividend System with a Surcharge on the first slice of income from other sources.

(1)   A pure Social Dividend System implies paying every citizen an adequate Social Dividend of, say, £100 and then taxing all other income (earnings, dividends, interest, rent, etc.) at, say 55 per cent for its finance.

(2)   A pure Conditional Benefit System implies offering to every citizen an adequate Benefit of, say, £100 but then deducting from the citizen's benefit 100 per cent of any other post-tax income which that citizen may receive, until the point is reached when the Conditional Benefit payable to him or her is reduced to zero. The finance of such a scheme might require a rate of tax of only, say, 25 per cent on all other sources of income in order to finance such limited amounts of Conditional Benefit as remain payable to those citizens whose other sources of post-tax income were less than £100. Such an arrangement is the exact equivalent of a Social Dividend of £100 financed partly by a combined rate of tax of 100 per cent on the first slice of a citizen's other sources of income (i.e. by the 25 per cent rate of income tax plus a Surcharge of 75 per cent on the first £100 of earnings etc.) and partly by a rate of tax of 25 per cent on all other sources of income in excess of the first £100 slice.

(3)   A Social Dividend scheme with a more moderate Surcharge on the first £100 of earnings etc., will lie in between the extremes of (1) and (2). Thus for example there might be a Surcharge of 15 per cent (instead of 75 per cent) on the first £100 slice of income together with a general rate of income tax of 45 per cent on all income other than the Social Dividend. In this case the combined tax rate payable on the first £100 slice of income would be 60 per cent (i.e. 45 per cent + 15 per cent) and on income above £100 would be 45 per cent.

In all three cases all citizens are guaranteed a basic standard income of £100, financed in Scheme (1) by a tax of 55 per cent on all other sources of income, in Scheme (2) by a tax of 100 per cent on all other sources of income below £100 and a tax of 25 per cent on all other sources of income above £100, and in Scheme (3) by a tax of 60 per cent on all other sources of income below £100 combined with a tax of 45 per cent on all other sources of income above £100. If a tax rate of 55 per cent on the great majority of incomes above the £100 adequate subsistence level is found to have an unacceptable disincentive effect on work and enterprise, a move from Scheme 1 to Scheme 3 may enable the rate of tax on higher levels of income to be reduced from 55 per cent to a tolerable level of 45 per cent. This would still enable those at the bottom end of the scale to supplement their basic £100 with 40 per cent of any other sources of income, whereas a move to Scheme 2 would reduce their total incomes to the dead level of £100, thereby eliminating all incentives and reducing their standards of living to the basic minimum. If a pure Social Dividend is too expensive, a Social Dividend with a Surcharge on low incomes may be much better both for incentives and for the distribution of income than a pure Conditional Benefit system.

The outstanding revenue effect of the Surcharge on the first slice of income is that all citizens at the upper end of the income scale pay what amounts to a fixed 'poll tax' (i.e. the Surcharge on £100), which will enable a considerable revenue to be raised from such citizens without any rise of the marginal rate of tax on their other sources of income. In this way additional revenue can be raised from the rich without any disincentive effects – indeed perhaps with some slight improvement in incentives to earn more in order to make up for the 'poll tax' loss of income.

The Agathotopians found that such a Surcharge greatly relieved the situation. But, of course, the greater the relief of disincentives at the top end of the income scale brought about by raising the Surcharge with its 'poll tax' effects, the greater the disincentive effects and the lower the raising of standards at the lower end of the scale. It remains a matter of great controversy in the Agathotopian community whether the inevitable disincentive effects of high tax rates either at the upper or at the lower end of the income scale in fact justified the setting of the basic minimum at the generous level required to satisfy the requirements of a fully adequate standard of living.

In a fifth stage of development of their Social Dividend regime the Agathotopians found an entirely new and revolutionary source of revenue which much relieved the situation. This source of revenue took the form of the socialisation of the beneficial ownership (without incurring any of the management) of some 50 per cent of the national wealth of the community, a change of such basic structural importance as to merit discussion as a wholly novel institutional feature of the Agathotopian economy.

(4) The Socialisation of the Beneficial Ownership (Without the Management) of One Half of the Island's Capital Assets as a Source of Revenue for the Finance of the Social Dividend

The Agathotopian State itself owns some 50 per cent of the capital wealth of the community and uses the revenue from the return on this capital to help to finance the Social Dividend. At present in the typical capitalist economy the State far from being a net owner of capital assets in fact is often on balance a debtor to the private sector of the community. The private sector owns more capital assets than the total real assets of the community because it owns also the net National Debt issued by the governmental sector to the private sector. In Agathotopia there is no net National Debt; in its place there is a net National Asset equal to one half of the real assets of the community. The private sector owns only one half of the real assets of the community instead of an amount of wealth equal to the whole of the real assets of the community plus the net National Debt of the governmental sector. The absence of a net National Debt and the additional ownership by the State of wealth equivalent to one half of the real wealth of the community means, of course, that the government loses the revenue from any taxes which would otherwise have been levied on the interest on the National Debt and on dividends or rents received on the other transferred assets. But there is a net gain equal to the post-tax return on what would otherwise have been a National Debt and on one half of the real assets of the economy, a revenue which is used in Agathotopia to help to finance the Social Dividend.

In Agathotopia, however, the government plays no direct part in the management of the partnership enterprises or other private concerns the capital of which it owns indirectly. There is a free and very vigorous competitive capital market and Stock Exchange on which private individuals and institutions freely deal in respect to the 50 per cent of the real assets of the community which they own. The government invests its ownership of the other 50 per cent of the community's real assets in competitive unit trusts and similar competitive investment institutions which merge the government's funds with the private funds in the search of a high yield on the funds so employed. Thus indirectly the Agathotopian government receives the yield on the Capital Share Certificates of various Labour-Capital Partnerships and on the capital resources of other private concerns without taking any direct part in the management of the economy's competitive private enterprises. It is indeed an unwritten rule of the Agathotopian economy that the government should leave the competitive market alone but that it should be the beneficial owner of a large part of the community's wealth so that the income from such wealth can be equally distributed to all citizens in the form of a Social Dividend.

To many of us living at present in a capitalist mixed economy this must appear a topsy-turvy form of nationalisation or socialisation of property. In the UK, for example, immediately after the Second World War the Labour Government carried out a widespread programme of nationalisation of private enterprises, Coal Mines, Steel, Transport, Electricity, etc. But in all these cases adequate compensation was paid to the private owners. The net result was that the government took over the management of the concerns while the previous private owners continued to enjoy the yield on the property indirectly in the form of interest on the new National Debt issued in compensation. The Agathotopian form of socialisation is to take over the yield on the property, but to leave the management in private competitive hands.

The Agathotopians are, however, experiencing one difficulty in achieving this divorce between management and beneficial ownership of socialised assets. There is a wide range of capital assets in owner-occupied dwellings, owner-managed farms, small partnership enterprises, etc. for the value of which there are no day-to-day quotations on the Stock Exchange or other similar capital market organisations. By investing its 50 per cent share of the total capital assets of the community exclusively in marketable assets the State threatens to swamp the Stock Exchange and similar organisations and to leave private owners of capital with only the range of less liquid non-marketable assets to hold. This threatens one of the basic objectives of the Agathotopian economy which is to have a flourishing and flexible private capital market of a kind which will make it possible for private enterprise easily to market its capital assets. The Agathotopians desire the Stock Exchange and similar markets for capital assets to have a very large private component.

For this reason they are considering the possibility of devising a form of tax which will enable them in effect to transfer part or the whole of the State's beneficial ownership of marketable Stock Exchange assets into beneficial part ownership of all capital assets whether marketable or non-marketable. To acquire an indirect participation of, say, 10 per cent in the beneficial ownership of all assets the procedure would be as follows. There would need to be a valuation of all real income-bearing assets. The State would pay a subsidy to the owner of each such asset of 10 per cent of its value. The funds needed for this subsidy would be obtained by the sale of part of the excessively large State holding of marketable assets. Thereafter all assets would be subject to a 10 per cent tax on their net income yield, there being an agreed formulation for the rate of yield to be assumed for tax purposes on owner-occupied dwellings and similar assets. This tax on the yield of all income-bearing real assets would be subject to 100 per cent initial tax allowances, in the sense that all owners of such assets could deduct from the gross yield earned on the assets not only the cost of maintaining and replacing the assets but also the cost of acquiring additional real assets of this kind. On the other hand, the taxable yield on such assets would also include any proceeds from the disposal of such assets. The implication of this system wold be that the State acquired a 10 per cent participation in the ownership of all such assets, having 'purchased' this ownership by a subsidy to the owners on the first take-over and later by a remission of tax equal to 10 per cent of the cost of new additional assets. The State would then receive in revenue 10 per cent of the net yield on any such assets.[13]

(5) Budgetary Problems in Agathotopia and the Complexity of Agathotopian Fiscal Policy

In Agathotopia there are three exceptional features which, in comparison with the experience in a typical capitalist mixed economy, impose a heavy burden on the central government's budget. (i) There is a very heavy burden to carry in the form of the payment to all citizens of a Social Dividend on a scale adequate to support a decent standard of living. Even after allowance for the abolition of all other forms of social benefit this constitutes an extremely heavy addition to public expenditure in comparison with the normal expenditures on social benefits in a typical capitalist mixed economy. (ii) In addition the Agathotopian budget needs on average year after year to run a budget surplus on current account; in a growing economy it is necessary for the Agathotopian State to acquire new capital assets equal to one half of the nation's total savings, so as to maintain its beneficial ownership of one half of the country's growing national wealth. (iii) Moreover, it needs to raise revenue from some other source to make up for the fact that the Agathotopian income tax regime exempts all savings from tax in order to make easier the accumulation of capital wealth by the poorer members of society.

In order to keep marginal tax rates as low as possible the Agathotopians do all they can to prevent erosion of the tax base. Thus they impute a realistic taxable rent to the enjoyment of the owner-occupied dwellings and owner-managed farm lands; and, in their savings-exempt income tax, any capital gains which are realised for expenditure on consumption are automatically included in the tax base. They enjoy considerable administrative savings through the abolition of social benefits of a kind which depend upon the policing of specific conditions such as involuntary unemployment or genuine sickness; but they have used much of these resources to monitor the black economy, tax evasion of every kind being much better policed and much more heavily penalised than in the UK. In their general economic policies they concentrate on taxing that which is socially undesirable rather than subsidising that which is socially desirable, traffic congestion being tackled by exceptionally heavy taxation of the congesting use of private cars rather than by the subsidisation of public transport. They protect the countryside by taxing its obnoxious treatment rather than by subsidising farmers to produce unwanted supplies. They obtain a substantial revenue from a tax on expensive advertisement which they regard as a social nuisance and a waste of resources; in their opinion, it represents a mutually destructive and therefore ineffective means by which producers attempt to poach customers from each other in a way which, unlike a reduction of selling prices, confers no real benefit upon the consumers; it merely persuades them to vie with each other in the purchase of things which they would not otherwise want and which in many cases they cannot really afford. On business concerns they levy what corresponds to a Corporation Tax, from which Discriminating Labour-Capital Partnerships are exempt.

In addition to these general principles the Agathotopians have introduced three special measures in an attempt to alleviate the exceptionally heavy charges which it has to meet. (i) They raise a substantial revenue from the taxation of capital wealth. This takes two forms: (a) they levy a low annual tax on all personal holdings of wealth above a low exempt level and (b) they impose an important tax on all transfers of wealth by gift or bequest above a low exempt level. (ii) By maintaining a socialisation of the beneficial ownership of a net National Asset equal to one half of the nation's total wealth they avoid budgetary expenditure equal to the post-tax payments of interest on what in a typical capitalist mixed economy might have been the net National Debt, and gain the post-tax yield on its net National Asset. (iii) They raise a substantial Surcharge on the first slice of all personal incomes other than the tax-free Social Dividend.

However, in spite of these three substantial alleviations the Agathotopians have been able to maintain the adequate Social Dividend regime only at the expense of a fairly high general rate of savings-exempt income tax.

In addition to these exceptional fiscal burdens on the Agathotopian budget the fiscal regime in Agathotopia has to face an exceptionally complex task. In the capitalist economy, as in Agathotopia, appropriate wage-setting institutions are needed to prevent increased expenditures on goods from causing an inflation of money costs and prices rather than an increase in output and employment. Then the setting of rates of interest through Monetary Policy and of rates of tax and public expenditure through Fiscal Policy needs to be jointly designed so as to achieve a steadily growing but uninflated total of money demands for goods and services with an acceptable division between present consumption and capital accumulation.

This is, of course, not the sole interest in Fiscal Policy in the capitalist mixed economy. In particular the actual forms and levels of government expenditure and of tax revenues within any given Budget Balance are considered in their effects on at least two further macroeconomic issues, namely the general effects on the Distribution of Incomes and on the Incentives to Work, Enterprise and Investment.

In the Agathotopian economy all these same financial instruments and objectives are operative. But Fiscal Policy is still further complicated by an Agathotopian interest not only in the growth of the total capital assets of the economy but also in the distribution of the beneficial ownership of such assets as between the private and public sectors. In essence while the capitalist economy is concerned with a single Wealth Target (e.g. the community's total capital assets) the Agathotopian economy is concerned with two Wealth Targets, the total accumulation of assets and the distribution of the ownership of such assets as between the private and public sectors.

To meet this twofold wealth objective the Agathotopians try to distinguish between those taxes which are likely to be paid largely at the expense of the taxpayer's real consumption (such as the savings-exempt income tax) and those which are likely to be paid largely at the expense of the taxpayer's savings or holdings of wealth (such as the tax on transfers of wealth). By controlling the size of its budget surplus the Agathotopian government aims to control the growth of its own holding of wealth; by choosing a suitable mix of consumption and capital taxes in the composition of the necessary revenue it aims at achieving simultaneously the desired level of private savings. They do not expect perfection. The level of any social dividend; the level of any special levy on the first slice of income or expenditure; the level of government expenditures on defence, health, education, and other services; the structure, rates and progression of rates of tax on savings-exempt income, on wealth and on transfers of wealth; all these they realise will have effects on distribution, on incentives and on the provision of both public and private savings. They are continuously revising a structured package of these various items in order to provide not a perfect distribution of income and wealth, nor a complete absence of economic disincentives, nor the ideal level of total savings, nor its ideal distribution between public and private savings but rather to find the least undesirable package of imperfect distribution, imperfect incentives, imperfect level and imperfect distribution of saving between public and private savings. Agathotopia is a Good Place to live in, but it is, alas, not Utopia.

IV   THE TRANSITION TO THE PARTNERSHIP ECONOMY

In the island of Agathotopia the acquisition by the State of one half of the economy's wealth is already past history. It occurred more than a century ago and the trauma of the event has been totally forgotten. The institution is just taken for granted. If however, we in our capitalist mixed economies wished to reach an Agathotopian type of economy, how could we make the transition? In particular how could we make the transfer of the beneficial ownership of the National Debt plus one half of the real wealth of the community from the private to the public sector of the economy?

One possibility might be a once-for-all cataclysmic Capital Levy by which a given amount of wealth, on a progressive scale according to the size of the individual private holdings of property, was transferred from private to public ownership. This would involve a gigantic social revolution. History suggests that the immediate uncompromising forcing of major changes on this scale against fiercely held opposition inevitably leads to unforeseen disastrous results. Situations of traumatic change may arise for other reasons. At the end of the Second World War it was reasonable to consider the possibility of a large-scale Capital Levy to rid the country of a large part of the National Debt incurred during the war. But a vast once-for-all transfer in normal times could have disastrous effects upon the stability of society.

This means that the transition to Agathotopian arrangements is going to take a long time. Some form of continuing budget surplus will be needed in order gradually to redeem National Debt and to acquire instead a net National Asset. In so far as private savings are considered to be insufficient to meet the national wealth target, it is appropriate that the budget surplus should be raised by taxes which restrain private consumption. In so far as private savings are considered to be adequate, shift of wealth from the private to the public sector can be achieved by financing the budget surplus from taxes which are likely to be paid out of private savings or holdings of wealth. In either case the interest on National Debt will gradually fall and/ or the return on National Assets will gradually rise. The ever greater budgetary ease can then be used partly to improve a Social Dividend payment and partly to raise the annual budget surplus and thus to speed up the process of transfer of property. There is great virtue in compound interest. It can set in motion a reliable gradual improvement in social welfare. The first steps on the journey should be the hardest.

The approaches to the other Agathotopian institutions can all be taken gradually. Labour-Capital Partnerships can be developed gradually at the enterprise level. Reforms of taxation of income and of transfers of wealth can be introduced by stages so as to encourage a wider spread of the ownership of property. A Social Dividend can be started on a very moderate scale financed out of the abolition of existing personal allowances under the income tax, by the reduction of other social benefits, and by some moderate increases of tax rates supplemented at some stage with an element of special levy on the first slice of other income. If the journey is taken at a gentle pace, one can hope ultimately to reach Agathotopian conditions without too much strain on the way.

APPENDIX A   FACTORS RESTRICTING THE REPLACEMENT OF RETIRING WORKER PARTNERS

In the main text it was argued that the adoption of the rule of redistribution for the treatment of the pure-profit of retiring worker partners and, to a lesser extent, the adoption of the rule of cancellation for this purpose might impede the expansionary forces in a Discriminating Labour-Capital Partnership. The young recently engaged partners might oppose the engagement of new partners in order to restrict the number of future potential recipients of any pure profit which was released by older worker partners on their retirement.

The purpose of this Appendix is to analyse this potential motive for restriction in the case of the rules of redistribution and of cancellation. We illustrate these forces by examining a particular example of the occurrence of pure profit in a Discriminating Labour-Capital Partnership.

In Table 4.1 we consider a partnership in which there are m teams of working partners of equal sizes. Team m was engaged at the beginning of this year (Year 1), team $m - 1$ was engaged last year, team $m - 2$ was engaged two years ago; and so on. Team 1 will retire at the end of this year. For many years up to and including Year–1 this partnership has covered its costs but has made no pure profit so that each term of workers has been receiving a zero pure profit as indicated in the column headed Year–1. In Year 0 there is a sudden but lasting improvement in the performance of the partnership; a large pure profit is made; each working partner's share of this pure profit amounts to B' as shown in the column headed Year 0.

At the beginning of Year 1 the old Team 1 retires, each of the other teams moves one step up the team index, leaving team m to be replaced by a new team which on the discriminatory principle does not share in the existing pure profit. Each of the other $m - 1$ teams receives in addition to its existing pure profit of B' a supplement equal to $(1 - \sigma)/(m - 1)$ of the B' which is surrendered by the retiring team 1 of Year 0. In this expression σ measures the proportion of the benefit which seeps to holders of Capital Share Certificates. Thus σ will be zero if (as with the rule of redistribution) all the retiring team's pure profit is distributed in equal amounts among the remaining worker partners and will be equal to $\overline{\sigma}$, the ratio of Capital Share Certificates to total Share Certificates, if (as with the rule of cancellation) the retiring team has simply to surrender for cancellation all its holding of Labour Share Certificates. With $B = B'\mu_1$ and $\mu_1 = (m - \sigma)/(m - 1)$, the distribution of pure profit among the worker partners will in Year 1 be as shown in the column headed Year 1.

The purpose of Table 4.1 is to consider the future prospects of those teams of 'old hands' who were already engaged in this partnership in Year 0. We are accordingly concerned only with the fortunes of those teams which lie above the heavy line sloping up Table 4.1 diagonally from left to right.

At the beginning of Year 2 team 1 of Year 1 will retire releasing a pure profit of B to be distributed among the other $m - 1$ teams of Year 1. One of the beneficiaries of this redistribution will be the team of 'new hands' engaged at the beginning of Year 1 and lying below the heavy diagonal line in Table 4.1. Teams 2 to $m - 1$ of Year 1 will have become teams 1 to $m - 2$ of Year 2, each with $B + B(1 - \sigma)/(m - 1) = B\mu_1$.[14]

Table 4.1 Redistribution of Labour Pure Profit with Replacement of Retiring Team

$$B = B^t\mu_1 \qquad \mu_1 = 1 + \frac{1-\sigma}{m-1} = \frac{m-\sigma}{m-1}$$

Team \ Year	−1	0	1	2	3	4	...	m − 2	m − 1
1	0	B'	B	$B\mu_1$	$B\mu_1^2$	$B\mu_1^3$	...	$B\mu_1^{m-3}$	$B\mu_1^{m-2}$
2	0	B'	B	$B\mu_1$	$B\mu_1^2$	$B\mu_1^3$	...	$B\mu_1^{m-3}$	
3	0	B'	B	$B\mu_1$	$B\mu_1^2$	$B\mu_1^3$			
...	0	B'	...	...	...	...			
m − 3	0	B'	B	$B\mu_1$	$B\mu_1^2$				
m − 2	0	B'	B	$B\mu_1$					
m − 1	0	B'	B						
m	0	B'							

By a similar process the amount of pure profit for the remaining teams of 'old hands' will develop as shown in Table 4.1 for future years up to Year $m - 1$.

In Table 4.2 we start off with the same story as in Table 4.1 for all years up to and including Year 0; but we suppose now that at the beginning of Year 1 a decision had been taken to reduce the size of the partnership by one team by not replacing the retiring team 1 of Year 0. Thus in Table 4.2 after Year 0 production will be carried on by only $m - 1$ teams instead of m teams. If the marginal revenue product of the missing team had been more than its cost, its absence would mean some reduction in the partnership's pure profit. If we suppose that the absence of a single team caused a loss of total pure profit to the partnership of $\tilde{B}$, then $\tilde{B}(1 - \overline{\sigma})$ of this would be loss of pure profit to the working partners, so that there would be a loss of pure profit to each team of workers of $\delta = \tilde{B}(1 - \overline{\sigma})/(m - 1)$. In Table 4.2 accordingly for Year 1 we record each team of 'old hands' as enjoying a pure profit of $B - \delta$ instead of B as in Table 4.1.

Clearly the 'old hands' will suffer an immediate loss of pure profit if absence of the new team (which on the discriminating principle would have been paid only its cost) causes some reduction in the total pure profit available for distribution. But in future years this loss will to a smaller or greater extent be balanced for the 'old hands' by a gain from the fact that the pure profit enjoyed by a retiring member will be divided among only $m - 2$ instead of $m - 1$ teams. This development is shown in Table 4.2 which differs from Table 4.1 in only two respects: first, that each team of 'old hands' starts in Year 1 with a pure profit of $B - \delta$ instead of B; and, second, that a retiring working member's pure profit is distributed among $m - 2$ instead of $m - 1$ other teams so that $\mu_1 = 1 + (1 - \sigma)(m - 1) = (m - \sigma)/(m - 1)$ is replaced by $\mu_2 = 1 + (1 - \sigma)/(m - 2) = (m - 1 - \sigma)/(m - 2)$.

We can now use Tables 4.1 and 4.2 to compare the difference of the future prospects of any given team of 'old hands' at Year 1 as between the case of Table 4.1 in which it is decided to replace the retiring team and the case of Table 4.2 in which it is decided to reduce the future size of the partnership by one team.

Let $\rho = 1/(1 + r)$ where r is the rate of interest at which working partners discount the future. In this case the Present Value of its pure profit for team $m - 1$ in Table 4.1, to be expected at the beginning of Year 1 as the team moves up the heavy diagonal line, is

$$B\left\{1 + \rho\mu_1 + (\rho\mu_1)^2 + \cdots + (\rho\mu_{1)})^{m-2}\right\} = B\frac{(\rho\mu_1)^{m-1} - 1}{\rho\mu_1 - 1} \tag{1}$$

The corresponding value for the $m - 1$ team of Year 1 on Table 4.2 is

$$(B - \delta)\frac{(\rho\mu_2)^{m-1} - 1}{\rho\mu_2 - 1}.$$

Similar expressions can be found to express the present expected value of future pure profit for the pth team of Year 1 on Tables 4.1 and 4.2 by substituting in equation (1) the number of years' service still expected in the partnership (namely, p) for the number of years service expected by the $m - 1$ team (namely, $m - 1$).

Thus we can generalise by saying that the contraction of the partnership's worker membership by the failure to replace team 1 at the end of Year 0 should improve the future prospects for team p at the beginning of Year 1 if

Table 4.2 Redistribution of Labour Pure Profit without Replacement of Retiring Team

$$B = B'\mu_1 \qquad \mu_1 = 1 + \frac{1-\sigma}{m-1} = \frac{m-\sigma}{m-1} \qquad \mu_2 = 1 + \frac{1-\sigma}{m-2} = \frac{m-1-\sigma}{m-2} \qquad \delta = \frac{\widetilde{B}(1-\widetilde{\sigma})}{m-1}$$

Team \ Year	−1	0	1	2	3	4	…	m − 2	m − 1
1	0	B'	$B-\delta$	$(B-\delta)\mu_2$	$(B-\delta)\mu_2^2$	$(B-\delta)\mu_2^3$	…	$(B-\delta)\mu_2^{m-3}$	$(B-\delta)\mu_2^{m-2}$
2	0	B'	$B-\delta$	$(B-\delta)\mu_2$	$(B-\delta)\mu_2^2$	$(B-\delta)\mu_2^3$	…	$(B-\delta)\mu_2^{m-3}$	
3	0	B'	$B-\delta$	$(B-\delta)\mu_2$	$(B-\delta)\mu_2^2$	$(B-\delta)\mu_2^3$			
…	…	…	…	…	…	…			
m − 3	0	B'	$B-\delta$	$(B-\delta)\mu_2$	$(B-\delta)\mu_2^2$				
m − 2	0	B'	$B-\delta$	$(B-\delta)\mu_2$					
m − 1	0	B'	$B-\delta$						

$$(B-\delta)\frac{(\rho\mu_2)^p-1}{\rho\mu_2-1} > B\frac{(\rho\mu_1)^p-1}{\rho\mu_1-1}$$

i.e. if

$$\frac{\delta}{B} < \left\{1 - \frac{(\rho\mu_1)^p-1}{\rho\mu_1-1} \middle/ \frac{(\rho\mu_2)^p-1}{\rho\mu_2-1}\right\}. \tag{2}$$

The outcome clearly depends upon whether or not the relative sacrifice of total worker's pure profit due to the reduction in the number of teams (δ/B) is outweighed by the advantage of having the pure profit of retiring members in future years distributed over a smaller of beneficiaries ($\rho\mu_2 > \rho\mu_1$).

We have already noted that $\delta = \check{B}(1 - \bar{\sigma})/(m-1)$ so that we can write

$$\frac{\delta}{B} = \frac{\check{B}(1-\bar{\sigma})}{(m-1)B} \tag{3}$$

where $\check{B}$ is the excess of the Marginal Revenue Product over the cost (W) of one team, $\bar{\sigma}$ is the ratio of Capital Share Certificate to total Share Certificates, and $m-1$ measures the number of teams over which the loss of pure profit to the workers must be spread.

But $B = \mu_1 B' = B'(m-\sigma)/(m-1)$ as depicted in Table 4.1. If we write $B' = \beta W$ where W measures the cost element in the payment to a worker team so that β measures the ratio of the initial pure profit per team of workers (B') to the team's cost (W) we can rewrite equation (3) as

$$\frac{\delta}{B} = \frac{\check{B}}{W} \cdot \frac{(1-\bar{\sigma})}{(m-\sigma)\beta} \tag{4}$$

so that the condition for the team p to gain by the contraction of the membership as expressed by the inequality (2) can be rewritten as:

$$\frac{\check{B}}{W} < \frac{(m-\sigma)\beta}{1-\bar{\sigma}} \left\{1 - \frac{(\rho\mu_1)^p-1}{\rho\mu_1-1} \middle/ \frac{(\rho\mu_2)^p-1}{\rho\mu_2-1}\right\} \tag{5}$$

The term $\check{B}/W$ on the left hand side of (5) measures the relative excess of a team's marginal revenue product over a team's cost and this, if the number of teams is large, can be regarded as an approximate indication of the proportionate excess of a worker's marginal revenue product over a worker's cost. If worker partners had been taken on until the worker's marginal revenue product had been reduced to the level of the worker's cost, $\check{B}/W$ would be zero and it would clearly be in the interests of existing worker partners to restrict the size of the workers' membership. But as the number of worker partners was reduced the marginal revenue product of a worker would be raised, and it would be in the interest of the pth team of workers to vote for such contraction until $\check{B}/W$ were raised at least to the critical level indicated in (5).[15]

The critical condition in (5) depends basically upon the discriminatory principle that any new team is engaged in the first place at a remuneration which is equal to its cost, although the other pre-existing teams may in addition be enjoying various levels of pure profit. It is of interest to contrast the critical value of $\tilde{B}/W$ in (5) with the critical value of $\tilde{B}/W$ which would need to be reached to make it unattractive for existing worker partners to restrict the membership in a Non-Discriminating partnership; in such a partnership all worker partners, new and old, would receive 'equal pay for equal work' which implies that any available profit would be shared equally among them.

In such a Non-Discriminating partnership the pure profit team would be increased by the non-replacement of a team so long as the loss of worker pure profit caused by the reduction of one team $\tilde{B}(1 - \bar{\sigma})$ were less than the existing pure profit per team B'. With $B' = \beta W$ this means that in a Non-Discriminating partnership the condition (5) for the pth team to gain from a restriction of the number of teams would be replaced by the condition.

$$\frac{\tilde{B}}{W} < \frac{\beta}{1 - \bar{\sigma}} \qquad (6)$$

which would also be relevant for the prospective fortunes not only of the pth team but of any one of the existing teams.

In Table 4.3 we give some numerical examples of the implications of the conditions expressed in the inequalities (5) and (6). We assume that the working life a working partner in any given partnerships is 20 years so that $m = 20$ and that the partnership is 20 per cent capital-intensive in the sense that the ratio of Capital Share Certificates to Total Share Certificates is 0.2. Thus $\mu_1 = (m - \sigma)/(m - 1) = 19.8/19 = 1.042$ and $\mu_2 = (m - 1 - \sigma)/(m - 2) = 18.8/18 = 1.044$ in the case in which all Labour Share Certificates of retiring members are surrendered and cancelled; and $\mu_1 = 20/19 = 1.053$ and $\mu_2 = 19/18 = 1.056$ in the case in which the pure-profit Labour Share Certificates of retiring members are not cancelled but are distributed among the remaining worker partners. We assume further that the rate of discount of future benefits by worker partners is 5 per cent per annum so that $\rho = 1/1.05$ and that in the initial situation of Year 0 the amount of pure profit per worker was 20 per cent of the cost element in the working partners income so that $\beta = 0.2$.

The following features may be noted:

Table 4.3   Critical Values of $\tilde{B}/W$ below which Restriction of Number of Worker Partners would be Attractive

		$\sigma = 0$	$\sigma = 0.2$
Discriminating Partnership	$p = m - 1 = 19$	0.125	0.098
	$p = m/2 = 10$	0.0625	0.049
Non-Discriminating Partnership		0.25	0.25

With $m = 20$, $\rho = 1/1.05$, and $\beta = 0.2$.

(1) All the critical values of $\tilde{B}/W$ are > 0. That is to say that if there is no excess of Marginal Revenue Product over Cost for the marginal team it will in all cases be attractive to worker partners to reduce the size of the membership. Since there is no immediate loss of total pure profit, it will always be of interest to existing worker partners to have to share the profit of retiring members over a smaller number of remaining beneficiaries.

(2) There will therefore be a critical positive value for $\tilde{B}/W$ which is necessary to remove the motive for restriction of numbers. This critical value is in every case higher in a Non-Discriminating Partnership than in a corresponding Discriminating Partnership. Thus we may conclude that the adoption of the principle of discrimination will lead to an expansion of the number of working partners, but that in those cases in which the pure profit of retiring members reverts in whole or in part to the remaining partners, there will remain obstacles to the complete expansion up to the point at which the marginal revenue product of an additional partner is reduced to the cost of a new partner.

(3) However, the critical value of $\tilde{B}/W$ which will make restriction of numbers attractive in a Discriminating Partnership, is lower for existing partners who have few more years of service than for existing partners who have many more years of service (i.e. in the table for workers with 10 years of service ahead it is roughly only half as high as for those with 19 years ahead). The older working partners have a smaller prospect of gaining from the retirements of still older partners than is the case with the younger partners. Indeed, as can be seen clearly from Table 4.2 the partners who are on the point of retirement will have no incentive to oppose the employment of a new team unless that team's marginal revenue product was actually lower than its cost (i.e. unless $\tilde{B}$ and so δ were negative). If $\tilde{B}$ is positive those on the point of retirement would certainly lose if the team is not engaged, because they will have nothing to gain from the redistribution of any pure profit enjoyed by their younger colleagues.

(4) This fact that the attractiveness of restriction of entry of new partners will be greater to younger than to older partners means that there may be an important difference of interest within the working membership. Thus in Table 4.3 the majority of members (teams up to the tenth team) would vote for expansion so long as $\tilde{B}/W$ was greater than around 6 per cent, whereas the youngest members of the team would vote for expansion only if $\tilde{B}/W$ were over $12\frac{1}{2}$ per cent.

(5) The existence of seepage of the pure profit of retiring worker members to the benefit of capitalist members ($\sigma > 0$) will reduce the advantage to the worker members to restrict numbers, since they have less to gain from the pure profit of retiring members. In Table 4.3 the rise of seepage from 0 to 20 per cent will substantially reduce the critical level to which $\tilde{B}/W$ may fall without leading to a desire to restrict the engagement of new working partners. Even more important is the fact that as the years pass the incentive for restriction will diminish until it completely disappears as the seepage of pure profit to the capitalist members progressively reduces the amount of labour pure profit available for the future benefit of younger members. This important feature is not shown in Tables 4.1, 4.2, or 4.3 which refer only to the position of the pth team immediately after the first appearance of the labour pure profit.

(6) Inequalities (5) and (6) show clearly the fundamental importance of the factor β in determining the level of the critical value of $\tilde{B}/W$ in all cases. A doubling of β (the proportion of initial pure profit to cost) will in all cases double the level of the

critical value of $\tilde{B}/W$. The greater the amount of pure profit available for future redistribution, the greater will be the attraction to restrict membership.

(7) Table 4.3 does not itself show the effect on the critical level of $\tilde{B}/W$ of a change in the discount rate r and so of the factor ρ. But from Tables 4.1 and 4.2 it can be clearly seen that if the future was discounted at an infinite rate all members of the partnership would be opposed to restriction unless δ were zero or negative. If δ (and so $\tilde{B}/W$) were positive every member would suffer the immediate loss due to the reduced total of pure profit resulting from the loss of one team's marginal contribution to the total pure profit. In fact the higher the rate of discount, the smaller will be the attraction of any future increase in pure profit per member arising from the future distribution of retiring members' pure profit among a smaller number of beneficiaries.

It is clear from the above analysis that the incentive to expand employment can vary very greatly according to the particular conditions of the particular partnership. For example in a case in which there was much workers' pure profit to distribute (a high β), no seepage to capitalists ($\sigma = 0$), and a low rate of time discount by working partners (a high ρ), the critical value of $\tilde{B}/W$ could be very high.

There is, however, one aspect of the problem which has so far been neglected and which in fact suggests that the degree of restriction on the size of a partnership's working membership will be less than has been suggested by the preceding analysis in this Appendix. We have treated W in this Appendix as a measure of the remuneration which must be paid during his first year of service to a newly engaged working partner. But if this partner has a prospect of receiving a considerable pure profit bonus in future years (i.e. if the present value of the engagement is exceptionally high) he may well be prepared to enter the partnership at an exceptionally low initial reward, i.e. an exceptionally low value of W and high value of $\tilde{B}$. But this will raise the actual level of $\tilde{B}/W$; it will mean that the loss of pure profit to the existing partners if they do not engage the new partner will be exceptionally high.

However, if the capital market is very imperfect and the newly engaged working partner cannot borrow on good terms to make up for an exceptionally low starting remuneration, he may not be willing to accept an exceptionally low value of W. But this is only another way of saying that the working partners' rate of time discount is exceptionally high; and this in turn (instead of raising the actual level of $\tilde{B}/W$ through setting an exceptionally low level of W) will lower the critical value below which the existing $\tilde{B}/W$ must lie if there is to be a given attraction to restrict the working membership. Either way the restrictive influence is diminished.

In all cases it would appear that a Discriminating Labour-Capital Partnership would be less restrictive than a Non-Discriminating Partnership. But on the face of it, it would appear that a Capital Company would be even less restrictive than any Discriminating Partnership which operated on the rules of redistribution or of cancellation. At any given single level of W this would be true, since the owner of a Capitalist Company unlike the working partners of the Discriminating Partnership would have an incentive to expand employment so long as $\tilde{B}/W > 0$. This analysis rests, however, on the assumption that both the Capitalist Company and the Discriminating Partnership are confronted with the same value for W. In fact, as has been argued in the main text, the existing working partners (the insiders) in a Discriminating Labour-Capital Partnership will welcome outsiders who demand a low level of remuneration, whereas the insiders in a Capitalist Company will demand that outsiders be employed only a high level of pay.

APPENDIX B   THE CHARACTERISTICS OF VARIOUS SOCIAL DIVIDEND SCHEMES

This Appendix is devoted to a description of the structure of different types of Social Dividend scheme. In order to compare the merits and demerits of the various schemes, it is useful to assume that each scheme is self-financing in the following sense. Each scheme will involve additional budgetary expenditure for the payment of the Social Dividend. It is assumed throughout this Appendix that the additional revenue needed to balance the budget is raised by increasing the rates of Income Tax, all other tax rates and governmental expenditures remaining unchanged. All adult men and women are assumed to be assessed separately both for Income Tax and for receipt of social benefit, whatever their family circumstances; and children are all assumed to count as, say, one half an adult for receipt of social benefits.

A taxpayer's receipt of income from earnings and return on capital wealth before tax and social benefit will be called his or her Unadjusted Income, and after deduction of tax and payment of social benefit will be called his or her Adjusted Income. We examine in this Appendix three kinds of adjustments to income which are specially designed to maintain the standards of living of those with little or no other income.

(1) Personal Tax Allowance

With a normal income tax regime we assume that a first slice of Unadjusted Income which we call the Personal Tax Allowance is exempt from income tax and that the same standard rate of tax is applied to every taxpayer's Unadjusted Income less Personal Tax Allowance.

(2) Conditional Benefits

Cash benefits may be paid to citizens in certain specific conditions, e.g. if the citizen is unemployed or sick. Or a cash benefit may be paid on condition that the recipient's receipt of any Unadjusted Income is deducted from the benefit. Both these types of social benefit we will call Conditional Benefits; but we will confine our analysis to the second type. Thus we may suppose that £100 is paid to a citizen who has no Unadjusted Income, but that this benefit is reduced pound for pound as his Adjusted Income rises from £0 to £100 at which point it is discontinued.

(3) Unconditional Benefit or Social Dividend

If however a cash benefit is paid at a fixed rate to every taxpayer regardless of the level of his or her Unadjusted Income or of any other circumstances, we will call this a Social Dividend.

In general throughout this Appendix we will assume that any Personal Tax Allowance, Conditional Benefit, or Social Dividend are all set at the same rate which is regarded as what is needed to enable a single adult citizen to maintain an adequate standard of living. We shall use this as the unit of measurement of income.

Thus a citizen with an Unadjusted Income of 3 is a citizen whose pre-tax earnings and income from capital wealth are three times the minimum level assumed necessary to maintain an adequate living standard.

In Figure 4.1 the line *OBC* would depict the situation under an Income Tax regime with a Personal Tax Allowance equal to 1 unit and a rate of tax of 25 per cent on all Unadjusted Income in excess of this 1 unit. With Unadjusted Income on the horizontal axis and Adjusted Income on the vertical axis, the line *OBV* would represent the level of Adjusted Income in the absence of any tax. With a Personal Allowance of 1 unit and a subsequent tax rate of 25 per cent the Adjusted Income moves up the line *OB* at a slope of 1 in 1 and from *B* moves up the line *BC* with a slope of 3 in 4. If the Personal Tax Allowance of 1 unit were replaced by a Conditional Benefit of 1 unit the Adjusted Income line would become the heavily marked line *ABC*. For all persons without any Unadjusted Income at the origin *O* a Conditional Benefit of *OA* would be paid and this would be reduced pound for pound as the citizen's Unadjusted Income moved up the line *OB*. At the point *B* the Conditional Social Benefit would have been reduced to zero and from *B* onwards the levy of tax would reduce the slope of *BC* to 3 in 4. In what follows we shall be comparing other regimes with this Conditional Benefit Regime and shall accordingly repeat the line *ABC* on all the following diagrams.

All citizens to the right of point *M* with Unadjusted Incomes above 1 unit will be paying tax, the revenue from which will lie in the horizontal hatched area {≡} between the lines *BV* and *BC*. All citizens to the left of point *M* will be receiving

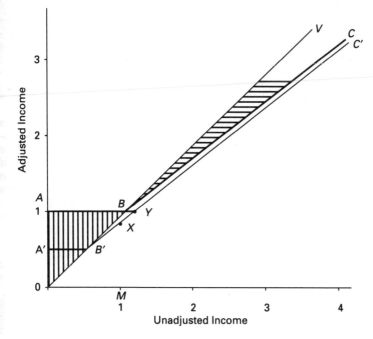

Figure 4.1

some Conditional Benefit, the expenditure on which will lie in the vertically hatched area { ||| } between the lines *AB* and *OB*. We are simply assuming that given this Conditional Benefit and the other elements of government expenditure (defence, health, education, etc.) and given the other sources of government revenue (VAT, etc.) an income tax rate of 25 per cent is sufficient to balance the budget. This simple assumption is chosen solely for illustrative purposes.

Indeed the choice of this low rate of 25 per cent should not be allowed to give the impression that to pay a universal Conditional Benefit at an adequate rate and to raise the Personal Tax Allowance up to this same adequate rate is anything but a very expensive policy. At the origin *O* are concentrated all those children, pensioners, sick, or unemployed who have no other sources of income; and this will include the unemployed who might be able to earn something less than 1 unit of income but who have no incentive to take such work as their pay would simply be deducted from the Conditional Benefit. Between *O* and *M* are all such citizens who have a small return from other sources. The bill for paying a Conditional Benefit at what is considered a fully adequate rate can be a very heavy one.

Moreover there is an additional cost if this involves raising the Personal Tax Allowance up to the same adequate level of 1 unit. Suppose, for example, that the Personal Tax Allowance had previously been set and were maintained at *OA'*, i.e. at half the fully adequate Conditional Benefit. The citizens' post-tax income would then move up the line *OB'C'*. Up to the point *X* this inadequate income would be supported by the Conditional Benefit along the line *AB*. If now the Conditional Benefit were cut off at the point *B*, a citizen's Adjusted Income would fall abruptly from *B* to *X* as his or her Unadjusted Income rose from below to above the level *OM*. This would represent an unacceptable 'marginal tax rate' of more than 100 per cent; by earning more the citizen would reduce his or her spendable Adjusted Income. To prevent this anomalous situation the range of Unadjusted Income over which Conditional Benefit would be payable would have to be extended from *AB* to *AY*, so that Adjusted Income moved over the line *AYC'*.

Within the triangle *B'BY* the State would neither gain nor lose net revenue. If Income Tax were payable at source citizens would be taxed in this area, but at the same time the payment of Conditional Benefit would have to be increased to offset the increased payment of tax. This would constitute a tiresome administrative arrangement with the authority in charge of Conditional Benefits paying out money for the recipients to pay over to the tax authority. But at the expense of this crude transfer of tax into benefit in this limited region, the maintenance of the Personal Tax Allowance at only half the level of the Conditional Benefit would raise a very substantial additional revenue for the State without any rise in the rate of tax above the existing rate of 25 per cent. The revenue whose loss would be avoided by not raising the Personal Tax Allowance up to the level for the Conditional Benefit would lie in the area between the lines *BC* and *YC'*. To the right of the point *Y* the additional revenue can be represented as a 'poll tax' equal to *BX* raised on all taxpayers with Unadjusted Incomes greater than *AY*.

In the remainder of this Appendix we will confine our attention to cases in which the Personal Tax Allowance under any Conditional Benefit regime is equal to the full Conditional Benefit of 1 unit. But it should be borne in mind that arrangements with a lower Personal Tax Allowance are possible and can introduce a very substantial alleviation of the budgetary problem.

We turn next to the consideration of Social Dividend regimes. Figure 4.2 displays the hideous increase in excess expenditure which would be involved if the Conditional Benefit of Figure 4.1 were simply turned into an unconditional Social Dividend without any increase in the rate of tax. The line *ABC* is repeated from Figure 4.1 and shows the citizen's Adjusted Income under a Conditional Benefit, Personal Tax Allowance, and rate of tax which is assumed to balance the budget. The dashed line *ADE* now represents the Social Dividend regime. Every citizen receives the Social Dividend of *OA* and then on the whole of his or her Unadjusted Income pays a tax of 25 per cent so that the line *ADE* slopes up at 3 in 4 from the starting point *A*.

As a result of the change to the right of the points *D* and *B*, that is to say for all citizens whose Unadjusted Income exceeds 1 unit, every citizen receives as it were a 'poll-subsidy' equal to $\frac{3}{4}$ of a fully adequate standard of living of 1 unit, an amount which is measured by the excess of *DE* over *BC*.

This extra expense falls in the vertically hatched area { ||| } between *DE* and *BC*. Indeed for such citizens it is as if they received a full Personal Tax Allowance (*MB*) and in addition a fixed 'poll subsidy' (*BD*). This 'poll-subsidy' is equal to one $\frac{3}{4}$ of the Social Dividend because $\frac{1}{4}$ is in fact paid away in tax on the first unit of the citizen's Unadjusted Income.

This result can be clearly seen by extending the line *CB* until it cuts the vertical axis at the point marked *A″*. It can at once be seen that for all taxpayers to the right of *M* with Adjusted Incomes on the line *BC* it is quite indifferent whether the regime

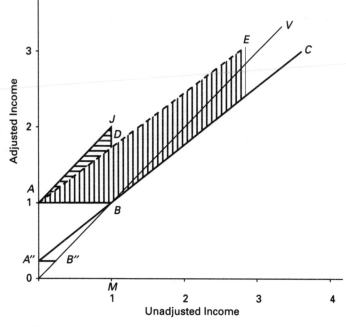

Figure 4.2

consists of a tax-free Personal Allowance equal to MB plus a tax of 25 per cent on all Unadjusted Income in excess of MB or whether the regime consists of a tax-free Social Dividend of OA'' plus a tax of 25 per cent on all Unadjusted Income without any tax-free Personal Allowance. The movement from the line BC to the higher line DE would in the latter case result simply from an increase in the Social Dividend of $A''A = BD$.

To the left of BD there will be some additional government expense on social benefits in the area ADB for those citizens (e.g. old-age pensioners with some small income from capital or private pensions) who are already in receipt of Conditional Benefit.[16] There will, on the other hand, be some small offset in additional revenue in the triangle AJD due to tax paid on small earnings by persons who previously had no incentive to go out to work as long as their Conditional Benefit was reduced pound for pound, but now have some incentive to accept available low earnings of which they will retain 75 per cent.

It is patently clear from Figure 4.2 that if the budget was balanced on the Conditional Benefit regime on the line ABC it would be hideously in deficit on the Social Dividend line ADE, if the rate of Income Tax were left unchanged at 25 per cent. One way of tackling this deficit would be to raise the rate of Income Tax, an adjustment which can be depicted by swinging the line ADE of Figure 4.2 in a clockwise direction. The result of raising the rate from 25 per cent to 50 per cent is then shown in Figure 4.3, where the line AD_1E_1 rises at a slope of 1 in 2 (since half of income is left untaxed) instead of the slope of 3 in 4 of Figure 4.2.

With the regime of Figure 4.3 all citizens to the right of point F (i.e. all citizens with Unadjusted Incomes greater than three times the Social Dividend) are worse off under the Social Dividend arrangement than they would have been under the Conditional Benefit regime of Figure 4.1. What they gain in having a tax-free Social Dividend is more than offset by the higher rate of tax on their Unadjusted Incomes. From these citizens the State receives a net additional revenue in the horizontally hatched area between FC and FE_1 to the right of point F. To the left of point F citizens with positive Unadjusted Incomes gain more from the tax-free Social Dividend than they lose from the rise in the rate of tax; and the shift from the Conditional Benefit regime to the Social Dividend regime involves extra expenditure within the triangle AFB. For all citizens with zero Unadjusted Income (e.g. most children) there is no change in the State's expenditure. In the triangle AJD_1 there may be some moderate addition of revenue from the taxation of the low earnings of persons who under the Conditional Benefit regime had no incentive to work, but now seek work since they can retain 50 per cent of their pay.

Whether or not the raising of the rate of tax to 50 per cent would suffice to cover the cost of the Social Dividend scheme depends upon the distribution of the population of citizens along the Unadjusted Income horizontal axis. If there are many citizens to the right and few to the left of F, the additional revenue will be large relative to the additional expenditure. Among other factors this depends essentially upon the generosity of the level chosen for an adequate standard of living. If this basic unit of income was chosen to be equal to $\frac{1}{3}$ of the average Unadjusted Income per head of the population, there would lie as much income to the right of F producing a net excess of revenue over expenditure, as would lie to the left of F producing a net excess of expenditure over revenue.

Let us suppose that the Social Dividend regime of Figure 4.3 with a 50 per cent rate of tax does balance the budget. Comparing the two regimes (the Social Divi dend regime on line AD_1E_1 and the Conditional Benefit regime on line ABC) we can describe the difference as follows: both regimes start by giving the taxpayer 1 unit of income (he or she starts at point A instead of point O); the Social Dividend regime then taxes all additional income at 50 per cent; the Conditional Benefit regime then 'taxes' the first unit of additional income at 100 per cent and any further additional income at 25 per cent.

There is a second clear distinction between the effects of the two regimes. The Social Dividend regime has a much more marked equalising effect upon the distribution of Adjusted Incomes than does the Conditional Benefit regime. A shift from the latter to the former reduces the Adjusted Incomes of the better-off citizens to the right of F and raises the Adjusted Incomes of all the less well-off citizens to the left of F.

There is thus a stark choice between (i) a high degree of equalisation of standards, and a possible excessive degree of disincentives to work and enterprise from a Social Dividend regime with a 50 per cent marginal rate of tax on all Unadjusted Income and (ii) a markedly lower equalising effect combined with a reduction of the marginal rate of tax to 25 per cent on the vast majority of potential earners to the right of point M at the cost of a 100 per cent marginal rate of tax on those to the left of M.

There are, however, two types of regime which are, as it were, blends of Conditional Benefits and Social Dividends. They offer a possible selection of intermediate positions with equalising effects and marginal tax rate effects which lie

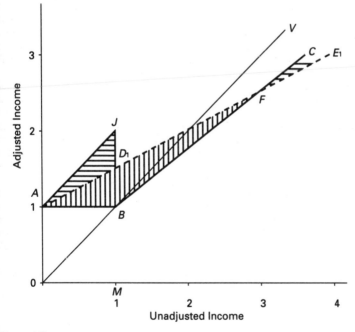

Figure 4.3

between the two extremes presented by Conditional Benefit and Social Dividend
regimes. The first possibility is to raise the rate of tax on the first unit of Unadjusted
Income above the basic rate of tax on the rest of Unadjusted Income but without
raising it to 100 per cent; this solution is depicted on Figure 4.4. The second
possibility is to pay a Social Dividend at a rate less than 1 unit (e.g. at a rate of 0.85
of an adequate standard of living) and to top this up to a fully adequate level by
adding a Conditional Benefit (e.g. at a rate of 0.15) which will in turn be diminished
pound for pound as the citizen receives any Unadjusted Income; this solution is
illustrated in Figure 4.5.

In Figure 4.4 the line ABC represents once more the regime with a Conditional
Benefit of 1 unit and a rate of income tax of 25 per cent, while the line AD_1E_1 is a
reproduction of the line AD_1E_1 of Figure 4.3 and represents the regime with a Social
Dividend of 1 unit and a rate of income tax of 50 per cent. The line AD_2E_2 represents
a Social Dividend regime in which the rate of income tax has been reduced from 50
per cent to 45 per cent, this reduction being offset by an additional Surcharge of 15
per cent on the first unit of each citizen's Unadjusted Income. Thus there is a
combined levy of 60 per cent (45 per cent + 15 per cent) on the first unit of
Unadjusted Income so that the line AD_2 rises at a slope of 2 in 5 (i.e. representing the
40 per cent of Unadjusted Income left after the combined tax of 60 per cent). From
D_2 to E_2 the slope rises to 55 per cent, representing the proportion of income
remaining after the tax of 45 per cent. It so happens that with this particular
combination of Surcharge and reduced general rate of tax the D_1E_1 and D_2E_2 lines

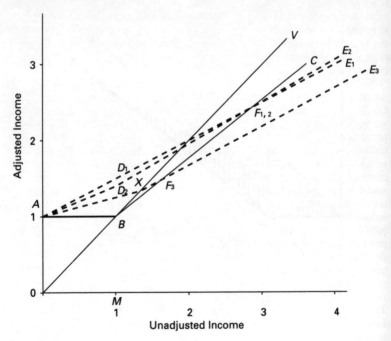

Figure 4.4

cut the BC line at the same point $F_{1,2}$, so that at a level of Unadjusted Income of 3 units a citizen would have the same standard of living under all three regimes.

With this change in Social Dividend regimes there would be a saving of State expenditure to the left of the point $F_{1,2}$ in the area between the lines $AD_1F_{1,2}$ and $AD_2F_{1,2}$ and there would be a reduction of State revenue to the right of point $F_{1,2}$ in the area between the lines $F_{1,2}E_2$ and $F_{1,2}E_1$. There is no reason to believe that this saving of expense would be exactly equal to the loss of revenue; whether or not this would be so depends upon the density of population at various points along the horizontal Unadjusted Income axis. But the imposition of a Surcharge on the first slice of Unadjusted Income can be a very powerful budgetary tool. It would certainly be possible to raise the Surcharge up to a level at which a 45 per cent general rate of tax would be sufficient to cover the cost of the Social Dividend scheme. At the extreme a Surcharge at a level which raised the combined rate of tax on the first unit of Unadjusted Income to 100 per cent would cause the AD_2 line to coincide with the AB line so that the general rate of tax could be reduced to 25 per cent on our assumption that such a rate would be sufficient to finance a Conditional Benefit of 1 unit.

Nor is it essential that the first slice of income on which a Surcharge is levied should be confined to the first unit of Unadjusted Income. The line AXE_3 in Figure 4.4 represents a case in which (i) the general rate of tax is 45 per cent (as is the case of AD_2E_2), (ii) the Surcharge is 30 per cent causing a combined rate of tax of 75 per cent on the first slice of income, and (iii) the first slice of income on which surcharge is levied is raised from 1 unit to $1\frac{1}{3}$ units, this being the point at which the revenue from the combined rate of tax of 75 per cent on Unadjusted Income will just serve to repay the whole of the citizen's Social Dividend. By comparing the way in which the line AXE_3 lies below the line AD_2E_2 one can see how effective a Surcharge regime can be in raising revenue without raising the marginal rate of tax on the majority of taxpayers.

In Figure 4.5 we turn to the other form of blend between Conditional Benefit and Social Dividend, namely an inadequate Social Dividend topped up by a reduced Conditional Benefit. We compare this new blend with the Surcharge regime which we have just discussed. Thus the line AD_2E_2 in Figure 4.5 is simply a reproduction of the line AD_2E_2 of Figure 4.4 and represents a regime with a Social Dividend of 1 unit combined with a 45 per cent rate of tax on all Unadjusted Income together with an additional Surcharge of 15 per cent on the first unit of Unadjusted Income. We compare this line with the line AGD_2E_2 which represents a regime with an inadequate Social Dividend of OH topped up by a Conditional Benefit of HA with a tax rate of 45 per cent on all Unadjusted Income without any Surcharge on the first unit of such income. We have chosen to set the new rate of Social Dividend at a level ($OH = 0.85$) which leaves all citizens to the right of the point D_2 in exactly the same position under both regimes. What they would lose from a reduction of Social Dividend from OA to OH they would gain by the removal of the Surcharge of 15 per cent on the first unit of their Unadjusted Income.

To the left of the point D_2, however, there is a marked changed and the citizen's Adjusted Income is shown by the kinked line AGD_2 in place of the straight line AD_2. To the right of the point G the retention of 55 per cent of a citizen's Unadjusted Income more than makes up for the inadequacy (HA) of his or her Social Dividend and no supplementation of post-tax Unadjusted Income by Conditional Benefit is needed. But up to this point G, Conditional Benefit must be paid at a decreasing rate

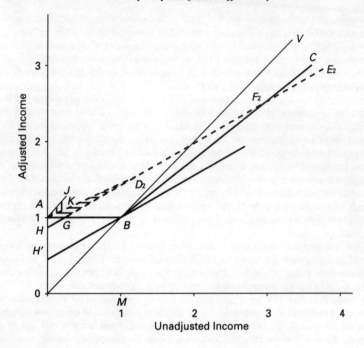

Figure 4.5

to supplement the deficiency of Social Dividend plus 55 per cent of Unadjusted Income.

Within the triangle AD_2G the budget would gain from saving on Social Dividend more than it lost on the elimination of the Surcharge; but this budgetary saving would be accompanied by some loss of revenue within the triangle AJK due to the discouragement of low earnings up to the point G. We assumed in the discussion of Figure 4.4 that the budget can be balanced on the kinked line AD_2E_2. It follows, therefore, that if there were a net budgetary saving by choosing the regime AGD_2 instead of AD_2, it should be possible to finance a Social Dividend somewhat greater than OH. This possibility would, however, be very restricted. Any rise of the point H would cause the point D_2 on the AGD_2 regime to rise above the point D_2 on the line AD_2. This would represent a great loss of revenue equal to a corresponding 'poll-subsidy' to all the taxpayers to the right of point D_2. In fact by choosing an adequate Social Dividend together with a Surcharge on the first unit of income instead of an inadequate Social Dividend together with a Conditional Benefit but without any Surcharge, one can improve the condition of the poorer members (in the triangle AD_2G) together with some removal of disincentive to the lowest earners (in the triangle AJK) at the expense, at the worst, of a very small additional 'poll tax' on the less needy citizens.[17]

Figures 4.1 to 4.5 serve only to give a description of the structural features of different institutional forms of Conditional Benefit, Social Dividend, and Income Tax Regime. By observing along the horizontal axis the level of a citizen's Unadjusted Income one can read off up the vertical axis what would be the citizen's Adjusted Income after deduction of Income Tax and addition of Conditional Benefit or Social Dividend. But this in itself gives no indication of the total net budgetary revenue or expenditure resulting from the given regime; that depends upon the number of citizens at each point of Unadjusted Income.

In particular the diagrams in themselves say nothing about the direct effect of the institution of any particular form of regime upon any particular citizen's Unadjusted Income. The institution of a particular regime may well cause a citizen to change his or her so-called Unadjusted Income before it is subject to the Tax-Benefit Adjustments depicted in the relevant diagram. Such changes in a citizen's so-called Unadjusted Income are likely to be most pronounced under the straightforward Social Dividend scheme of Figure 4.3. In that regime the citizen is given a fully adequate fixed tax-free Social Dividend, the receipt of which will make him or her have a less urgent need to earn additional income. Moreover, for all better-off citizens this substantial fixed income will be combined with a high marginal rate of tax on any additional earnings and this increases the effort required to obtain any given level of post-tax spendable income. The Social Dividend reduces the need for additional spendable income and the higher rate of tax increases the cost of obtaining additional spendable income. Together the two changes will lead to a disincentive to earn additional income. This disincentive will cause the citizen to produce a lower level of so-called Unadjusted Income before it is subject to the particular Tax-Benefit regime of Figure 4.3. Each such citizen will have a lower so-called Unadjusted Income and will be subject to less tax than would otherwise have been the case.

In discussion of Figures 4.1 to 4.5 no reference was made to these possible disincentive effects of the different schemes. The only incentive effects to which reference was made were the encouragement which a shift from Conditional Benefits to some form of Social Dividend might give to citizens at the lower end of the income scale to go out to earn a low income. In such cases the scheme might lead to some improved incentives and so to some increased earnings and increased budgetary tax revenue. But for the great majority of citizens the various Social Dividend schemes are liable to cause substantial disincentive effects leading to a substantial reduction of governmental revenue. In comparing the pure Social Dividend scheme of Figure 4.3 with the pure Conditional Benefit scheme of Figure 4.1 we assumed for purely illustrative purposes that there would be a need for a rise in the rate of tax from 25 per cent to 50 per cent. Some part of this rise in rate of tax must be attributed to the disincentive effects leading to a reduction in the total level of taxable incomes.

There is a second set of factors affecting incentives and disincentives which must be borne in mind. Figures 4.1 to 4.5 are all drawn on the assumption that it is total Unadjusted Income which is subject to Income Tax. But in sections III of the main text it is suggested that the basis of tax should not be total Unadjusted Income (U) but only Unadjusted Income less net Savings (U–S). Figures 4.1 to 4.5 can then remain unchanged if we measure (U–S) instead of U along the horizontal axis. The corresponding height up the vertical axis will then measure the citizen's expenditure on consumption (C).[18]

The exemption of savings from Income Tax will of course reduce the revenue raised in tax in all cases in which citizens are saving any part of their income. We have assumed in section III of the main text that this loss of revenue is made good by additional taxation on wealth or on the transfer of wealth by gift or bequest. But how much lost revenue from Income Tax must be replaced by additional revenue from Capital Taxation will depend not only upon the level of savings which would have occurred if savings had not been exempt from tax, but also upon any effects of the exemption of savings from tax on the incentive of citizens to earn more or less income or to save more or less out of any given income. It is not possible in this simple appendix to consider in detail the nature or extent of these possible secondary incentive effects of the introduction of exemption of savings from tax. But in general there is no reason to believe that they will be very great in one direction or the other in the case of the better-off citizens.

But at the bottom end of the scale there is one important effect to be noted. The exemption of savings from tax means that any citizen who earns more and saves all the additional Unadjusted Income will not pay any additional tax; and as depicted in the diagrams this result is true of the lowest incomes even under a Conditional Benefit scheme. The level of income OA in Figure 4.1 is the Conditional Benefit which will be paid at the origin O when $U-S$, and not necessarily U, is zero. So long as a citizen consumes no more than OA (i.e. saves all his or her Unadjusted Income and lives only on the Conditional Benefit OA), the citizen will continue to receive this unchanged amount of Conditional Benefit. All citizens, however low their earnings, have, even under a Conditional Benefit scheme, some incentive to earn since they can without any loss of consumption save the whole of those earnings with the intention of building up their Unadjusted Income until it exceeds OA. From this point on they will be in a position to use part of their Unadjusted Income in order to raise their level of consumption, any excess of Unadjusted Income over the basic level of OA being subject only to the general rate of Income Tax even if none of it is saved.

For this reason there will be a very strong incentive indeed under a Conditional Benefit scheme for the whole of low earnings to be saved, since otherwise they will be 'taxed' 100 per cent by an equivalent reduction of the Conditional Benefit. There will be a strong, though somewhat less decisive, incentive under the Surcharge scheme of Figure 4.4 for any low incomes to be saved. Any such savings will exempt the saver of low income from the Surcharge as well as the general tax rate on all such savings; but the prospective yield on such savings will be taxed only at the general rate of tax if it is spent later when the saver has built up his or her income to a level above the basic Social Dividend level. If it is desired to promote the equalisation of the ownership of wealth by promoting the savings of those with little property while taxing the wealth of those with much property, the effects of a Conditional Benefit scheme or Social Dividend cum Surcharge scheme under a Savings exempt Income Tax regime should be borne in mind.[19]

In Figures 4.1, 4.3, 4.4 and 4.5 we have depicted the following regimes:

Regime 1   A Conditional Benefit of 1 unit with a Rate of Income Tax of 25 per cent on the line *ABC*.

Regime 3   A Social Dividend of 1 unit with a Rate of Income Tax of 50 per cent on the line AE_1.

Regime 4   A Social Dividend of 1 unit with a Rate of Income Tax of 45 per cent
plus a 15 per cent Surcharge on the first unit of Unadjusted Income on
the line AD_2E_2.

Regime 5   A Social Dividend of 0.85 of a unit with a Conditional Benefit of 0.15
of a unit and a Rate of Income Tax of 45 per cent on the line AGD_2E_2.

All these Regimes are assumed to be such as will preserve a balanced governmental budget without any change in other governmental taxes or expenditures.

One may summarise the relative merits and demerits of these various forms of
Social Benefit or Social Dividend schemes under the following four headings:

(1)   Incentive Effects
(2)   Redistributive Effects
(3)   Risk-Bearing Effects
(4)   Administrative problems

(1) Incentive Effects

The different schemes have very different incentive effects at the top and the bottom
ends of the income scale. Regime 1 has the least disincentive effects at the top end
of the scale where it provides what corresponds to a Social Dividend of only OA''
in size (see Figure 4.2) combined with a low marginal rate of tax 25 per cent. But
it has the greatest possible disincentive effects at the bottom end of the scale where
it threatens to tax away 100 per cent of all earnings. At the other extreme Regime 3
has the worst disincentive effects at the top end of the scale with a high Social
Dividend of OA combined with the highest marginal rate of tax of 50 per cent; but
it has the least unfavourable disincentive effects at the bottom end of the scale.
Regime 4 is a compromise, reducing moderately the disincentives of Regime 3 at
the top end and those of Regime 1 at the bottom end of the income scale. Regime 5
has the same disincentive effects as Regime 4 for those at the top end of the scale
and it extends these moderate disincentive effects further down the income scale
(over the range GB in Figure 4.5); but this it does at the expense of reintroducing the
absolute disincentives of Regime 1 for those at the very bottom of the income scale
(over the range AG in Figure 4.5).

This summary needs some modification if one is dealing with an Income Tax
Regime which exempts savings from tax. In particular the absolute or heavy disincentives at the bottom of the scale in Regimes 1, 4 and 5 will be modified in that
any income which is earned will escape the excessive marginal rates of tax of 100
per cent or of general rate plus surcharge if the income is saved.

(2) Redistributive Effects

The redistributive effects of Regime 1 can be very great. They consist of raising
sufficient revenue at the expense of all those above OM on the income scale in order
to raise up to the level OA the incomes of all those with incomes below OA, as can
be seen in Figure 4.1. All the other regimes have even greater redistributive effects
than Regime 1. The excess redistributive effects of Regimes 3 and 4 can be seen

from Figure 4.4 where the distribution of Adjusted Income is represented by the line *ABC* for Regime 1, by AD_1E_1 for Regime 3, and AD_2E_2 for Regime 4.

Both Regime 3 and Regime 4 have greater redistributive effect than Regime 1 since in both cases those to the right of point *F* are worse off than with Regime 1 while those to the left of *F* (other than those clustered at the origin with zero Unadjusted Incomes) are all better off than with Regime 1. But the redistribution effect of Regime 3 is greater than that of Regime 4 since those to the right of point *F* are better off while those to the left of *F* are worse off with Regime 4 than with Regime 3. Regime 5 has substantially the same overall redistributive effect as Regime 4 except that with Regimes 5 those near the bottom of the income scale are likely to fare somewhat less well.

(3) Risk-Bearing Effects

There remains the argument in favour of a Social Dividend scheme that it will make it more acceptable for workers to accept partnership arrangements under which their earnings will vary with the fortunes of the partnership enterprise, if they have some element of fixed income to fall back on. A Social Dividend certainly has an effect of this kind but the effect is a limited one. Its extent is illustrated by the figures in Table 4.4.

In considering the results shown in Table 4.4 there are two factors to be taken into account. If a citizen's Unadjusted Income falls by 10 per cent there are two ways in which the impact on the Adjusted Income will be mitigated. In the first place, the greater the ratio of the fixed Social Dividend to his or her other income, the smaller will be the percentage fall in his or her Adjusted Income. In the second place, the higher the marginal rate of tax, the greater the amount of any loss of pre-tax income which is absorbed by paying a smaller amount of tax to the government. Thus for all income above the basic standard level of unity, the percentage fall in Adjusted Income is smaller (i) the nearer the Unadjusted Income approaches unity (since the fixed Social Dividend becomes a larger proportion of total income as one moves from income 4 to income 2), (ii) the higher the marginal rate of tax (as one moves from Regime 1 through Regimes 4 or 5 to Regime 3), and (iii) the higher the Social Dividend (as one moves to Regimes 3, 4 and 5 from Regime 1 with its low 'notional' social Dividend of *OA"* as shown on Figure 4.2). Below unit income the risk depends upon the structure of the Regime. It is totally absorbed by the government's adjustment of Conditional Benefit in Regime 1. It is absorbed by tax plus

Table 4.4   The Percentage Fall in a Citizen's Adjusted Income Resulting from a 10 per cent Decline in Unadjusted Income

Level of Unadjusted Income	0.5	2	4
Regime 1	Nil	8.6	9.2
Regime 3	2.0	5.0	6.7
Regime 4	1.8		
Regime 5	2.4	5.6	7.3

surcharge in Regime 4 and by tax alone without Surcharge in Regime 3 and by a still lower rate of tax in Regime 5. But if Unadjusted Income were $\frac{1}{4}$ or less, the relevant rate of tax for Regime 5 would rise to 100 per cent and the whole of the fall in Unadjusted Income would be absorbed by tax as in Regime 1.

(4) Administrative Problems

If Conditional Benefits depend solely upon a citizen's Unadjusted Income (as is the case in all the Regimes discussed in the Appendix) there are no administrative problems concerned with the determination whether a citizen is sick, involuntarily unemployed, etc. The one determining factor is the level of his or her Unadjusted Income.

If, however, the Income Tax Regime is one which exempts net Savings from tax, it will be essential to assess Unadjusted Income and Savings separately for each individual citizen. The kinks in tax liability at the level *OM* in Regimes 1 and 4 and at the level *AG* in Regime 5 could raise additional administrative tasks. For this reason the pure Social Dividend Regime 3 would be administratively the simplest. Indeed if the Income Tax Regime did not exempt Savings and if the rate of tax were constant at 50 per cent over all ranges of Unadjusted Income there would be no need for individual assessment. The administrative problem would be simply to pay the fixed Social Dividend to all citizens and to raise, at source if possible, a 50 per cent rate of tax on all Unadjusted Income.

The best way to summarise the main points is as follows. The higher the Social Dividend and the higher the general rate of tax imposed to finance it, the greater will be the beneficial effects on the equalisation of Adjusted Incomes and on the mitigation of risk-bearing. But both the rise in the Social Dividend (which enables people to enjoy a given income without earning so much) and the higher marginal rate of tax (which reduces the net return on any additional earnings) will tend to reduce economic incentives for work and enterprise. In the choice of policies these results must be weighed against each other.

Notes

1. Section II of the present chapter is a revised and much enlarged version of chapter VI of my book *Alternative Systems of Business Organisation and of Workers' Remuneration* (Allen & Unwin, 1986) and of section 7 of my pamphlet 'Different Forms of Share Economy' (Public Policy Centre, London, 1986). Section III is a revised and much enlarged version of the paper which was presented at the afternoon session of the conference held in Rome in March 1988.
2. Published by Giangiacomo Feltrinelli Editore, Milan, 1989.
3. In economists' jargon it can be noted that the discussion in the text is about the relationship between a factor's cost and its marginal revenue product, and not about the relationship between its cost and the value of its marginal product.

4. Or perhaps not quite the best of all possible arrangements. Agathotopia (the Good Place) is only one of the group of Topian Islands which includes also Ameinotopia (the Better Place), Aristotopia (the Best Possible Place), Utopia (the Non-existent Perfect Place) and, beyond Utopia, Cacotopia (the Bad Place), Caciotopia (the Worse Place) and Cacistotopia (the Worst Place). There is great excitement among the Topians because the Utopians have suggested that they introduce a common currency and harmonise their rates of tax. Many Agathotopians, including my old friend Professor Dr Semaj Edaem, are very worried as to how far they can go without endangering the survival of the rather distinctive Agathotopian economic institutions and policies.

5. Alternative treatments of the Labour Share Certificates of retiring worker partners are discussed in a later section.

6. See Theodor Hertzka, *Freeland, A Social Anticipation* (Chatto & Windus, London, 1891).

7. See Professor Mario Nuti, 'On Traditional Cooperatives and James Meade's Labour-Capital Discriminating Partnerships'. Paper presented at a Conference of the Lega Nazionale delle Cooperative e Mutue, Rome, March 1988.

8. In Appendix A the factors affecting the restrictive forces due to the rules of redistribution and of cancellation are discussed and illustrated in greater detail.

9. See, for example, Dr Ernest Fehr, 'The Labour-Capital Partnership: Reconciling Insider Power with Full Employment', paper presented to the International Economic Association Conference on 'The Economics of Partnership: A Third Way', September 1991.

10. In this chapter we do not deal with the liquidation of Labour-Capital Partnership. As far as voluntary liquidation is concerned, in the case of a large concern with many capitalist shareholders it is practicable to rule that voluntary liquidation should be arranged only with the agreement of the majority of worker partners as well as of the majority of capitalist partners. In this case there would have to be some reasonable agreed treatment of the interests of the worker partners. But in the case of, for example, a one-man capitalist setting up a retail shop and taking on assistants as worker partners endowed with Labour Share Certificates, it would be unreasonable – indeed perhaps impracticable – for the worker partners to be able to prevent the one-man owner from retiring and taking his capital out of the business. The Agathotopians seek for such cases some rule which requires the capitalist partner on liquidation of the business to devote some share of the value of the concern's assets to the compensation of the worker partners.

11. Cf. Maurice Allais, chapter IV.1 of *L'Impôt sur le Capital et La Réforme Monetaire*, Hermann Editeur (Paris, 1977).

12. The characteristics of the various Social Dividend schemes are discussed in greater detail in Appendix B at the end of the main text.

13. This method of dealing with the problem has been suggested to Professor Semaj Edaem by Mr Martin Weale of Cambridge University. See also chapter 12 of the report on 'The Structure and Reform of Direct Taxation' by a committee set up by the Institute for Fiscal Studies (Allen & Unwin, 1978).

14. If $\sigma = 0$ and the whole of the pure profit of a retiring worker partner is

distributed among the remaining worker partners, in the form of an equal distribution among them of the number of shares of the retiring number which are not needed to meet the cost of hiring the new replacement worker, the distribution shown in the table is precisely accurate. But if $\sigma = \overline{\sigma}$ the distribution of the benefit of $B(1 - \overline{\sigma})$ among the remaining $m - 1$ partners will not be strictly equal at $B(1 - \overline{\sigma})/(m - 1)$. This is so because the distribution of benefit will now take place not by a distribution of an equal number of share certificates to all remaining worker partners (as with the rule of redistribution), but instead (as with the rule of cancellation) by rise in the rate of dividend on all share certificates of which a proportion $B\,\overline{\sigma}$ will go to the holders of Capital Share Certificates. The remaining proportion $B(1 - \overline{\sigma})$ will be distributed among the existing worker partners not equally, but in proportion to their holdings of Labour Share Certificates. One team of these partners (namely the newly engaged team m of Year 1) will hold fewer share certificates (only enough to cover their cost) than the other remaining $m - 2$ teams of Year 1 which will hold an additional number of shares corresponding to their pure profit. The $B\mu_1$ of Year 2 should in this case be somewhat larger. This inaccuracy will be of importance only in those cases in which pure profit is large relatively to cost.

15. For purposes of simplicity of algebraic exposition the story of a contraction of workers' membership has been told in terms of the non-replacement of one whole team. But in fact the restriction would probably take the more gradual form of a reduction in the number engaged in each individual team as it was replaced. In any resulting steady state one could once again reach a new situation in which there were m teams with each team being smaller in number so that $\tilde{B}/W$ would be higher and could satisfy the critical condition indicated in (5).

16. If x is a citizen's Unadjusted Income in this range the state pays $1 - x$ under the Conditional Benefit Scheme. With the Social Dividend scheme the State pays 1 unit in Social Dividend but receives in tax tx, a net charge to the State of $1 - tx$. The additional charge to the State is thus $(1 - tx) - (1 - x) = x(1 - t)$.

17. Figure 4.5 the line $H'B$ is drawn parallel to the line HD_2 and thus measures what a citizen's Adjusted Income would be with a Social Dividend of OH' and a tax rate of 45 per cent. It is clear that for the point G to lie to the left of the point B any Social Dividend must be greater than OH'. In other words in order that an inadequate Social Dividend should help to relieve pressure on the payment of Conditional Benefit it must exceed OH', which corresponds to the value at the general rate of income tax of a Personal Tax Allowance (OM) which is equal to the Conditional Benefit (MB).

18. If U = Unadjusted Income, D = Social Dividend, B = Conditional Benefit and T = Total paid in tax, the amount available to the Citizen to spend or save (i.e. $C + S$) must be equal to $U + D + B - T$. Thus

$$C = U - S + D + B - T.$$

If the basis of tax is $U - S$, $T = t(U - S)$, so that

$$(U - S)(1 - t) + D + B = C,$$

which is what is measured up the vertical axis in each diagram, when $(U - S)$ is measured along the horizontal axis. When $U = S$, i..e at the point O on the horizontal axis, we will have $C = D + B$. So that D or B measures the level of consumption which is attainable if the whole of the unadjusted income is saved.

19.   Figure 4.1 to 4.5 do not indicate what would happen if $U < S$, so that $U - S$ were negative. The diagrams cover all the cases in which $U - S$ is zero or greater than zero. A situation in which $U - S$ were negative would be one in which a citizen was saving more than his or her total Unadjusted Income, i.e. was saving part of his or her Conditional Benefit or Social Dividend. Consumption would fall below the basic adequate level unless D or B were raised to cover the excess saving.

5 The Building of the New Europe: National Diversity versus Continental Uniformity*

FOREWORD

The David Hume Institute was very glad to welcome Professor Meade to its list of authors with the publication of his Hume Paper *Agathotopia: The Economics of Partnership* published in 1989 for the Institute by Aberdeen University Press. In that much-acclaimed work, he set out his ideas on the study of industrial organisations which would best accord with a harmony of interests between workers and capitalists.

Although well known for his explorations in reconciling capitalism and socialism, he is professionally even better known for a long list of treatises and articles on international trade theory and policy. Indeed, it was this aspect of his work that won him the Nobel Prize in Economics in 1977. The Institute has now been twice blessed, for Professor Meade has paid it the compliment of asking it to publish his views on how to reconcile the preservation of a large measure of freedom within individual countries within the European Community with economic cooperation of a far-reaching character between them. In an important sense, this chapter is a sequel to his earlier Hume paper for it deals, *inter alia*, with the question as to whether the kind of economic experiment outlined in *Agathotopia* could be conducted by individual countries within the European Community itself.

---

* First published in 1991 by The David Hume Institute as Hume Occasional Paper No. 28, and presented in January 1991 as a special lecture at a University of Rome Conference on 'Building The New Europe', the proceedings of which conference were published in 1992 as *Building the New Europe, Volume 1: The Single Market and Monetary Unification*, edited by Mario Baldassarri and Robert Mundell (Macmillan).

Although the Institute has to offer the usual disclaimer that it has no collective view, its supporters and readers of this chapter will immediately recognise its importance as a contribution to the present debate on the future of Europe.

GORDON HUGHES
Executive Director
David Hume Institute

I INTRODUCTION

This chapter is concerned solely with certain internal economic aspects of the relations between the member countries which may come together to build a New European Community. It does not deal with any of the political problems involved nor with any of the political or economic aspects of the relationship between the New Europe and the rest of the world. Within these limitations it is argued that there is a potential clash of far-reaching importance between two distinct major objectives. On the one hand, it is maintained that there are at present exceptionally strong reasons for preserving a large measure of freedom for the various countries of Europe to experiment in different diverse forms of liberal economic policies and institutions. On the other hand, it is maintained that there are powerful arguments in favour of building a strong centralised union structure to control and unify certain economic policies and institutions in order to attain certain clear communal objectives. Some clash between these two principles is inevitable. But must one of these principles be for practical purposes abandoned in favour of the other or is some set of workable arrangements possible which will achieve the main advantages of both principles?

II THE DEMISE OF COMMUNISM

In this chapter it is simply assumed that the New Europe should be built so as to be capable of incorporating the ex-communist countries of Eastern Europe, including perhaps ultimately Russia itself. The incorporation of such countries would, it is generally agreed, be dependent upon their having successfully switched from basic dependence upon a command-economy structure to basic dependence upon a structure of competitive free-enterprise market arrangements.

In discussing the economic implications of this requirement that members of the New Europe should promote competitive free-enterprise market structures, it is useful to distinguish between the advantages of free enterprise and the advantages of competition. Free enterprise implies that there are certain risk-bearing entrepreneurs who are free to take decisions to maximise the profit which they can obtain from the enterprise which they direct. One way of increasing profit is to reduce the cost of producing whatever is being produced. Free enterprise may thus be welcomed as offering high incentives to produce efficiently in the sense of getting as large an output of products as possible from any given input of factor resources.

Competition strengthens this incentive to produce efficiently since otherwise the profit of the enterprise may be threatened by the lower cost and selling price of competitors' products. In addition a competitive search for profit brings with it a quite different social advantage in so far as it attracts resources into the production of goods for which consumers express the highest values by offering the highest prices and into methods of production which employ the plentiful and thus the cheaper rather than the scarce and therefore more expensive factors of production.

Such are the economic advantages of a free-enterprise competitive market structure. But in certain situations serious monopolistic conditions are inevitable. In the case of a free-enterprise monopoly, such as a privatised national railway network, profit may be increased, not only by using a given amount of resources as efficiently as possible but also by restricting the input of resources and the output of products in order to enjoy an excess profit by raising the selling prices of the products and squeezing the prices paid for the factor inputs. In this case the social advantage of using inputs efficiently may be more than offset by the social disadvantages of restricting the inputs and outputs of the monopolised concern. If the business had been nationalised and run by official managers under instruction to produce as much as possible subject to being able to sell the product at a price which covered the market cost of the factor inputs, outputs of products and inputs of factors might be increased more nearly to the socially optimal levels; but the profit incentive to maximise output per unit of input would be weakened. In such a case is a privatised free-enterprise market or a nationalised socialist market structure to be preferred?

Subject to some basic questions of this kind one may in general greatly welcome the extension throughout Europe of competitive free-enterprise market structures wherever they are possible. From this it is very often implicitly if not explicitly inferred that a restriction of membership of the New Europe to countries which effectively promote competitive free-enterprise market conditions removes any need for diversity in the national economic policies and institutions in the New Europe. Capitalism, it is contended, has knocked Socialism out. All members of the New Europe will have familiar capitalist market economies. We can, therefore, concentrate attention on building a centralised union structure which helps these more or less uniform national capitalist structures to work harmoniously and efficiently together.

I believe this conclusion to be totally false. It is clear that, even in the absence of the problems raised by integrating the ex-communist countries into a New Europe, there is need for much experimentation in developing liberal capitalist economies. Neither the extreme Thatcherism of the United Kingdom nor even the successful Social Market of Germany can be regarded as the end of the road in a search for the best form of liberal economy. It would be a grave obstacle to progress if changes in these structures could be tried out only on a uniform basis in every European country simultaneously.

But the transition of the ex-communist economies of Eastern Europe from a 'Socialist' to a 'Capitalist' way of life does raise these issues in a very clear way. When 'Capitalism' versus 'Socialism' is the subject of political discussion in the countries of Western Europe 'Socialism' is normally held to exhibit one or more of the three following features: (i) the State Ownership and Planned Management of the Land and Capital resources of the community together with extensive State regulation of, and intervention in, many activities which remain in private hands, (ii) a great emphasis upon State measures to ensure a more Equal Distribution of income and standards of living, and (iii) Social Security, including the certainty of earning a living in conditions of Full Employment.

III THE OWNERSHIP, MANAGEMENT AND REGULATION OF THE COUNTRY'S CAPITAL WEALTH

There is in fact almost an infinity of various diverse ways in which the production of goods and services may be organised, planned and managed. I will mention only six typical varieties.

Variety One may be called Command Socialism, where there is a central economic plan instructing production units what to produce and what resources to use for their production and how to allocate their output to consumers. It is not competitive; it does not rely on free enterprise; and it makes no use of a market.

Variety Two may be called Market Socialism. With this system there is no competitive free enterprise, since all productive enterprises are State owned and established or disestablished by the central authority, the State owning all the capital invested in the various firms. But the managers of the firms are instructed to produce as much as they can, subject to covering their costs at current market prices of their imports and outputs, prices being adjusted so as to clear all markets.

The remaining four varieties of productive structures could meet the full requirements of a competitive free-enterprise market structure.

Variety Three may be called the Capitalist Company structure and is the familiar textbook pattern for the discussion of Capitalism. There is private ownership of capital resources with freedom to establish a new firm. In the firms the owners of the capital resources appoint the management. Labour is hired by the Capitalist Company at an agreed fixed rate of pay and the employer-owners of capital bear the risk by receiving what income is left over from the market sale of the output of the firm after the payment of labour and other hired factors of production.

Variety Four is the Profit-Sharing Capitalist Company in which the textbook Capitalist Company is modified by granting to workers, in addition to any element of fixed wage, a share in the residual profits of the firm, but with the owners of the Capital still engaging the workers and making the main decisions about the working of the firm.

Variety Five may be called the Labour Cooperative in which Capital and Labour reverse their roles. The workers hire the capital resources used in the firm; they manage the firm and take all decisions about its policy; and they bear the risks by accepting as their pay what income is left over from the sales revenue of the firm after paying the agreed sums for the hire of capital, land, and other productive resources.

Variety Six may be called the Labour-Capital Partnership. The firm is run by partners some of whom contribute work to the firm and some risk-bearing capital. The partners share in the management and risk-bearing of the firm and they divide the residual profit of the concern between them in predetermined shares according to the amount of work and/or risk-bearing capital which they put into the firm. In this structure neither capital hires labour nor labour hires capital, but worker and capital partners together decide on the management of the firm including decisions about the terms on which new worker or capital partners should be engaged by the firm.

There can, of course, be many mixtures of these various forms of competitive free-enterprise market structures. In any one economy there may be some Capitalist Companies, some Profit-Sharing Capitalist Companies, some Labour-Managed Cooperatives, and some Labour-Capital Partnerships. Moreover a single firm may be constructed on a mixture of forms. For example in a Labour-Capital Partnership some workers may be hired by the partners at a fixed wage and some capital funds may be lent at fixed interest to the partnership by outsiders who are not partners.

The existence of certain Socialist elements in the production processes adopted by the members of a New Europe cannot be ruled out of court. Thus a nationalised railway network could be operated on full Market Socialist principles, selling its products and buying its inputs in an uncontrolled free market. Even elements of Command Socialism will inevitably exist in socialised activities producing such public goods as Defence and Law and

Order and may well by choice be adopted in other activities such as those of a National Educational System or a National Health Service in which the outputs are not subject to market sales but are produced and allocated according to a central plan, but in which various degrees of Market Socialism or indeed of full competitive free-enterprise may be adopted for the supply of various ingredients into these services.

Moreover, so-called socialist intervention in the management of a country's economic resources can include not only those cases in which the resources are owned and/or operated directly by some State organisation. It covers also many forms and instances of State intervention by means of regulation and control of private concerns operating otherwise in a free market. Town and Country Planning, the control of Monopolistic Mergers between private companies, the setting of maximum prices, and the quantitative restriction of the output of pollutants are examples of such interventions.

Clearly not all elements of State ownership, management, fiscal interventions and direct regulation of industrial and similar activities can be ruled out in the economies of New Europe. There are many possibilities for legitimate diversity and experimentation in mixtures of different forms of structure within an economy which is generally based upon the principles of competitive free-enterprise markets.

IV THE DISTRIBUTION OF INCOME AND WEALTH, SOCIAL SECURITY AND FULL EMPLOYMENT

The other main features with which the ideology of the old Socialist countries of Eastern Europe may be associated are the Distribution of Income and Wealth, Social Security and Full Employment. These ideas are so closely interconnected that it is convenient to discuss them together.

All European governments take some measures to relieve the poverty of those citizens who are destitute and indeed to effect some measure of general redistribution of income and wealth. But there are a number of questions to be asked. First, there is the question of degree. At what point, if any, do egalitarian measures become such a soaking of the enterprising rich and subsidisation of the idle poor as to prohibit membership of a community built on the principle of free enterprise? Second, can the measures normally employed in the present Capitalist countries be usefully supplemented by measures of a more Socialist type? Third, how far can any diversification of national experiments in redistributive and other social policies be accommodated in a New European economic community?

The varieties and the implications of different redistributive and other social measures are so numerous that it is impossible to present a *catalogue raisonnée* of all possible experiments. I intend, therefore, to describe one country's particular experiment in combining a reliance on competitive free-enterprise markets with a somewhat socialistic apparatus for a more egalitarian distribution of income and wealth and for greater social security and fuller employment. I raise the question whether it would, in principle, be possible for this particular country, without any basic reformulation of these social policies, to join an economic community composed of the existing Western European countries. One can in this way well illustrate all the main problems of integrating different social objectives and experiments into a single economic community based on competitive free-enterprise markets.

The country which I have in mind is the Island of Agathotopia which I visited in 1988 and whose attempt to combine a reliance on competitive free-enterprise markets with a radical emphasis on these social objectives I greatly admired.[1]

The Agathotopians accept the fact that they cannot rely on competitive free-enterprise markets working efficiently unless they allow the markets to determine the price of the factors of production, that is to say, of capital, of land of different qualities in different regions, and of labour of various skills and training. It is only if the producers of goods and services can compete for the hire or purchase of the various factors of production that free markets will have the effect of attracting the factors of production into the industries and the methods of production that will produce the greatest amount of what the competing purchasers of the final products most desire to consume. The result will determine the incomes of the various owners of different resources of land and capital and of the various workers of different skills, training and localities. In particular the distribution of the revenue from the sales of manufactured products between return on capital and income of labour will depend upon the relative scarcity of labour and of capital resources, the degree to which consumers want goods and services which are capital-intensive or labour-intensive in their production, and the extent to which new technologies are relatively labour-saving or capital-saving. In their own economy the Agathotopians recognise the fact that these conditions are such that for the general range of industrial workers, apart from those with special skills or abilities, full employment depends upon the acceptance of a relatively low income from work. The demand for a higher rate of pay would involve a restriction of the demand for the labour, leaving some unfortunate workers in unemployment.

They have reacted to this situation in two ways.

First, they have taken a number of far-reaching measures to ensure that rates of pay are very responsive to labour market conditions and are very flexible in particular in a downward direction if that proves to be necessary to preserve full employment.

Second, they realise that it would have been impossible to move seriously in the direction of such flexibility in rates of pay if they had not taken equally far-reaching steps in providing for every citizen a basic income in addition to his or her income from work or from the ownership of wealth. Such a basic income constitutes a major instrument in the redistribution of income as well as being an essential element in mitigating the otherwise universal insistence on receiving a rate of pay sufficiently high to provide a given real standard of living.

To deal with the first of these two sets of problems the Agathotopians have a very extensive set of rules and institutions to promote competition through the outlawing of every kind of combination between individual productive units for the purpose of dividing the market, of maintaining prices or of preventing the entry of new competitors. Where any marked monopolistic power is unavoidable, as in the case of many public utilities, they set maximum levels for selling prices and other charges. They apply these same principles relentlessly to the labour market making it in effect very difficult for combinations of workers to take industrial action in order to prevent the management from employing additional workers at lower rates of pay.

In addition they have instituted a system of compulsory arbitration to settle any dispute about rates of pay in any sizeable productive unit, the arbitrators being required to set the wage at a level which will promote employment. This is designed not merely as an additional safeguard against pressures by inside employed workers for the raising of rates of pay above the level necessary to attract outsiders to the concern, but also to prevent employers with monopsonistic powers from keeping rates of pay below the level necessary to attract new labour to the concern.

The Agathotopians realise that none of these wage-fixing institutions can prevent capitalists and workers in any successful business from getting together to share an increase in their prosperity by raising simultaneously the wage rates and the dividends received by the firm's insiders rather than by reducing prices, selling a greater output and employing more workers to the advantage of deprived outsiders. They have tackled this problem in two ways.

First, to put some curb on such inflationary agreements among insiders they have introduced a scheme, covering all sizeable firms, under which any rise in the average rate of pay in excess of a given moderate norm is subject to an inflation tax.

Second, they have promoted a widespread structure of what they call Discriminating Labour-Capital Partnerships. The Agathotopians have a great preference for the partnership form of structure in which the worker's reward takes the form not of a contractual rate of wage but of a share in the concern's profit or rather in the net value added by the concern. They encourage it by means of extending certain tax privileges to such forms of industrial organisation. But the danger is that any such partnership which is especially successful and whose members are for that reason receiving returns on their partnership shares which exceed the market rates of return which are being earned elsewhere in the economy will have no incentive to expand their successful enterprise. To expand indefinitely by offering to additional partners the same share of profit which the existing partners are themselves enjoying would lead to a reduction of the incomes of all partners down towards the outside competitive levels.

The Agathotopians have met this problem by insisting that a Labour-Capital Partnership should receive favourable tax treatment only if it were ready to adopt what they call the principle of discrimination in their plans for expansion. In the case of a successful Discriminating Labour-Capital Partnership, this requires the partnership to offer to new partners whatever terms of membership are needed to attract them without any obligation to offer them terms which are as high as those already enjoyed in the existing exceptionally successful partnership. By this means a successful partnership, which ought in the public interest to expand, can attract new partners without any reduction of the incomes enjoyed by the existing partners. However, this principle of discrimination between the terms of engagement for existing and for new additional partners implies the abandonment of the principle of equal pay for equal work.

The Agathotopians have managed to operate a reasonably successful Full Employment policy by accompanying the measures for the downward flexibility of money wage payments so long as any substantial number of workers are unemployed with a combination of monetary and fiscal policies designed to maintain a steady 5 per cent per annum rate of growth of their money GDP, i.e. of the total of money expenditures on their domestic products.

They recognised that it was impossible to put into effect the general measures just discussed unless pay was supplemented by another source of income to offset the prospect of possible low and risky rates of pay. This purpose was in part achieved by the familiar means of State provision on

an equal basis to all citizens of education and health services. But in
addition to this they rely on two less familiar arrangements.

First, they devised their structure of taxation in such a way as to encourage a more equal distribution of ownership of private wealth and so of the
receipt of investment income. For this purpose they exempted all net savings from their income tax base by the simple process of adding to the tax
base all sales of capital assets and exempting from the tax base all purchases
of capital assets. But they combined this with a moderate annual wealth tax
on all holdings of capital assets above a given level together with heavy
taxation on transfers of wealth by gift *inter vivos* or by bequest on death.
The result was that citizens with little wealth could accumulate savings up
to a given level free of tax, while further accumulations by savings or by
transfers of wealth from other citizens were penalised.

Second, there are no personal or other tax-free allowances under their
income tax (other than the exemption of tax on net savings). But in place of
such personal allowances the State pays free of tax to every citizen a Basic
Income which depends solely upon the age of the citizen, a distinction
being drawn between the payment to a child or to an adult of working age
or to a pensioner.

This Basic Income is paid at a generous rate to every citizen, rich or
poor, and it thereby imposes an extremely heavy burden on the Agathotopian
government's budget. They have been prepared to accept the need for a
relatively high and progressive schedule of tax for their Savings Exempt
Income Tax and for their duties on transfers of wealth *inter vivos* and at
death. But such sources of revenue could not be sufficient to finance the
hideous expense of paying a substantial tax-free benefit to every citizen,
rich or poor. They have supplemented their tax revenue by three exceptional
measures.

First, the Agathotopians are very Green and have taken far-reaching
steps to curtail every form of pollution. They have refrained in every case
from doing this simply by issuing restrictions on the amount of any polluting element which any producer or other economic agent is permitted to
emit. Still less are they willing to use the methods of subsidising non-
polluting competitors of any polluting activity. They have in every case
acted by imposing a tax or other charge on polluting activities at a rate
sufficient to achieve the desired reduction of that activity. In those cases
where more direct quantitative regulation of a pollutant seems necessary
they have acted by auctioning to the highest bidders the quota rights to
produce the pollutant. They have in addition imposed an important tax on
advertisement of different kinds on the grounds that the extensive promotion of unnecessary consumerism is a form of social pollutant. They have

raised a very substantial revenue by these taxes and charges which are not merely revenue-raisers but whose indirect effects are wholly desirable.

Second, they have imposed a Surcharge on the first slice of each citizen's taxable income. The reason is as follows. Much the cheapest way of guaranteeing a minimum income to every citizen is to pay a Conditional Basic Income to every citizen but to withdraw the payment pound for every pound of other income received by the citizen. In this case no one receives any payment above whatever is needed to supplement his or her other income up to the basic minimum. The revenue needed for guaranteeing a Basic Income is minimised, but all incentive to earn additional income at the bottom of the scale is removed since such income is docked pound for pound as it is earned. An Unconditional Basic Income with no Surcharge, on the other hand, does not penalise earnings at the lower level, but it is intolerably expensive if it is paid at an adequate rate to every citizen, rich or poor. A Surcharge on the first slice of other income is a compromise. The need for other revenue is reduced at the cost of a partial, but only partial, extra disincentive against earning income at the bottom of the income scale.

Third, in marked contrast with the representative capitalist economies of Western Europe, the Agathotopians have no State National Debt. On the contrary they have a State National Asset. Over the past years by heavy taxation of a form which is paid out of private savings or private holdings of wealth they have managed to pay off any original National Debt and in addition to accumulate for the State a National Asset. The surplus capital funds thus accumulated are invested by the State through investment trusts and similar private financial institutions indirectly in private competitive free enterprises. The State does not manage these enterprises. It, like many a private rentier, merely enjoys the beneficial ownership of the profit made by private enterprise of one kind or another. The net result is that the State, instead of having to raise tax rates to pay interest on a National Debt, receives indirectly a substantial proportion of the yield on privately managed capital assets without having to raise tax rates for that purpose.

To reach this position the government in any capitalist country with an existing National Debt would have to go through a process of what may be called Topsy Turvy Nationalisation. If a private company is nationalised with an issue of National Debt to raise the funds to compensate the previous private owners, the State takes over the management of the concern but does not benefit financially from the ownership in so far as the interest payable on the National Debt is raised *pari passu* with the profits earned by the nationalised enterprise. But if on the contrary the capital funds are raised by an annual levy on private wealth and are then used to redeem the

National Debt or are invested by the State on the Stock Exchange indirectly in part ownership of a range of businesses which remain in private management, the State does not nationalise the management of any private enterprise but does acquire a partial beneficial ownership in a range of otherwise private concerns. It is to be noted that this process of Topsy Turvy Nationalisation would present a formidable fiscal problem for the Capitalist countries of Western Europe starting off with a large National Debt, whereas in the case of a Socialist country of Eastern Europe the result might well be achieved merely by refraining from selling the whole of the beneficial ownership of all the State-owned assets to the private sector.

There could clearly be a very great variety of experiments in this catalogue of institutions and policies for the promotion of flexibility of prices and rates of pay, for the maintenance of Full Employment, and for the redistribution of income and wealth in a competitive free-enterprise market framework, which I have illustrated from the Agathotopian experiment. The question arises whether diversification in this sort of experimentation would be compatible with the requirements of an effective economic union of the countries concerned. It is to the requirements of such a union and to the question of the degree to which such requirements would preclude national experimentation that I will now turn.

V   THE ROLE OF POLITICS AND OF EXTERNAL RELATIONS

This chapter is confined to a discussion of the distribution of *economic* functions *inside* a European Community between the national governments and the central community authorities. It purports therefore to exclude all considerations of political matters and of relations of the Community and its members with other parts of the world. These distinctions between the political and the economic and between the internal and the external problems of the New Europe are inevitably artificial. In fact in the final choice of designs for a New European Community both political and external aspects must play a very significant role.

No doubt it will, and should, be a requirement of the New Europe that the governments of the member countries, as well as the governmental authorities of the community itself, should be based on the political principles of liberal democracy. The design of such liberal democratic structures presents great problems and is of the utmost importance. But for the purpose of this chapter in discussing the distribution of internal economic functions between the national governments and the central community authorities we may simply assume that appropriate efficient governmental institutions exist at both the national and the central level to carry out the relevant internal economic functions.

But there are other important objectives of the political arrangements in a New Europe. The political structure may well be designed so as to produce what may be called Internal Cohesion between the member nations and External Influence *vis-à-vis* the nations of the outside world. In the present century two world wars have arisen as a result of the nations of Europe fighting each other; the cohesion that a political union might create can thus be very highly valued even if it carries with it little or no economic advantages – indeed even if it carried with it only economic disadvantages. Moreover political union can enhance the influence and power which the constituent members can exert in world affairs; and for this purpose it may be argued that it is not politically sufficient simply to promote a single market within Europe, but that political arrangements should be such as to enable Europe to exert a powerful unified influence over world political and economic institutions and policies.

These aspects of a New European political structure, namely their effects on Internal Cohesion and External Influence, inevitably have effects upon internal economic developments which in turn have implications for the distribution of economic functions between the national governments and the central authorities within a New European community. Defence arrangements provide an outstanding example. Suppose that Defence became a direct function of the New European Community. This (i) would promote Internal Cohesion by giving the various member nations a function which they had to perform jointly together, (ii) would increase their power and influence *vis-à-vis* the rest of the world, and (iii) by necessitating a large increase in the central authority's budget would greatly affect the internal distribution of economic functions between the national governments and the central community authority.

There are many other political and external institutional arrangements which have internal economic implications of this kind. The following are three examples. (i) The choice of a Customs Union rather than a Free Trade Area basis for a European Single Market, (ii) the Common Agricultural Policy of the European Community, and (iii) the proposals for a single currency in a European Monetary Union. All three of these institutions have two very important features.

First, they give the central political authority a task for the member countries to decide and administer jointly: a single set of imports levies in the case of the European Economic Customs Union; a single set of support prices and subsidies in the case of the Common Agricultural Policy; and a single structure of money rates of interest in the case of the European Monetary Union. Second, all of them draw a sharp distinction between the inside members and the outside foreigners, the insiders sheltering behind the common tariff against foreigners' products, or enjoying the agriculture subsidies which are not available to foreign farmers, or dealing in a single money which is distinct from the foreigners' money.

These features in all three cases promote the Internal Cohesion of the community and increase its bargaining power and other forms of External Influence *vis-à-vis* the rest of the world. But they also have important implications for the distribution of economic functions within the community: the Customs Union determines a single set of uniform harmonised imports duties and shifts revenue from the national budgets to the central budget; the Common Agricultural Policy implies, like Defence, a heavy centralised fiscal burden; and a Common Currency shifts the determination of monetary policies, such as the setting of rates of interest, from national central banks to a central monetary authority.

Thus in fact a complete disregard of political and external considerations is not really possible in considering the distribution of economic functions between national and central authorities within the New Europe. However, having looked this problem squarely in the face, we will pass on to consider that distribution with the minimum possible reference to the implications of political and external factors.

VI THE PRINCIPLE OF SUBSIDIARITY AND THE PARABLE OF THE AMBIDEXTROUS ECONOMIST

In the current discussion of economic decisions about European Union much reliance is often put on the principle of subsidiarity, namely the principle that, in the ascending hierarchy of authorities from paterfamilias to neighbourhood council to regional council to national government to European Community, anything which can be done well at a lower level should be left to that level and only those things which cannot be done well at the lower level should be assigned to decision and administration by a higher level of authority. This sensible Federalist doctrine can no doubt in many cases be of great help. I take environmental control as an example. Certain forms of pollution – or more generally of what economists would call external diseconomies – may be very local in their incidence, such as the noise emitted by various local activities. Other forms of pollution may be very widespread in their effects, such as the chemical pollution of the atmosphere or of sources of water, in which case a polluting activity in one locality may have its effect over a wide territory of a continent or even of the whole world. The principle of subsidiarity can then clearly point to the assignment of the control of the former type of pollution to a local or national authority and of the latter type to a European or World authority.

Much lip-service is paid to this doctrine of subsidiarity. But it is in fact in direct opposition to the idea described in the previous section that the Internal Cohesion of a New Europe can be strengthened by finding positive tasks for the central Community authorities to perform. On occasion one feels that the principle has for this reason been reversed and that the assignment of a given function to a Community authority is recommended provided that it can be efficiently performed at the centre and regardless of the question whether it could be equally well or even better performed at the national level.

But even in the absence of any anti-subsidiarity tendency of this kind, the application of this comforting principle of subsidiarity does not present a simple solution to the great majority of problems of clashes between the relative advantages of national diversification and continental unification. It will be my purpose in what follows to point out that time and time again there are certain clear advantages in leaving a matter to the unfettered choice of a national government and at the same time there are certain quite different but equally clear advantages in devising a uniform continental solution for the problem. In such cases the pros and cons of the various possible solutions must be weighed up against each other in making the final choice, the principle of subsidiarity playing the very minor role of suggesting that if the other pros and cons seem to be evenly balanced the chairman's casting vote, as it were, should go in favour of the national authority.

At this point I introduce the parable of the Ambidextrous Economist. President Truman, we are told, instituted a search for a One-Armed Economist so that when he sought advice on an economic decision he would not be told that on the one hand there was a case for, but on the other hand a case against, a particular decision. I believe that President Truman was at fault in this desire. Indeed, that very great President himself had, I believe, on his desk a placard which read 'The Buck Stops Here'. There is almost always a case for and a case against an economic decision; in such cases it is the duty of an economic adviser to explain the economic technicalities of the case for and of the case against; it is the duty of the President to decide between the two. In a number of instances where the case for or the case against a particular proposal seems to me to be overwhelming I will play the role of the President and decide what should be done. But I shall frequently play the role of the Ambidextrous Economist and will describe a number of cases where there is a much more evenly balanced clash between the case for national diversification and the case for continental uniformity. It is for the reader then to play the political role of the President and make the final choice between alternative solutions. One must not fall into the vulgar error of believing that an economic adviser is useless because he or she confines his or her advice to a statement of the economic case on the one hand for, and on the other hand against, a particular policy.

On this principle I shall proceed to discuss such possible clashes under two main headings which cover, I think, the two basic sets of problems which are the subject matter of current debate about European Economic and Monetary Union, namely the formation of a Single Economic Market and of a Single Monetary Unit.

VII   THE GENERAL NATURE AND ECONOMIC OBJECTIVES OF A SINGLE EUROPEAN MARKET

The general purpose is to remove all direct and indirect obstacles to the free movement of goods, services, capital and labour between the separate competitive free-enterprise market economies of the European countries so as to transform the whole into one uniform competitive free-enterprise market. The economic advantages expected from such a transformation are those so well expounded long ago by Adam Smith and Ricardo.

First, free trade in products between countries with different factor endowments will enable each constituent country to concentrate on the goods and services in the production of which it has a comparative advantage with the result of an increase in the total output of goods and services.

Second, free trade will extend the size of the total market for goods and services and thus enable a greater advantage to be taken of the reduced costs of production which may result from Adam Smith's division of labour in a large scale of production. In some cases a market of an extent no less than that offered by the whole European continent may be required to enable any one European producer to take full advantage of the economies of large-scale production. In other cases each separate European national market might be of sufficient extent to enable one or at the most a very limited number of national producers to take full advantages of the economies of scale. In such a case the organisation of a single market covering the whole European continent could ensure that there was much more effective competition in what would otherwise be a structure of national enterprises, each able to exploit monopoly powers in its own protected national market.

Finally, the freedom of movement of labour or capital from the localities in which it is relatively plentiful and cheap to the localities in which it is relatively scarce and expensive will supplement the cost-reducing effects of free trade in increasing the output of the products of labour and capital.

The action needed to construct such a single market would seem to be obvious, easy and straightforward. Remove all national or continental governmental obstacles to freedom of movement of goods, services, capital, and labour and the problem is solved. There is much truth in this simple prescription; but, alas, for reasons to which I have already alluded in earlier sections of this chapter, the answer is a good deal more complicated than that. There are at least three groups of basic reasons why simple *laissez-faire* is not enough.

The first general set of complicating factors can be grouped under the heading of those resulting from monopolistic conditions. Where economies of scale are so large relatively to the market that there is room for only one or two productive units to service the given market, free competition cannot be relied upon to produce the optimum output of the product. Producers will have some incentive to restrict output and to raise prices above cost because there is no room in the market for new competitors producing on a scale which would make their entry profitable. This phenomenon can take many forms ranging from that of a single railway network covering the whole geographical area to that of a small local producer protected by heavy cost of transport of products into his area from outside sources or protected by the attraction of a special brand name of the product.

A second general set of complicating factors can be grouped under the heading of external economies or diseconomies. By the term 'external diseconomies' economists describe situations in which a private producer or consumer imposes a social cost on society for which he or she makes no payment, the most obvious cases being those in which the activity causes some form of pollution the social cost of which does not enter into the market cost of the good as it is produced or consumed. By external economies the economist describes a situation in which some economic activity produces a social good for which the private producer or consumer obtains no market benefit, an example being the invention of some new unpatented product or method of production of which competitors can take advantage without making any market payment to help to meet the cost of the initial research involved in perfecting the invention. A single market will be working efficiently only if some means can be found of bringing these external social costs or benefits into account in determining what are the real benefits to society of producing one product instead of another or or using one method of production rather than another. But this involves some form of state intervention to tax or otherwise restrict activities with high

xternal diseconomies and to subsidise or otherwise promote those activi-
es with high external economies.

The third general set of complicating factors can be grouped under the
eading of Distributional Effects. As has already been argued at length in
ection IV of this chapter, an economy which is based on competitive free-
nterprise market arrangements will lead automatically to a given distribu-
on of income and wealth among the citizens of the community which may
ot be considered acceptable.

In all of these three cases of monopolistic conditions, of environmental
ollution and of the distribution of income and wealth, State intervention in
ie market may be needed. In all three cases the questions arise: How
nacceptable must the adverse effects become for positive intervention in
ie market to be legitimate? What forms should such interventions take?
nd should any such interventions be operated on diverse national prin-
iples or by a continental authority on a uniform basis?

In the next section I will try to illustrate the possible answers to these
uestions by applying them, very superficially I fear, to a select number of
ssues which are currently debated in connection with the building of a New
urope. In examining these specific questions I shall, on the principle of
ubsidiarity, assume that the starting point is that the Continental Authority
hould do nothing; it should rely upon *laissez-faire* to construct an effective
ingle Market. Starting from this basis I shall then ask whether in any
articular instance there is an economic case for active intervention at the
ontinental level, bearing in mind that such active continental intervention
iay take a positive or negative form. By negative continental intervention
mean that the continental authority merely prohibits the national use of
ertain policies, or institutions, e.g. it prohibits a national government from
iscriminating in favour of its own nationals in making contracts for gov-
rnmental purchases of goods and services. In the case of such negative
ontinental interventions the central authority must, of course, have certain
owers and procedures for ensuring that these prohibitions are respected by
ie national authorities. By positive continental intervention I mean the
esign by the central authority of a policy or institution which requires the
elevant positive action to be taken by the continental authority itself, as in
ie case of a common tariff of import duties or a common set of subsidies
n the case of agriculture. It is not easy to draw a sharp distinction between
egative and positive interventions by the continental authority; but the
istinction is, I think, sufficiently sharp to be a useful one.

The basic objective of a Single Market is, as has already been discussed,
o promote competition through freedom of movement of goods, capital and
abour. In the case of positive interventions in the Single Market which are

left to the decision of the national authorities, I shall draw a distinctio
between what may be called uncompensated and compensated freedom c
movement. The idea behind this distinction can be made clear by a simpl
example. There is a tax of 10 per cent in country A on a particular produc
In country B there is no tax. Uncompensated freedom of movement of th
good from B to A would mean the absence of any tax on the import of goo
by A from B, and this would give the producers of B a 10 per cei
'unnatural' tax advantage over the producers of the good in A. A 10 per cei
duty on the import of the good from B would represent what I would ca
compensated free entry for the good into A. This has real meaning becaus
a 20 per cent duty which would give A's producers a 10 per cent advantag
over B's producers would in my terminology mean that there was n
freedom of movement of the good, even though there might be no quan
itative quota restriction on the amount of the good that was permitted t
move from B to A. The application of the idea of compensated freedom c
movement is not at all easy, as I hope to show; but as a means of clarifyin
some of the basic underlying issues in the discussion of the treatment c
clashes between national diversity and continental uniformity it can,
believe, be useful.

VIII   SOME SPECIFIC SINGLE MARKET ISSUES

(1) Agriculture

Many relevant issues are raised by the Common Agricultural Policy, but
shall not discuss them in this chapter. My official reason for not doing so i
that it is impossible to consider the CAP without discussing the commerci;
relations of the members of the European community with outside nor
member countries; and I am strictly excluding relations with outside cour
tries from the scope of this chapter. An additional personal reason fc
excluding the CAP from this chapter is to avoid the apoplectic fit which
might suffer if I started to do so. I can claim to be one of the foundin
fathers of the GATT; I have always worked for movements towards free
dom of trade on a world-wide basis and have abhorred the construction c
tight regional discriminatory protective devices. That the governments c
the EC members should have risked endangering the whole future of th
GATT for the sake of the political votes of a group of uneconomic farmer
seems to me to be an unspeakable outrage. At this point I break my promis
not to discuss the external relations of the European Community by askin
the question whether the so-called Capitalist countries could not be enligh

ned enough to apply to their mutual trade the principles of competitive free-enterprise markets, the application of which they are welcoming so heartily for the ex-Communist countries.

2) The Social Charter and the Redistribution of Income and Wealth

On the principle of subsidiarity, as already explained, I start the examination of this wide range of labour market and other social interventions in the market on the assumption that such interventions should be left to the national governments and that the function of the European community in these matters is to ensure the free competitive movement of goods and of factors of production between the member countries. On examination there is much to be said for continuing to rely in the main on this principle in the case of these social measures.

There are great differences in the standards of living in the various member countries. Any attempt to lay down a meaningful minimum wage for all workers in the community as an equalising device at the lower end of the income scale would have disastrous effects. If such a regulation were strictly confined to the wage for labour it would be extremely unfair to a country which adopted the Agathotopian policy of tackling unemployment by combining a low wage with a high Basic Income from other sources or which adopted the profit-sharing principle of combining a low fixed rate of wage with a high share of profit for the workers. If an attempt were made to set a meaningful minimum, it would at least be necessary to include receipts from a Basic Income, from a share of profits or from other similar sources in the definition of the 'wage'. This together with other problems such as the treatment of part-time work through the decision whether it was the hourly rate of pay or weekly earnings to which the minimum referred would raise great administrative problems, the regulation and policing of which would require a considerable central bureaucratic staff.

But the basic argument against such central intervention does not depend upon these administrative problems. A minimum rate of pay which had any meaning for the member countries with existing high standards would be a device which protected them from being undercut by the products of member countries whose uncontrolled rates of pay would be below the minimum. As far as real differences in the productivity of labour in different European countries are concerned, it is freedom of movement of goods, of capital, of enterprise, and of workers between the countries which could provide a really effective equalising factor. The concentration of production on labour-intensive products in those countries where labour is plentiful and

on capital-intensive products in those countries in which capital equipmer
is plentiful, together with free exchange of the products between the tw
types of country, would promote total production as well as helping t
equalise earnings. And a similar tendency would result from the free flo\
of capital from economies in which it was plentiful into economies in whic
it was scarce and from the free migration of workers from economies i
which labour is cheap to economies in which it is expensive.

There is a similar strong argument for leaving questions affecting th
choice of institutions and other arrangements for wage-fixing and of th
structure of competitive production units to the decision of the nation
governments rather than to attempt to devise central regulations coverin
the participation of workers in the management of such units. Differer
countries may produce different mixes of what I have called Market Social
ism, Capitalist Companies, Profit-Sharing Companies, Labour manage
Cooperatives, and Labour-Capital Partnerships with different arrangement
about wage-fixing and about labour participation in the management of th
concerns. By ensuring free competition between them, the central Europea
authority can make its best contribution to the choice of the most appropri
ate structures.

There remains, however, one very important set of problems in this fiel
with which the simple attribution to the national governments of thes
social policies does not cope satisfactorily. Where differences in standard
of living are due to differences in real underlying economic conditions, th
proposed *laissez-faire* attitude of the central authority is likely to be th
appropriate answer. But such differences may themselves well be the resu
of differences in national regulations, institutions, and policies rather tha
of differences in the underlying supply, demand, and productivity of th
available economic resources. Suppose that countries A and B are ver
similar in their real underlying economic resources; that A has adopted
wide range of institutions and policies to redistribute income and wealth i
an egalitarian direction; but that B has interfered very little with the distri
bution of income and wealth which results from the free play of the com
petitive markets. Low-paid unskilled workers might migrate from B to A t
enjoy the favourable tax, social security, basic income advantages in A
while highly-skilled high-paid workers and successful entrepreneurs migh
migrate from A to B, carrying their capital funds with them, to enjoy th
relatively favourable tax treatment which they would receive in B. At th
extreme such a situation could lead to a most inefficient and undesirabl
concentration of all the poor low-productive factors in one country with al
the rich high-productive factors in the other.

One result might be that country A would decide to abandon or to modify its egalitarian interventions. Free competition between A and B in the Community market would have induced a convergence in national policies, in this case probably in the direction of scrapping egalitarian experiments.

A second possibility is that the central Community authorities should introduce regulations for the harmonisation of the relevant national institutions and policies. This would imply that some egalitarian intervention should take place but on the same scale and by the same means in all the national economies. This solution raises the great problems of deciding what the uniform scale and methods should be and implies the building of an effective central bureaucratic apparatus to administer and enforce the harmonised procedures. It also has the disadvantage of eliminating the possibility of diverse experimentation in the different national arrangements.

A third possibility is that the central Community authority should allow free national experimentation in these policies but should itself introduce and administer a positive form of egalitarian intervention of its own. For example it might itself raise a general community levy or tax of some form and use the proceeds to pay a modest Basic Income to all the citizens of the member countries. The national governments could be left to top this up with their different national schemes. Movements of people and capital would as before put a brake on the most extreme egalitarian experiments; but the existence of the modest Community scheme would mean that the outcome of the competition between the national experiments would be less markedly inegalitarian than would otherwise have been the case. This solution would permit more national experimentation and would involve a less complicated central bureaucratic apparatus than the solution through centrally administered full national harmonisation.

A fourth possibility is to allow complete national freedom of experimentation in this field but to attempt to offset the effects of competition between the different national schemes by modifying the forces of competition through the introduction of what I have called compensated freedom of movement of goods, capital, and workers. Workers would be free to migrate from country B to country A, but they would not enjoy the extra egalitarian benefits which were offered in A over and above those that were offered in B. Capital could flow from A to B but would remain subject to any extra egalitarian tax or other treatment to which it was subject in A.

I will return later to the question to what extent such compensated freedom is a practical possibility.

Meanwhile I claim the privilege of the Ambidextrous Economist and

leave the choice between these solutions of the problem to the reader'
Presidential decision.

(3) Norms and Standards of Health, Safety and Similar Reasons

The formation of a Single Market for the European Community clearly
requires the removal of national regulations of particular activities which
are designed simply to protect national producers, or traders, against the
competition of the producers and traders of other members of the community. But often the problem is not as simple as that. Thus imports of goods
may be controlled on the grounds that the foreign goods may carry with
them a threat to the health or safety of the consumers. Regulations excluding foreign banks or other financial institutions from providing their services in the domestic market may be imposed in order to protect local
standards of operation for the financial security of the creditors of the
institutions. Medical, legal, or other practitioners may be required for similar reasons to have acquired recognised national qualifications, often ob-
tainable only by lengthy and costly training.

Some national procedures may be protective of national producers without any other important justification, such as regulations which require
governmental procurement to give preference to national supplies. But
many regulations, while they have an important, perhaps a predominant
protective effect, may also have a legitimate and important purpose in the
protection of the consumer. This is a field in which there is a clear need for
Community action to ensure that necessary regulations exist to protect the
health, safety and security of consumers of goods and services without
imposing unnecessary protection to local suppliers. In fact a great deal of
tedious and detailed work has been done and is in the process of being done
to apply this principle to a large number of particular activities.

I shall not attempt to discuss these individual cases in this chapter
because this is a field in which, if one assumes that all are agreed on the
basic principle of a single market, there is no basic inevitable clash between
national and community interests. The only problem is to search for a
method which prevents the use of such regulations for national protective
purposes with the minimum of detailed community regulation. Wherever
possible, the best method for this purpose is the rule that member countries
should recognise the national norms and standards of each other. Country *A*
should allow free import of goods and professional services and personnel
from country *B*, provided these goods and services satisfy the norms and
standards which country *B* lays down for the consumption of country *B*'s
products in country *B*. This rule would have to be accompanied by some

basic Community minimum requirements which each country's national norms and standards would have to satisfy. But subject to that provision, the method allows the maximum possible national diversity of norms and standards with the minimum amount of central bureaucratic administration.

(4) Control of Monopolies

Another closely related but more difficult set of problems arises in cases in which important monopolistic structures are inevitable. In fact we live in a world of imperfect competition in which monopolistic elements are to be found in most, if not all, markets. Everyone is familiar with the danger that a monopolist may restrict output in order to raise the price of the product and to make an undue profit at the expense of the consumer. The basic weapon against such monopolistic action lies in a competitive economy in which there is freedom for new suppliers to enter the monopolist's market to take advantage of the monopolistic profits with the result of increasing supplies and bringing the price of the product down.

Why then does freedom of competition not suffice to remove all monopolistic activities? The answer lies in the phenomenon of 'increasing returns to scale'; in order to produce a good or service at a low cost one must have a sufficiently large market to be able to produce on an economically large scale. This principle applies over the whole range of activities from the village shop to the gigantic industrial combine. The village shop operates in a market which enjoys a modest protection due to costs of transport and of customer movements. The villager finds it cheaper to walk round to the village shop to buy a loaf of bread rather than to take the train or bus to the nearest large shopping centre. The village shop is thus able to charge a somewhat higher price than the neighbouring large shopping centre. No competing village shop enters a small village market because there is not room for two to be able to conduct the business on a scale which is sufficient to reduce the costs to a tolerable level. The same set of considerations on a very different scale will explain why there is room for only one or two producers of, say, cars, each able to preserve some degree of monopolistic profits. Low costs of production may require an assembly line which will handle a very large output; and the demand for cars may be such that there is room for only one or two assembly lines producing on an economic scale.

So long as the separate nations of Europe could take steps to protect their industries from competing imports, a good might well be produced separately in each country on a scale which was not sufficient to enjoy all the available cost-reducing advantages of a large-scale production. The re-

moval of national trading obstacles by the formation of the single marke
would then enable one country's production unit to undercut and expand a
the cost of another country's production unit or to merge voluntarily with
another country's production unit and to concentrate the two national pro
ductions into one production unit. In other words it might well result in the
concentration of the national units into one or two much larger units. The
result could be a real saving in cost for the Community as a whole combined
with a concentration of activity and profit in one central locality at the cos
of the other nations whose production units had been absorbed into the
concentrated central unit. Here is the possibility of a very real clash of
interest between the production of the good at the lowest possible cost for
the Community as a whole and the desire of a nation to avoid the danger of
becoming a deindustrialised depressed region and to maintain some diversity in its industrial structure. In view of these considerations what should
be the policies of the member nations and of the community?

A merger will have two effects. On the one hand, it will increase the
monopolistic powers of the merged concerns; on the other hand, the merger
by increasing the scale of operations of the single concern may well reduce
the costs of production of the combined output. Whether or not the merger
should be permitted must depend upon whether or not it is judged that in the
particular case the disadvantage of increased monopolistic power is or is not
outweighed by the opportunities for real cost reductions. But should the
judgement and control be a function of the national authorities or of a
central Community authority?

In so far as the proposed merger is confined to two or more concerns
operating in, and providing services for, a particular country it would seem
clear that on the principle of subsidiarity the decisions should remain with
the national authorities. It is arguable that even in the case of a proposed
merger between concerns operating in a number of national markets – and
it should be remembered that many large concerns are in any case multi-
nationals operating in many national markets – each nation should have
the power of preventing a merger of a concern located in its territory, even
when the merger concerns businesses located in other territories. Such a
power may be needed to preserve its industrial base and the diversity of its
enterprises. But on the other hand it would appear that in such cases there
should be a central Community authority to judge whether the whole
balance between increased monopoly power and reduced costs was such as
to make the merger desirable for the community as a whole. But in this case
the questions remain how far and by what means should the Community
authority take into account national interests in the diversity of their produc-

tive activities. The present Ambidextrous Economist does not know the answers and once more leaves the Presidential decisions to the reader.

Where a large-scale productive structure is needed in order to attain low and economic costs of production, a limitation of the misuse of the inevitable monopolistic power may be attempted through the control of the monopolist's selling price. A similar result may be achieved even more directly by the nationalisation of the enterprises concerned (as, for example, in the case of a country's generation and distribution of electricity), the managers of the nationalised concern being instructed to produce on as a large a scale as is compatible with setting prices at a sufficiently high level to cover costs plus a moderate rate of profit. In such cases there is a wide range of systems for price-fixing which may be available. Where increasing returns to scale are still operating, the average cost of producing a unit of the product will be higher than the marginal cost, that is to say, than the extra cost incurred by adding some additional units to the total output. The average cost will be lowered because the additional units of output add less to the total cost than the existing average cost. In such cases there is a strong case for charging prices on a discriminatory basis which allows some or all units of production to be sold at the low marginal cost while the average cost is covered by charging additional sums on some other basis.

Two examples may be given. The electricity supplied by a nationalised concern may be sold at a low marginal cost when it is exported to consumers in other countries where it can compete with and undercut the local producers and at a higher price to the domestic consumers. Alternatively the electricity may be sold to all consumers at the low marginal cost while a fixed standing charge based on some criterion other than the amount of electricity consumed is added to the electricity bill of each domestic consumer. The foreign importing country may be charging a single average cost price for all its output. It may, therefore, argue that discriminatory prices of the kind outlined in these two examples represent a case of dumping in which the exported electricity is sold at a lower price than that charged in one form or another to the domestic consumer. The question therefore arises whether there should be Community regulation over such national pricing systems even though they are designed to increase the sales and so to reduce the costs of the monopolistic producers. If so, should some Community action take the form of prescribing such pricing systems or of allowing the importing countries of such products to impose a compensating import duty equal to the excess of the export's average cost of production over the price charged for the export? The latter solution would allow a diversity of national experimentation in that a system of charging low marginal-cost prices to the units sold to its own domestic consumers could be applied in the exporting country while tax-inclusive average prices were charged in the importing country.

Finally, one may note that the monopolistic powers of some producers are positively maintained and reinforced officially by patent laws. Such arrangements are justified by the fact that the great costs of research and development of new products and of new methods of production would not be undertaken if the results could immediately be used by all competing producers without making any contribution to the cost of producing the invention. Patent rights give the inventor a monopoly of the use of the invention for a given period of years. The longer the period during which the monopoly profit from the protected use of the invention can be enjoyed, the greater the incentive to produce such inventions but the longer the period during which other producers and consumers cannot make use of the new knowledge. The question arises whether there should be any special Community regulations to prevent the misuse of the patent system by one member country at the expense of others through granting strict patent rights for excessive periods to its national inventors of what may be very simple innovations. It is questionable whether the situation needs any special Community regulation over and above the existing general international arrangements in this field.

(5) Externalities and Environmental Problems

Interventions of one kind or another in the workings of competitive free-enterprise markets are needed in those cases in which there are social costs or benefits involved in the activity which are not charged or paid in the workings of the private price mechanism. The cost of pollution of the air or the sea or river water by the discharge of deleterious gases or chemicals of one kind or another is a most important example which is of great topical interest.

Where it is possible without too much difficulty, there is great merit in controlling such pollution by a system of taxes or other charges or levies on the amount of pollution which each individual polluter is causing. If the polluter is taxed at so much per unit of the socially harmful gas or chemical which his or her activity causes it is equivalent to a simple supplement of the private production costs – of capital, raw materials, and labour – which the activity entails. Such a form of intervention has all the merits of competitive free-enterprise market arrangements. It leaves private producers and consumers in competition with each other to choose what they will produce and consume, including in the costs and prices in the market the social as well as the private costs of production. The social costs are charged on those who are doing the social damage and this gives them an incentive to change their methods of production which matches the social need for them to do so. But at the same time it allows for the fact that some polluters will be able to change their methods of production more easily and with less loss of output than others. To avoid the tax, those who can change easily will change more than those who can change only at a great private cost; and it is economically sound that, if the discharge of a harmful element is to be reduced to a given tolerable level, the reduction of the discharge should be undertaken by those who can most easily do so.

Finally this method of control of pollution has an outstanding advantage over other methods of direct regulation; it raises tax revenue for the government in question. All governments need tax revenue. Most forms of taxation carry with them some undesirable disincentive effects such as the possible effects of a progressive income tax on the incentives and opportunities of entrepreneurs to expand their businesses. But levies on pollution constitute a method of tax which not only raises revenue but does so in a way which improves economic incentives in competitive free-enterprise market conditions.

Unfortunately, however, the application of the method of taxing the polluter can present grave administrative costs and technical difficulties. It requires some physical and administrative means for measuring the amount of pollution caused by each polluter. Such measurement may be technically difficult or even impossible. In such cases it may be possible to restrict the amount of pollution by more crude means. For example, it might be laid down that one particular polluting method of production should in all cases be prohibited. Such a regulation might reduce the polluting element to an unnecessarily low level and would make no distinction between those who could reduce pollution at little cost and those who could do so only at great cost. Direct and crude regulation of this kind should be employed only where the administrative and other costs of charging pollution taxes are too high.

So much for the methods of environmental controls. One must also draw a distinction between the cases in which a private polluting activity affects only the social costs in a local region of one country and those cases in which the polluting activity affects social costs over a wide area which includes many countries. We may start with a sharp distinction between an activity which affects only one member country of the European Community and an activity whose social costs affect all the countries of the Community.

The principle of subsidiarity suggests that in the case of a purely local environmental social cost (as in the case of Town and Country Planning of the use of land resources or of noise abatement in a given locality) the responsibility of control should lie with the national government, which would be free to use whatever method of control it chose to use. In the case of an activity which pollutes on a European continental scale the argument for using a Community pollution tax is very strong in all cases in which such taxation is a practical possibility. For the reasons already given it would represent the appropriate method for supplementing a European continental structure of competitive free-enterprise market arrangements. It would also have the great advantage of providing the central Community with a tax revenue. But where a continental pollution could not be controlled by a continental pollution tax, the function of the central Community authority could be reduced to a determination of the quantitative extent to which each member should reduce its emission of the pollutants, leaving it to each national government to determine the means by which its quantitative target should be attained.

But the scope of polluting activities is not confined to those which affect one member country alone and those which affect all the European member countries. Some polluting activities (e.g. the discharge of chemicals into a river) may affect some but not all of the member countries of the Community, or may affect a group composed of one or more member countries together with one or more non-member countries (e.g. the discharge of chemicals into a river flowing through a number of different countries). This suggests that schemes of pollution control may be best devised between groupings of countries which may differ in their composition and which may or may not contain countries which are, as well as countries which are not, members of the European Community.

This subject of environmental control is, as everyone now knows very well, of the greatest importance but it is at a very early stage of discussion and application. I myself feel unable to say more than that those forms of environmental pollution which affect all or a majority of the European countries raise problems of the kind which I have described and which certainly call for appropriate treatment by a central Community authority.

(6) Harmonisation of Taxes and Subsidies

It is in the setting of taxes and subsidies that the most difficult and important clashes between national and continental interests can occur. The general problem is clear. If one decides to build a perfect Single Market in which no governmental interventions have any effect in distorting the relative advantages of producing or consuming one nation's product rather than another's or of working or of holding capital or of living in one national area rather than another, there must be complete harmonisation of all taxes or subsidies throughout the area of the Single Market. Otherwise there will inevitably be some distortion of choice. On the other hand such complete and perfect tax harmonisation would remove all possibility of effective diversity in the national designs of economic institutions and policies.

The problem of finding an appropriate balance between legitimate and illegitimate diversity of national fiscal arrangements raises an extremely wide range of very complicated issues. It is possible in this chapter only to scratch the surface of the problem by giving a few simple examples of the sort of issues involved.

Taxes which are laid simply on a nation's import or a nation's export of a particular good or service should be clearly ruled out by a general Community regulation against such national protective devices. But indirect taxes on the whole national consumption or on the whole national production of a commodity are not in the same way obviously protective.

An indirect tax which is levied on all domestic production of a product with exported production paying no tax but all imports being subject to the tax, is clearly a tax on domestic consumption regardless of the source of the taxed good. Similarly an indirect tax which is levied on all production whether it is consumed domestically or is exported but without levying any tax on imports of the products, is clearly a tax on domestic production of the taxed good regardless of its destination. In order to prevent the most obvious protective uses of indirect taxation it is clear that a national indirect tax should be either a tax on the national consumption whatever the source of the good or a tax on the national production whatever the destination of the product.

But such a simple rule would not suffice to rule out the design of structures of indirect taxes which in fact had a very marked protective effect. For example, in the case of VAT which is a tax on national consumption, harmonisation would mean that the tax must be imposed on all items of consumption at the same uniform rate of tax. But in the interests of diversification it can be argued that the different nations should be permitted to differentiate between their scales of VAT and of other indirect taxes as between one class of goods and another. The legitimate grounds for such differentiation might be (i) on distributional grounds (i.e. to tax expenditure on luxuries more heavily than expenditures on necessities) or (ii) on environmental grounds (i.e. on the grounds that the consumption of the good caused an environmental evil). However, if complete freedom of choice of tax scales were permitted, there would be nothing to prevent all goods which were imported in large quantities by the nation being taxed at exceptionally high rates which would give an incentive to the home consumers to shift their purchases away from foreign on to domestic products. For example, in the UK a heavy consumption tax on wine and a low tax on beer could encourage the British habit of swilling home-brewed beer instead of sipping French wines.

A similar problem arises with the indirect taxation of production. If a nation levies particularly high rates of tax on products which it does not export and particularly low rates on products which it does export, it would in fact be paying the equivalent of a subsidy on its exports.

Considerations of this kind raise the question whether and, if so, how and to what extent the member nations should be required to consult with, and possibly to acquire the consent of, some Community authority with regard to the structures of their indirect taxes. One conceivable procedure would be (i) to allow freedom to the constituent member countries to impose their own rates of indirect taxes, (ii) to require them in any case to define and treat each such tax as either a tax on consumption regardless of origin of the good or as a tax on production regardless of destination of the production, (iii) to allow other member countries to appeal to some Community body on the grounds that a member's structure of indirect taxes was in fact having an undue discriminatory effect on the offending member's imports or exports, (iv) to require the accused member to justify its structure on certain clearly defined grounds such as a desirable redistribution of income or the protection of the environment, (v) to produce an award by the Community body as to the degree of unjustifiable tax or subsidy there was on the complaining members' imports or exports of particular types of goods and (vi) to allow the injured members on the basis of 'compensated freedom of movement of goods' to offset the effect of the unjustifiable tax or subsidy by an offsetting subsidy or tax on their own imports from or exports to the offending country. But the question remains whether or not any procedure of this kind could possibly be made workable.

I turn now from Indirect to Direct Taxes and Subsidies. In this category one may include Taxes on Income, on Wealth, and on Capital Transfers and Subsidies to income such as the payment of Social Benefits of one kind or another. In so far as these taxes or subsidies are levied on, or paid to, residents of a given nation and in so far as persons never change their residence, there are no insuperable problems involved in failing to harmonise the structure or rates of the various national regimes. There would need to be an agreed Community system of double tax relief which ensured that it was the tax regime of the country in which the taxpayer was resident which was operative in the case of any transaction. Thus if a taxpayer resident in country *A* received income in respect of work done or capital invested in country *B*, the income would be subject to *A*'s Income Tax and would not be charged under *B*'s Income Tax regime. Similarly Wealth held in *B* by a resident of *A* would be subject to *A*'s Wealth Tax and would not be charged under *B*'s Wealth Tax; and Country *A*'s Social Benefits would be paid to residents of *A* and *B*'s to residents of *B*. However in the case of a Capital Transfer Tax there could be a problem. Suppose some capital were transferred from a resident of *A* to a resident of *B*. If the Capital Transfer Tax of *A* was payable by the benefactor and that of *B* was payable by the beneficiary, there would be a case of double taxation. Whereas if the Capital Transfer Tax was payable by the beneficiary in *A* and by the benefactor in *B* both parties would be exempt from tax.

In this last case there would need to be some Community agreement about the way in which this kind of situation should be treated; and there could be other cases for which special rules would have to be agreed, for example for the treatment of the income of a Discretionary Trust some of the potential beneficiaries of which might be residents of *A* and others residents of *B*. But in general the principle of applying the tax regime of the country of residence of the person liable to pay the tax would be clear in its application. The problem would be simply that of avoiding evasion. For this purpose Community procedures for cooperative action between the various national revenue-collecting authorities could be most helpful. In the extreme, if there was a single Community revenue-collecting administration applying the various national regimes on behalf of the various national governments, the opportunities for tax evasion would be greatly reduced.

So far so good. But as has been already shown in the discussion of social problems, differences in fiscal arrangements for the redistribution of income and wealth may give rise to very serious problems in a Community in which there is free movement of persons between the various member countries. Egalitarian country *A* with a high Basic Income might attract all the poor, inefficient, or idle citizens while incentive-minded country *B* attracted all the rich, efficient and active members of society together with their capital resources.

Movement from one place of residence to another is, of course, not costless, particularly in a continent in which languages differ from country to country. Some degree of diversity in tax regimes would be possible without leading to great movements of taxpayers. But if fully free uncompensated changes in residence were allowed, this would set a very effective limit to the degree of diversity in national tax regimes which was practicable. Those who advocated egalitarian measures on a large scale would have to persuade all – or at least the most important – nations of the Community to make more or less simultaneously the same sort of tax

changes, the extreme version of which would imply complete tax harmonisation and the complete disappearance of experimental national diversity.

But may there not be some form of compensated freedom of movement
of persons which would increase the feasibility of national diversity in tax
regimes? Theoretically there is one simple rule which would solve the
whole problem, namely a rule that while persons were free to change their
actual residences they could not change their legal residence for purposes of
direct-tax regimes. Thus a national of *A* who had migrated to *B* would still
be taxed under *A*'s tax regime. If such a rule were possible, the problem
would disappear. Citizens would still have an economic incentive to move
from *A* to *B* if and only if their pre-tax incomes were greater in *B* than in *A*.
The taxes which they would pay would depend upon *A*'s tax schedule, but
presumably the actual revenue would accrue to *B*'s government, since the
persons concerned would now for all intents and purposes be citizens of *B*
enjoying the advantages and responsibilities of that country. It is perhaps
not inconceivable that in the end, particularly if there were a single Community administration for the collection of the member countries' direct
taxes, a solution somewhat on these lines might be possible. But it does not
sound like a political possibility at the moment. I must leave it to the reader
to consider whether there are more feasible methods of introducing some
rough compensatory measures which would offset in part or whole some of
the undesirable effects of diverse direct-tax regimes. Or would the existence
of large diversities in national fiscal policies for redistribution of income
and wealth necessitate the continuation of direct controls over migration
between the member nations?

Such undesirable tax effects are to be expected not only as a result of the
differences in the redistributive effects of taxation which I have just discussed. If country *A* exempts all net savings from its Income Tax and
thereby turns it into a tax on consumption expenditures, while country *B*
operates a straightforward Income Tax, there will be an incentive for
citizens to be residents of *A* while they are saving for the future and their
expenditure is low and to become residents of *B* when they are living on
their past savings and their expenditures are greater than their income. Does
this mean that *A* and *B* must jointly decide to operate either an Income Tax
or an Expenditure Tax? Or could the citizens be treated as not having
changed their legal residence for tax purposes when they move from *A* to *B*?
Or could some rougher form of tax compensation be devised so that they
pay some penalty on what they have saved tax free in *A*, when they move
to *B*?

There are other forms of tax which I have not discussed and which raise
similar problems. For example, a Corporation Tax is a tax on profits, i.e. on

a form of income, which is payable not by a person but by a corporation. Differences in rates and structures of such a tax may thus affect incentives to expand production in one plant in *A* rather than in another plant in *B*, and in the case of a multinational company operating both plants it will give rise to incentives to keep the companies' accounts in such a way as to concentrate the profit return in the lower-taxed plant, for example, by selling intermediate products at an exceptionally high price when they move from the low-taxed to the high-taxed plant. Once again the question arises whether tax harmonisation is on balance desirable in order to remove these unwanted incentives.

This discussion of tax harmonisation has been very superficial, but it is hoped that it has served to show how basically important the question is in the search for a balance between the requirements of national diversity and continental uniformity.

IX EUROPEAN MONETARY UNION

A very special case of possible conflict between the merits of diversity and uniformity arises in the monetary field in choosing between a single European currency and a European set of national currencies with variations in the rate of exchange between them.

There are certain clear advantages in having a single European currency. The most obvious and familiar of these is the saving of the cost and inconvenience involved in having to change a domestic currency into a foreign currency for purposes of foreign trade, tourism, capital investment and other forms of transaction with foreigners, together with the ease of making comparisons between domestic and foreign prices and costs. Closely allied to this is another advantage, namely the removal of the uncertainty as to what the future rates of exchange will be between a domestic currency and various other currencies. The exporter of goods from *A* to *B* who contracts to produce them at a given price in *B*'s currency will bear no exchange rate risk if *B*'s currency is the same as *A*'s, but will bear a serious risk if *B*'s currency may depreciate in terms of *A*'s currency over the period of the contract; and in the absence of offsetting measures foreign exchange rates are notoriously volatile in their fluctuations.

For some countries membership of a Community with a single currency – or with monetary arrangements like the ERM which greatly restrict exchange rate variations – may enable the country to resist inflationary pressures. For example, suppose that a country is threatened with a high rate of inflation because of upward thrusts of money wage costs due to its wage-setting institutions. It may find it politically easier to take the necessary restrictive monetary and fiscal measures to fight such inflation if these measures are essential to maintain a given agreed exchange rate for its currency in terms of its competitor's currencies than if the restrictive measures are taken merely to avoid the rate of national inflation from rising above some nationally determined target level. There may be little or no real economic difference between the two methods. A given degree of restriction of money expenditures with the same consequential degree of recession and unemployment may be needed in both cases to break the wage cost-push inflation. The difference is basically a political one. The preservation of an internationally agreed exchange rate mechanism may be a more persuasive and credible argument than the prevention of a national index of inflation from rising above a target level and may thus have a greater effect in inducing wage bargainers to set less inflationary wage rates.

But probably the strongest argument in favour of a single European currency has little or no economic content but is straightforwardly political. A single currency gives the Community authorities a very important positive function to perform jointly – namely, the issue and administration of a single non-inflationary currency – in a way which distinguishes the countries concerned sharply from the outside world. Thus, like a flag it presents to the world a great symbol of unity. Such considerations may well be by far the most important ones in the case of a European Monetary Union with a Single Currency, but they are not basically economic.

But a structure of separate national currencies with the possibility of variations in the rates of exchange between them also has certain clear advantages. The first of these is the much greater ease of making any necessary adjustments between the general level of money prices and costs in one country and in another. Such situations may arise in a number of ways. Suppose that countries *A* and *B* concentrate on two different types of tradeable products, *A* concentrating on the manufacture of consumer goods and *B* on machinery and similar capital equipment. Suppose that the world demand for *A*'s product falls and for *B*'s product rises. Equilibrium in the world markets will require a general fall in the price of *A*'s products relatively to *B*'s products. Or suppose that *A* and *B* are producing very similar manufactured goods in competition with each other, but that *A*'s money wage costs have risen more rapidly than *B*'s. Such a development might occur through a higher rate of increase of output per head in *B* than in *A* or from a difference in institutions and customary procedures for the fixing of money wage rates, leading to a higher rate of increase of money earnings per head in *A* than in *B*. In either case a reduction of the general level of money prices and costs in *A* relatively to those in *B* is needed to restore *A*'s competitive position.

If *A* and *B* share the same currency, the process of readjustment requires an absolute reduction in *A*'s and/or an absolute rise in *B*'s money prices and costs. Such adjustments will be brought about in the markets by a slow and piecemeal procedure with the fall in the demand for *A*'s products causing reduced output and unemployment separately plant by plant in a whole range of industrial plants and companies. This process must continue on a scale sufficient to lead gradually to the necessary reduction in the general level of money prices and costs, while the rise in the demand for *B*'s products gradually causes a plant-by-plant rise in *B*'s money wages and policies. If, however *A* and *B* have different currencies, the whole adjustment can be achieved without a prolonged period of plant-by-plant adjustment and without unemployed resources in *A* by means of a single once-for-all depreciation of *A*'s currency in terms of *B*'s.

In deciding whether *A* and *B* should share a single currency or should retain separate national currencies the merits of exchange-rate variations as an instrument of adjustment between the two countries must be set against the merits of a single currency in reducing costs and uncertainties in transactions between the two countries. There are at least four important factors to be considered in assessing the relative merits of the two exchange-rate mechanisms.

First, the greater is the size of any national or regional economy, the greater is likely to be the value of its internal transactions relative to the value of its transactions with the outside world. For this reason the relatively small economy will suffer relatively bigger transactions costs from having a separate currency of its own, monetary transactions with outsiders being large relatively to monetary transactions with insiders. A separate currency is more appropriate, the larger is the volume of internal transactions relative to external transactions.

Second, in deciding whether to join a monetary union sharing a single currency with other countries, a country should take into account the structures of its own economy and of the economies of the other members of the monetary union. The smaller the probability of a need for the real terms of trade between its products and the products of the rest of the union to be adjusted from time to time (i.e. for the price of its products to vary relatively to the price of the products of the rest of the union), the smaller would be the relative merits of retaining its own separate national currency.

Third, the greater the flexibility of its own money costs and prices in response to changes in demand and supply, the smaller would be the advantages of retaining its national currency. A particular and important example of this is the ease with which its wage-fixing institutions and procedures allow money-wage costs to rise and fall in its various industries and occupations as a result of an increase or decrease in the demand for labour at each point in the economy. The greater the flexibility, the less the need for exchange-rate variations as a means of adjustment of a general disequilibrium.

Fourth, the greater the ease of movement of labour and capital from regions in which there is an inadequate demand for their services to regions in which they are scarce and fully employed, the less need will there be for a reduction in the prices of the factors of production in the former regions relatively to their prices in the latter regions and the less, therefore, the need for a depreciation of the former currency in terms of the latter.

There is one other important merit in having a set of different national currencies. A currency must be managed by the relevant monetary authority with some set of financial objectives in view. One such objective – and it is often considered to be the only objective – will be the prevention of inflation or at least the prevention of the rate of inflation from rising above a moderate target level. But there are many ways of measuring the degree of inflation. The commonest measure is the rate of increase of a price level. But there are many different price levels. To take the ordinary cost of living index has grave dangers. For example, suppose there to be a sharp rise in the price of imported oil which enters into the cost of production of the economy's consumer goods and services. In order to prevent an inflation of the cost of living, wage costs will have to be reduced absolutely by an amount necessary to offset the rise in the cost of the oil inputs. It would be difficult enough to resist an absolute rise in wage rates to offset the rise in the cost of living due to the increased cost of imported oil. But to obtain an absolute reduction in money wage rates sufficient to offset the rise in the price of oil might well need a restrictive financial policy on a scale which would cause a very large recession and growth in unemployment in order to cut wage rates sufficiently. Exactly the same problem would arise if it was decided to raise the rate of VAT or of other indirect taxes as a means of raising revenue. To offset the resulting rise in the cost of living would require an absolute reduction of money wage rates.

A more appropriate price index might be an index of the costs of production of the economy's output of goods and services exclusive of costs of imported raw materials and of indirect taxes (i.e. a GDP deflator). Such an index would not require an absolute reduction of wage costs to offset any rise in the price of imports or in indirect taxes. But it might still be liable to lead to serious recessions and unemployment. Suppose there were a rise in the price of imported oil which was allowed to lead to a rise in the cost of living rather than needing to be offset by an absolute reduction in wage rates. It would still be necessary to prevent the rise in the cost of living from leading to the absolute increase in wage rates which might be demanded in order to offset the rise in the cost of living. To prevent such increases in money wage costs there might have to be a serious recession and cutback in the demand for labour. To obtain an immediate reversal of a 1 per cent rise in wage demands might involve an immediate cutback, for example, of 5 per cent in the demand for labour.

There is another measure of wage inflation which would call for a much less drastic cutback in the demand for labour in such conditions. This alternative would be to control the rate of rise in the total value of home production of goods and services exclusive of imported materials and of indirect taxes instead of controlling the rate of rise in the price per unit of such output (i.e. to substitute the total money GDP for the GDP deflator). Any undesired increase in money wage rates by raising the money price of output would, of course, raise the total money value of the output by a corresponding amount. But to obtain an immediate reduction of 1 per cent in the value of total output could not at the worst lead to more than a 1 per cent reduction in the demand for labour. A 1 per cent reduction in the value of total output would be brought about by a 1 per cent reduction in the level of output and employment even if there were no responses at all in reducing the money wage rate and the money cost-price of output. For this reason taking the money GDP instead of a price level would be liable to cause much less sudden and sharp variations in the levels of output and employment. It would thus reduce the risks involved in joining a full monetary union with a single currency for a country whose institutions and procedures led to rather rigid wage-rate settlements.

There are thus many possible measures of inflation. A set of different national currencies would thus make room for a greater diversity of national experiments in the control of inflation, not only by allowing for different levels for any given inflation target but also by the choice of different methods of measuring inflation. In particular it would not rule out an experiment with an index of money GDP instead of a money price index as setting the inflation target. But if different countries were maintaining different inflation targets, there would have to be a possibility for at least moderate adjustments in their exchange rates.

There is one other important set of financial considerations which have important implications for the choice between a single uniform European currency and a set of independent national currencies. It should be the objective of the financial authorities not only to keep the economy on a given Inflation Target (whether this be a Price Target or a Money GDP

Target), but also to keep the economy on what may be called a Wealth Target. This latter target might take the form simply of maintaining a certain Budget Balance between the government's tax revenue and its current expenditures on goods and services, in order to avoid the possibility of the government simply eating up the country's Wealth by borrowing all private savings to finance a governmental excess of current spending. Alternatively, the Wealth Target might aim at keeping the level of Public plus Private Savings at a given target level. Whatever precise indicator is chosen for the Wealth Target – and there is every reason to regard diversity of national experiment in this sphere as being in itself a desirable feature – there will then be two policy instruments (namely, Monetary Policy controlling the Rate of Interest and Fiscal Policy controlling the Rate of Tax) available to aim at the two financial targets (namely the Inflation Target and the Wealth Target, whatever precise form these may take).

It is often taken for granted that the obvious course is to assign the use of the monetary weapon solely to the control of the monetary target (e.g. to raise or lower the rate of interest as it is desired to lower or to raise the rate of Price Inflation) and the use of the fiscal weapon solely to the control of the wealth target (e.g. to raise or lower the rate of tax as it is desired to raise or lower the Budget Balance). But this is a mistaken idea. Monetary restriction will reduce the amount of expenditures on goods and services. This reduction in demand will help to reduce prices, but it will also reduce the incomes of those producing the goods so that not only the revenue from indirect taxes will fall as the result of lower sales but the revenue from direct taxes will also fall as a result of lower expendable money incomes. Thus monetary restriction will lower the Inflation index and will also lower the tax revenue and thus the Budget Balance indicator. Fiscal restriction in the form of a rise in the Rate of Tax will raise the Budget Balance but it will also lead to a fall in demand for goods and services and thus to some fall in the rate of Price Inflation. Thus both financial weapons will affect both financial target. The way to use them efficiently so that both targets are maintained simultaneously is to use them jointly and simultaneously to produce the jointly desired effect on both targets. To use them with separate assignments, setting monetary policy to control Price Inflation without any consideration of its effect on the Budget Balance and setting fiscal policy to control the Budget Balance without any consideration of its effect on Price Inflation, is at its best a very clumsy and inefficient procedure which will enable the two targets to be reached only after a prolonged process of adjustment and readjustment. At the worst if Fiscal Policy is relatively more effective as a controller of Price Inflation and Monetary Policy relatively more effective as a controller of the Budget Balance, the independent operation of monetary policy to control Price Inflation and of fiscal policy to control the Budget Balance will lead to a disastrous instability of the system.[2]

The first solution would be to settle for a system of independent national currencies so that each national authority could control both its monetary and fiscal policies for the joint control of its own Inflation and Wealth targets. This would necessitate some degree of flexibility between the nations' exchange rates, though it would be perfectly possible and desirable to devise a set of European rules and institutions for the conduct of foreign exchange policies which prevented unnecessary volatility in exchange rates but allowed for those moderate exchange rate variations which will be needed to harmonise the diverse national financial targets.

The second solution would be to institute a single European currency to be shared by all the member countries with a single European Central Bank to administer its issue, but at the same time to centralise a sufficient part of the fiscal operations of the European Community in a centralised Community budget in order to enable Community monetary and fiscal authorities jointly to design a joint monetary-fiscal policy for the control of Inflation, while paying proper regard to the need not to upset national fiscal plans for the maintenance of their wealth targets. Such a situation might automatically result if for other purposes the European Community needed to develop its own considerable budget and tax revenue, as for example would be the case if joint expenditure on a single defence force became part of the Community's function. But in the absence of such a development one would need to endow the Community with a Community rate of tax (such as a Community VAT) which it could vary in order to help to regulate the total of money expenditures in the Community, but the revenue from which would be assigned to the various countries in which the revenue was raised. What needs to be avoided is a European Central Bank issuing a single European Currency with the sole object of maintaining an Inflation Target in terms of that currency but without regard to any fiscal effects, the independent national budgets being subject to a scattered set of independent fiscal authorities acting without any regard to the inflationary or deflationary effects of their decisions.

I will cease the Ambidextrous waving of my two arms and reveal my Presidential decision which is to advocate something on the lines of the British proposal for the issue of an additional European currency which, following their notation, I will call a Hard ECU. It seems to me to be a good way of reconciling as well as one can the conflicts which I have mentioned between the merits of a single European currency and of a set of independent national currencies.

Let me quickly state the main features of the proposals as I would like them to be made. Let there be a European Central Bank with the responsibility of issuing a new currency, the Hard ECU. Its duty would be to control the issue so as to stabilise in terms of the Hard ECU an index of the rate of Price Inflation or alternatively, as I would prefer, an index of the rate of growth of the Community's total Money GDP. Any member country or group of member countries could adopt the Hard ECU as their national currencies thus forming a full monetary union with the European Central Bank as their single operative central bank. Any other member country would be free to link its currency to the Hard ECU in a way designed to rule out unnecessary fluctuations in the Hard ECU value of its national currency but to permit such exchange rate variations as were planned to maintain equilibrium between its own plans for Inflation Control in terms of its own currency and the European Central Bank plans for its Inflation Control in terms of the Hard ECU. Such planned variations would need to have the agreement of the European Central Bank authorities. Personally I think that they might often take the form of a planned crawling peg between the national currency and the Hard ECU, changes in the rate of crawl being agreed from time to time with the European Central Bank.

Such a system would allow for the early formation of a full monetary union by those countries which were ready and desired immediately to do so, for a period of adjustment for those who wished to do so but were not ready to do so, and for a continued use of a suitably controlled but variable linkage with the Hard ECU for those countries who wished to maintain indefinitely the experiment of having one currency for domestic purposes and another currency for foreign transactions for one reason or other, such as a choice of different forms of Inflation or Wealth Target or a continuing divergence in wage and price setting mechanisms. The whole system would be a remarkable example of a new monetary experiment without, one would hope, nations which opted for one form of use of the Hard ECU being regarded as superior or inferior to those who opted for another.

A more detailed set of rules for such a Hard ECU solution of the European Monetary Problem is described in the immediately following Appendix to this chapter.

APPENDIX: THE BASIC FEATURES OF AN INDEPENDENT 'HARD ECU'

The following are 12 basic features of the Hard ECU arrangements described in the last paragraphs of the main text.

(1) Every currency system requires a Legal Tender by means of which obligations expressed in terms of the currency must in the last resort be met. The Legal Tender consists of Hard ECU bank notes.

(2) These bank notes are issued by a European Central Bank (ECB) with a strong independent Governor and Board of Directors.

(3) The initial assets and liabilities of the ECB are constituted in the following way. The National Central Banks (NCBs) pay into the ECB a proportion of their holdings of Gold and Foreign Exchange in return for Hard ECU deposit liabilities of the ECB. The assets of the ECB are further augmented by the payment into the ECB of Bonds or Bills denominated in Hard ECUs and issued by the National Governments and/or the NCBs of the constituent member countries in return for holdings of ECB Hard ECU deposit liabilities. The constituent governments guarantee the solvency of the ECB.

(4) All accounts, transactions, assets and liabilities of the European Community and of all its institutions and organisation are denominated in Hard ECUs. All tax payments or other payments by the National Governments to the Community's budget are thus payable in Hard ECUs.

(5) At the outset the existing ERM obligations of the National Governments are continued with the exception that the existing exchange-rate grid is abolished and is replaced by an obligation to peg each national currency to the Hard ECU with the existing permitted margins of fluctuation. The grid which sets a separate linkage between each pair of national currencies is a clumsy method of controlling exchange rates. It was preferred to a direct linkage of each national currency with the existing Soft ECU because the grid required no currency to depreciate unduly in terms of any other currency (including the hardest currency in the group), whereas a linkage with the Soft ECU required only a performance no worse than the average of the currencies in the group. The existence of a Hard ECU makes the grid system unnecessary.

(6) The ECB sets an interest rate structure at which it will negotiate to borrow or lend Hard ECUs in transactions with the NCBs, the National Governments, the Community Organisations and a wide range of other financial institutions both inside and outside the Community.

(7) The obligation of the ECB is to raise or lower its interest rate structure in terms of the Hard ECU so as to stabilise an Inflation Index measured in terms of Hard ECU prices. This index could be a Price Index covering the total output of goods and services of all the member countries, or, preferably, an Index of the Money Value in terms of Hard ECUs of that total output of goods and services. For the construction of such indices national values would be converted into Hard ECU values at the current market rates of exchange.

(8) The obligations of the NCBs would be to preserve their ERM pegs on the Hard ECU by appropriate adjustments in their interest rate structures in terms of their own National currencies.

(9)   The Governor and Board of Directors of the ECB would not include the Governors of the NCBs. There would thus be no grey area of mixed responsibilities. The ECB would be responsible for setting Hard ECU interest rates to control inflation in terms of the Hard ECU. The NCBs would be responsible for setting national currency interest rates to maintain their pegs on the Hard ECU.

(10)   It is essential that the ECB should be aware of the inflationary or deflationary effects of current fiscal policies and that Fiscal Authorities should be aware of the inflationary or deflationary effects of current monetary policies on their tax bases and so on their budgetary revenues. For this purpose there would be a process of continuous consultation between the monetary and fiscal authorities of the Community in order to coordinate monetary and fiscal policies so as to devise a joint strategy in control of inflation and of Budget Balances.

(11)   The setting-up of this ECB structure could be regarded as Stage Two of the Delors Report. The member countries which were ready and wished to do so could fix their pegs on the Hard ECU rigidly and irrevocably and could then adopt the Hard ECU in place of their national currencies. The NCBs of such countries would then become the local offices of the ECB. The system would be so flexible that not all member countries need adopt this full EMU solution at the same moment. Indeed a single country could at any time elect in agreement with the ECB to adopt the Hard ECU as its national currency.

(12)   Any member country which wished to do so could continue indefinitely to link its currency with the Hard ECU without ruling out any possible future changes in the exchange rate between its national currency and the Hard ECU. For example, it could simply maintain its existing ERM obligations under which any change in its peg would have to be agreed with the ECB. New forms of linkage with the Hard ECU could be devised to replace the ERM type of linkage. For example, a crawling-peg type of adjustment might be appropriate in certain circumstances. But the overriding rule would be that membership of the ECB group would be conditional upon the member country maintaining a linkage of its currency with the Hard ECU on terms which were accepted as suitable by the ECB.

Notes

1.   A more detailed account of my visit to Agathotopia may be found in Chapter 4 of the present volume. For the purpose of the present chapter it is not necessary to enquire into the details of the island's existence and other institutions nor to ask whether any European country would in fact ever be likely to act quite like the Agathotopians. The only relevance for the present chapter is to provide a list of many measures any one or combination of which a European country might wish to adopt.

2.   The dangers and disadvantages of assigning Monetary Policy exclusively to the control of Inflation and Fiscal Policy exclusively to the control of Budget Balances are increased by the formation of a Monetary Union with a single currency. The formation of the Union will cause much of the foreign trade of

each constituent member nation to be transformed into the domestic trade of the Union so that the ratio of foreign to domestic trade is much reduced. This has a double effect. (1) The fall in leakages of expenditures on imported goods causes the multiplier to be higher in the Union. This means that both Monetary Policy and Fiscal Policy are more effective in controlling domestic expenditures and so in controlling both Inflation and the tax base. But Fiscal Policy unlike Monetary Policy becomes less effective in controlling the Budget Balance. With a higher multiplier, a given rise in the rate of tax will have a larger effect in decreasing consumption expenditures and thus in restricting the tax base; and this will reduce the tax yield from any given rise in tax rate. (2) When interest rates are raised to fight Inflation, any consequential appreciation of the rate of exchange will have a smaller effect in reducing the cost of living in the Union in which the price of imports is a smaller component of the cost of living price index. This factor will reduce the effect of Monetary Policy on Inflation. For these two reasons the relative effects of Monetary Policy on Inflation and of Fiscal Policy on Budget Balances will both be reduced by the formation of the Union, so that the case for exclusive assignment of Monetary Policy to the control of Inflation and of Fiscal Policy to the control of Budget Balance is doubly weakened.

6 In Praise of Slowth: or The Agathotopian Treatment of the Environment as a Common National Asset

I INTRODUCTION

In 1955 my wife founded a society which she called SPES or 'The Society for the Promotion of Economic Slowth'. Its purposes was to spread a ray of hope in a world in which the physical environment was being pillaged and in which the social and political environment urged us all to strive to possess a number of goods which we did not really need and which we packaged and dissipated in the most wasteful manner. The society has flourished with its valuable, indeed unique, membership; and I am now myself faced with the difficult decision whether I should apply for membership with, I admit, the ambition of becoming its economic adviser.

Indeed, I find myself at present in a most deplorable, uncertain, ambivalent frame of mind. If the authorities predict an upturn in economic growth with a fall in unemployment and with rises in the production of manufactured goods for export and for home consumption, in consumer purchases of ironmongery of various kinds, in the number of cars and their mileage and in the consumption of various fuels, how should I react? Do I rejoice at the prospect of greater wealth and prosperity for this country which has been doing less well than it should in these respects? Or, given the dire prophesies of many well-informed scientists and other authorities, do I despair at the prospect of still greater strain on an overburdened environment with at least the possibility of very frightening consequences?

In order to take a rest in this troubled state of mind I spent a short holiday in the Island of Agathotopia. There, with the help of my old friend Professor Dr Semaj Edaem, I constructed a model for the economic behaviour of a country like my own which was faced with this frightening dilemma. I now reproduce it and seek advice as to whether I should submit it to the founder of SPES with an application for membership of that society.

The following is my blueprint for the treatment of this problem.

II THE ASSUMED PRODUCTION FUNCTION

The purpose of the present model is to illustrate how the existence of an external commonly shared environmental atmosphere may limit the operations of any competitive production process. For this purpose we start by assuming the existence of the simplest possible perfectly competitive system of production which takes the following form.

We assume labour to be the only factor of production in this competitive process with a working population of N individuals each of whom is working ℓ hours per week, so that

$$L = N\ell \tag{1}$$

where L measures the total labour input into the production process. This total input of labour is distributed over a large number of competing 'labour-employing firms'. We assume that the size of the individual firm does not itself affect the output per unit of labour in the firm.

On this assumption we can write

$$q = \ell \frac{Q}{L} \tag{2}$$

where q represents the amount produced by any individual worker, ℓ represents the amount of work done by any one individual worker, and Q represents the total output of the competitive production process, so that Q/L represents the amount produced per unit of work done throughout the whole economy.

It is the level of Q/L which will be affected externally by the common environment in which the competitive process is carried out. This effect we represent by

$$\frac{Q}{L} = L(A - L) \tag{3}$$

With this formula, as illustrated by Figure 6.1, increasing returns to scale at first lead to a rise in output per unit of labour input as more labour (L) is applied to give a common environmental atmosphere (A). But after a certain point the average productivity of labour (Q/L) declines as the common atmosphere becomes more and more choked with productive activity.

From equation (3) one can derive the community's production function, namely:

$$Q = L^2(A - L) \tag{4}$$

and the marginal productivity of labour, namely:

$$\frac{dQ}{dL} = L(2A - 3L) \tag{5}$$

This production function can be depicted in a familiar diagram (Figure 6.1).

It has the following features:

(1) As L increases from low values, both marginal and average productivity rise with marginal productivity greater than average productivity.

(2) At $L = \frac{A}{3}$, marginal productivity ceases to rise and starts to fall.

(3) At $L = \frac{A}{2}$, marginal productivity falls to equal average productivity which reaches its maximum at this point.

(4) At $L = \frac{2A}{3}$, the scarcity of A exercises such a limiting pressure that the marginal productivity falls to zero and Q reaches its maximum value.

(5) Between $L = \frac{2A}{3}$ and $L = A$ the pressure on the atmosphere is so great that total output declines as more inputs of L are applied to it, until at $L = A$ output is reduced to zero.

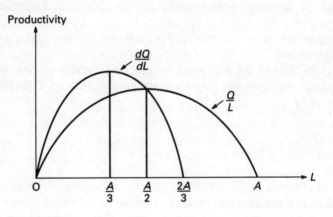

Figure 6.1

(6) Throughout this story there are very marked increasing returns to scale in A and L. From (4) we see that $\frac{\partial Q}{\partial A} = L^2$ so that $A\frac{\partial Q}{\partial A} + L\frac{\partial Q}{\partial L} = 3L^2(A-L) = 3Q$. Thus, to pay to the owners of A and to the the owners of L rewards equal to the values of their marginal products would require three times as much output as they were in fact producing, which is an index of the high degree of increasing returns to scale.

In fact, this is an unrealistic feature of the function. Increasing returns to scale are likely to be very important when the scale of output is low; but as the scale increases with an increase in size of the market more and more of the opportunities for a further division of labour will be used up. When the scale is sufficiently large for there to be a great deal of competition between units of production each of which is large enough to enjoy to the full the advantages of the division of labour, it would be possible to operate a market in which there are constant returns to scale with total output being just sufficient to pay to each factor of production including the atmosphere, a reward equal to the value of its marginal product. The following form of a production function

$$Q = \left(\frac{\alpha L}{\alpha + L}\right)^2 L^\theta (A-L)^{1-\theta} \tag{6}$$

has in a general form all the first five desirable properties of the function given in equation (4); but it has in addition the desirable sixth property that the economies of large-scale production fade out as the scale of operations increases. Differentiation of equation (6) gives $A\frac{\partial Q}{\partial A} + L\frac{\partial Q}{\partial L} = \frac{3\alpha + L}{\alpha + L}Q$ which falls from $3Q$ to Q as L rises from 0 to ∞.

In spite of the attraction of equation (6), we will use equation (4) as the production function throughout this chapter, because its use involves much less algebraic clumsiness than occurs with the use of equation (6). Reference will, however, be made to some relevant results which would have been significantly different if equation (6) had been used.

III THE STRUCTURE OF THE ECONOMY

Each of the competing 'labour-employing firms' described at the beginning of section II employs units of labour at a uniform money wage rate (w) and sells its output at a competitive selling price (p) where

$$p = \frac{wL(1+t)}{Q} = \frac{w\ell(1+t)}{q} \tag{7}$$

With a competitive wage (w) per man-hour the labour-cost per unit of output is $\frac{wL}{Q}$. There is a VAT-like tax (t) levied on this cost so that the competitive selling prices of output (p) is $\frac{wL(1+t)}{Q}$.

$$\left. \begin{aligned} B &= twL \\ b &= \frac{twL}{N} = tw\ell \end{aligned} \right\} \tag{8}$$

The total revenue (B) raised by the tax (t) is twL. This is distributed as a basic income (b) to each of the N individual members of the community so that the individual's total potential money income (m) is expressed by

$$w\bar{\ell} + tw\ell = m \tag{9}$$

where $w\bar{\ell}$ measures the money income which an individual could earn by taking no leisure and twl the basic money income distributed to each individual regardless of how much he or she earns. Thus $w\bar{\ell} + tw\ell$ is the individual's total potential money income which can be spent on leisure $(\bar{\ell} - \ell)$ at a price w or on goods (c) at a price p.

IV THE INDIVIDUAL'S CONSUMPTION FUNCTION

The individual citizen has a potential money income (m) as expressed in equation (9) which he or she can spend either on buying leisure at a money price (w) (i.e. by forgoing the earning of an income of w) or on buying products at the current market price (p). We illustrate our model by assuming the simplest possible demand function, namely that the individual spends a fixed fraction λ of potential income on leisure and remaining fraction $(1-\lambda)$ on goods, so that

$$w(\bar{\ell} - \ell) = \lambda m \tag{10}$$

and

$$pc = (1-\lambda)m \tag{11}$$

where c = the amount of goods consumed by the individual.

This in fact assumes that the consumer's price and income elasticities of demand for leisure and goods are both equal to unity. If income (m) goes up by 1 per cent, the consumer's expenditures on leisure and goods will both go up by 1 per cent. If the price of goods (p) goes up by 1 per cent, the amount of goods consumed (c) will go down by 1 per cent.

From equations (7), (9), (10) and (11) one can derive

$$\bar{\ell} - \ell = \lambda(\bar{\ell} + t\ell) \tag{12}$$

and

$$c = \frac{q(1-\lambda)}{\ell(1+t)}(\bar{\ell} + t\ell) \tag{13}$$

From equation (12) one can derive

$$\ell = \frac{(1-\lambda)}{1+t\lambda}\bar{\ell} \tag{14}$$

and $\bar{\ell} - \ell = \dfrac{\lambda(1+t)}{1+t\lambda}\bar{\ell}$ (15)

thus expressing the amount of work done per head (ℓ) and the amount of leisure enjoyed per head ($\bar{\ell} - \ell$) in terms of $\bar{\ell}$, λ and t.

Using equations (12), (13), (14) and (15) one can derive

$$c = q \tag{16}$$

Consumption of goods per head is equal to production per head as a result of the proceeds of the tax on consumption being redistributed as an addition to spendable basic income. In what follows we will employ the term q to express either consumption per head or production per head indifferently as the case may require.

From equations (14) and (15) it can be seen that a rise in the rate of tax (t) will lead to a reduction in the amount of work done per head (ℓ) and a rise in the amount of leisure enjoyed per head ($\bar{\ell} - \ell$). When the rate of tax is raised the real purchasing power of the individual's money incomes remain unchanged in the sense that any rise in the market price of goods is exactly offset by an increased receipt of basic income. Citizens could continue to purchase the same quantities of goods and leisure as before. But as can be seen from equation (7) a rise in t will raise $\dfrac{p}{w}$, the price of goods relative to the price of leisure, so that there will be some incentive to substitute the cheaper leisure for the more expensive goods.

V   THE OPTIMUM TAX LEVEL AND THE CLOSE OF THE SYSTEM

So much for the individual's reaction to the level of t. It remains to consider what is the optimal level at which the authorities should set the tax rate.

In fully competitive conditions, the output produced on the Common National Asset A by the competing labour firms would be sold at its average cost (namely, $\frac{wL}{Q}$) but is marginal labour cost would be different (namely $\frac{wdL}{dQ}$. If the marginal cost were greater than the average cost, a VAT-type tax can be set on the average cost to raise the selling price of the product up to its marginal cost in order to remove any incentive to produce on a larger-than-optimal scale. We would then have

$$\frac{wL}{Q}(1+t) = \frac{wdL}{dQ} \tag{17}$$

Using the expressions for $\frac{Q}{L}$ and $\frac{dQ}{dL}$ in equations (3) and (5) this gives

$$t^* = \frac{2L-A}{2A-3L} \tag{18}$$

where t^* represents the socially optimal rate of tax. It may be noted that t^* is a positive quantity if $\frac{2}{3}A > L > \frac{A}{2}$, that is to say, if L lies within the range of values for which on Figure 6.1 the marginal productivity of labour is positive but is less than its average productivity.

Since $N\ell = L$ (equation (1)) and $\ell = \frac{1-\lambda}{1+t\lambda}\bar{\ell}$ (equation (14)) we could write equation (18) as

$$t^* = \frac{2N(1-\lambda)\bar{\ell} - A(1+t^*\lambda)}{2A(1+t^*\lambda) - 3N(1-\lambda)\ell} \tag{19}$$

It is clear from equation (19) that with A and λ given, the value of t^* is determined by the value of N. But with the values of t and N given, the whole system is determined. With $\bar{\ell}$ given, ℓ and so $L = N\ell$ are deter-

mined by equations (14) and (1). With L given, Q, $\dfrac{Q}{L}$ and $\dfrac{dQ}{dL}$ are determined by equations (3) (4) and (5). With a constant w, p is determined by
equation (7), and b and m are determined by equations (8) and (9).

VI THE CRITICAL ROLE OF THE SIZE OF THE POPULATION

Unfortunately to derive from equation (19) the value of t^* in terms of N
would result in a not very illuminating solution of a clumsy quadratic
equation. By differentiation one can, however, determine the direction and
the form of the effect of a change in N on the other variables in the system,
given that t is always set at the optimal value t^* given in equation (18). This
process is described in an Appendix to this chapter. Here we confine
ourselves to the following catalogue of the signs of the various relationships:

$$\frac{d\ell}{dN} \text{ is } < 0, \text{ but } \frac{dL}{dN}, \frac{dt^*}{dN}, \frac{dB}{dN}, \frac{db}{dN} \text{ and } \frac{dQ}{dN} \text{ are all } > 0.$$

There is a critical value of N which will cause the optimal tax rate t^* to
be zero. We know that if $L = \frac{A}{2}$ output per unit of labour is maximised and
marginal productivity equals average productivity, as can be confirmed by
an inspection of equations (3) and (5) and as illustrated in Figure 6.1. At this
point $t^* = 0$, as can be seen from equation (18). But if $t = 0$ then from
equation (14) it can be seen that $\ell = (1 - \lambda)\bar{\ell}$ so that $L = N(1 - \lambda)\bar{\ell}$. Thus
at this point $L = \frac{A}{2} = N(1 - \lambda)\bar{\ell}$, so that

$$N = \frac{A}{2(1 - \lambda)\bar{\ell}} \tag{20}$$

This is the critical value of N at which producers can be allowed freely
to compete on the Common Atmosphere where their untaxed unsubsidised
earnings (i.e. their average product) will be equal to their marginal product.
One way of expressing the situation is that their individual activities present
no element of external economy or diseconomy. When one producer produces more this will not raise the average output and so the income of others
(because the economies of scale no longer are dominant) and it will not
reduce the average output and so the income of others (because the crowd-
ing out on the use of the Common Atmosphere has not started to dominate).

VII THE WELFARE STATE WITH A HIGH POPULATION

Suppose next that the population grows beyond this critical level of $N = \dfrac{A}{2(1-\lambda)\bar{\ell}}$. To maintain balance between an individual's net real rate of pay and his or her marginal product the optimal rate of tax must be raised from zero to a positive level $\left(\dfrac{dt^*}{dN} > 0\right)$ because the increased population will result in a larger total amount of activity in the Common Atmosphere $\left(\dfrac{dL}{dN} > 0\right)$ in spite of some reduction in work per head of population $\left(\dfrac{d\ell}{dN} < 0\right)$. This will cause the marginal product of labour to fall below its average product. An increase in an individual's activity will now entail an external diseconomy, since it will bring down the average product which is available to others. The rise in the tax rate to t^* combined with the payment of a fixed basic income to every individual will act as an appropriate disincentive on total economic activity on the Common Atmosphere.

We are now in a regime in which the State instead of owing a Net National Debt to its individual citizens owns a Net National Asset in the form of the Common Atmosphere. This is an asset which cannot in the nature of things be privatised by selling it in small parcels to individual private owners to internalise the existing external diseconomy associated with its current use. The State, however, can charge a rent for its use in the form of the optimal tax and can utilise the proceeds to pay a Basic Income to its citizens making each of them, as it were, the beneficial owner of a fraction of the Common Atmosphere.[1]

As N increases so these elements in the economic structure will become more and more marked. L will continually increase, ℓ will continually decrease, and t^*, Q, b and B will continually increase. The tax on the use of A and the receipt of basic income will become more and more marked as features of the economy. There will, however, be a ceiling to the rise of L, although L will continually rise towards that ceiling as N increases. From equation (5) and Figure 6.1 it can be seen that as L approaches $\frac{2}{3}A$, so the marginal product of labour approaches zero which means that the marginal cost of output approaches infinity. The rate of tax on the still finite average cost would need to approach infinity to equate it to the marginal cost. Indeed as can be seen from equation (18) t^* approaches infinity as L approaches $\frac{2A}{3}$. In effect L will never reach the limit $\frac{2}{3}A$. As N increases, L will continually increase. But as it gets near to the value $\frac{2}{3}A$, the rate of rise in t^* will be so great as to cause such a big reduction in ℓ that L increases less and less rapidly in response to any increase in N. ℓ will continually decrease, approaching, but never quite reaching, zero as N increases.[2]

VIII THE INCENTIVE SOCIETY WITH A LOW POPULATION

Let us return to the critical population $N = \dfrac{A}{2(1 - \lambda)\bar{\ell}}$ and consider the implications as N decreased below this value. The developments described above are all put into reverse. The marginal product of L rises above it average product. An increase in work by one citizen provides an external economy to the benefit of other citizens, as the increase in output increases output per head for the whole community. The optimal tax rate t^* becomes negative and takes the form of a subsidy on output to reduce the price of output to its lower marginal cost. The revenue needed to pay the subsidy is financed by a negative b, namely a fixed poll-tax or community charge. This poll-tax together with the subsidised price of output gives an incentive to sacrifice leisure for the consumption of a greater quantity of products.

As N decreases further and further below the critical level $N = \dfrac{A}{2(1 - \lambda)\bar{\ell}}$ all these phenomena increase in intensity. Total L decreases, although ℓ is rising; and the rate of subsidy $(-t^*)$ and the poll-tax or community charge $(-b)$ increase as the excess of the marginal product of L over its average product rises. There is once more a limit to these changes. As N approaches zero, so L approaches zero in spite of some limited rise in ℓ. From equation (18) it can be seen that as L approaches zero, so t^* approaches $-\frac{1}{2}$. It follows from equation (15) that the amount of leisure enjoyed by an individual will fall towards a lower limit set by a fraction of total $\bar{\ell}$ equal to $\dfrac{\lambda}{2 - \lambda}$. (I don't understand why!)

IX A COMPARISON OF THE TWO REGIMES

There are two main differences between the fiscal-economic regimes appropriate for a society with N above or for one with N below the critical level. The highly populated economy will have two features which are associated with a Welfare State, namely (i) disincentives to work marked by high taxation used to pay generous social benefits and (ii) an egalitarian fiscal regime in which revenue raised on the rich who consume more than the poor is used to pay an equal basic income to all citizens. In the economy with a low population there will be two features associated with the Thatcherite type of philosophy, where (i) special regard is paid to measures which promote incentives to work and effort at the expense of (ii) a less egalitarian distribution of income.

This brief contrast between the two types of fiscal economic regime should not be taken to imply that incentives to work efficiently are of no importance in a society with N above its critical level. It is clearly desirable that whatever goods are produced should be produced efficiently and economically with the expenditure of the minimum amount of labour; and for that purpose all the competitive incentives of profit maximisation can be called upon to play their part.

Moreover in the real world, though not in our present model, there is choice to be made between a large variety of different goods to be produced and of different methods to be employed in their production. In this situation it will be of special importance to give strong competitive incentives to select for production goods, and to devise and employ methods of production, which make the least demands upon the environmental atmosphere. This implies taxing different goods and processes at different rates according to the demands made on the atmosphere. This system must be designed to give incentives and to promote enterprise in the search for the least harmful goods and processes.

Such a use of economic incentives is compatible with a general bias in favour of the growth of production of goods without too much regard for their distribution if N is below the critical level, but in favour of greater leisure at the expense of growth of output of goods and greater concern about the distribution of what is produced if N is above that level.

X AN OPTIMUM POPULATION

But which of these two types of situation does one prefer? In brief, what is the optimal size of the population? The answer depends upon what criterion one chooses for definition of the optimum population.

If one regards the optimum population as that which will provide the highest rate of welfare per head of the population, it can be shown that the critical value of $N = A / 2(1 - \lambda)\bar{\ell}$ marks the optimum size of the population. This is the population in which the amount of physical product per unit of work done is maximised. Since leisure is wanted as well as physical product and since work done per head of population is itself a variable it may not appear obvious at first sight that the point at which output per unit of work done is maximised is necessarily the point at which welfare per head of population is maximised.

But that this is in fact so can be appreciated in the following way. Suppose that, with t^* always set at the level necessary to equate labour's reward with its marginal product, the population is above the critical level so that output per unit of work done was below the potential maximum. It would be possible, without changing the amount of work done per head of population, to reduce the population and so the total amount of work done until output per unit of work done was maximised. At this point each citizen's welfare would have been raised; each citizen is enjoying an unchanged amount of leisure since, *ex hypothesi*, work done per head is unchanged; and each citizen is consuming a greater product since output per unit of work done and so per head of population has been increased. By means of such a process of 'thought experimentation' one can see that the only position in which welfare per head could not be increased would be one in which N had the critical value of $A/2(-\lambda)\bar{\ell}$ and, with $t^* = 0$, all citizens had adjusted their work–leisure choice to obtain the best possible individual outcome.

But it may be questioned whether the maximisation of welfare per head of population is the best criterion of optimality. Would not a large population of very happy people be preferred to a small population of very happy people even if happiness per head were ever so slightly higher in the smaller of the two populations? If in some sense one is concerned with total welfare rather than with welfare per head, then the optimum population would exceed the critical level of $A/2(1-\lambda)\bar{\ell}$. Suppose the population were at this critical level. An increase in the size of the population would at first cause a very small fall in productivity; as can be seen from Figure 6.1 the fall in average productivity is at first negligible as one moves to the right from the highest point of the Q/L curve, though it becomes more and more marked the further one moves to the right. There will come some point (between the points $\frac{A}{2}$ and $\frac{2A}{3}$ on the diagram) at which the gain in total welfare by having a larger number of happy citizens is just offset by the loss of welfare per head of the existing number of citizens. But it remains clear that with a population which maximises total welfare rather than welfare per head, the economy would be one in which the Welfare State's disincentives to work and egalitarian social benefits would be more appropriate than unbridled incentives to work regardless of effects on the distribution of income.

XI CONCLUSIONS

How much mileage, if any, one can hope to get out of this chapter is very uncertain. It is certainly far removed from reality with its assumptions of perfect competition, identical qualities of all citizens, no governmental functions other than the one discussed in the chapter, no foreign relations with other economies, no capital goods or savings and thus no intertemporal distribution, and so on and so on.

In particular the discussion of a finely tuned optimal population size in a world in the less wealthy members of which there is a roaring uncontrolled runaway growth of population may seem positively perverse. Indeed, for the problems of such countries the analysis of the problem isolated in this chapter has a minimal, if not zero, relevance. The one claim that can be made is that the model highlights one aspect of one problem which is at present very relevant for the relatively wealthy, developed, industrialised countries of the world. But even in such cases it must be recognised that it ignores a host of other pressing problems.

APPENDIX

From equation (14) we obtain:

$$\frac{d\ell}{dt^*} = -\frac{\lambda\ell}{1+t^*\ell} < 0 \tag{A1}$$

From equation (18) we obtain:

$$\frac{dt^*}{dL} = \frac{A}{(2A-3L)^2} > 0 \tag{A2}$$

From equation (1), $L = \ell N$, we derive:

$$\frac{dL}{dN} = \ell + N\frac{d\ell}{dt^*} \cdot \frac{dt^*}{dL} \cdot \frac{dL}{dN}$$

$$= \frac{\ell(1+t^*\lambda)(2A-3L)^2}{(1+t^*\lambda)(2A-3L)^2 + N\lambda\ell A} > 0 \tag{A3}$$

so that

$$\frac{dt^*}{dN} = \frac{dt^*}{dL} \cdot \frac{dL}{dN}$$

$$= \frac{\ell(1+t^*\lambda)A}{(1+t^*\lambda)(2A-3L)^2 + N\lambda LA} > 0 \tag{A4}$$

and

$$\frac{d\ell}{dN} = \frac{d\ell}{dt^*} \cdot \frac{dt^*}{dN} = -\frac{\ell^2 \lambda A}{(1+t^*\lambda)(2A-3L)^2 + N\lambda\ell A} < 0 \tag{A5}$$

From equation (8), $b = tw\ell$, we derive:

$$\frac{db}{dt^*} = w\left(\ell + t^*\frac{d\ell}{dt^*}\right) = \frac{w\ell}{1+t^*\lambda} > 0 \tag{A6}$$

so that

$$\frac{db}{dN} = \frac{db}{dt^*} \cdot \frac{dt^*}{dN} = \frac{w\ell^2 A}{(1+t^*\lambda)(2A-3L)^2 + N\lambda\ell A} > 0 \tag{A7}$$

From equation (8) with $B = bN$ we obtain:

$$\frac{dB}{dN} = b + N\frac{db}{dN} = w\ell\left\{t^* + \frac{\ell NA}{(1+t^*\lambda)(2A-3L)^2 + N\lambda\ell A}\right\} > 0 \tag{A8}$$

From equation (5) with $\frac{dQ}{dL} = L(2A-3L)$ we derive

$$\frac{dQ}{dN} = \frac{dQ}{dL} \cdot \frac{dL}{dN} = \frac{L\ell(1+t^*\lambda)(2A-3L)^3}{(1+t^*\lambda)(2A-3L)^2 + N\lambda\ell A} \tag{A9}$$

which is > 0 since we assume $L < \frac{2}{3}A$.

Liberty, Equality and Efficiency

Notes

1. It must be remembered that we are assuming a production function in which there are serious economies of scale in terms of the two factors A and L. The tax will not raise enough revenue to pay the owners of A a rent which is as high as the value of its marginal product if, as we are assuming, L is in fact paid the value of its marginal product. The owners of A are simply getting what is left over after paying L the value of its marginal product. If however the form of production function given in equation (6) represented the conditions in an economy which was on a sufficient scale for the economies of large-scale production to have virtually faded out, the tax would in effect raise just the amount of revenue which would be needed to pay the owners of A a rent which was equal to the value of their marginal products.

2. All this assumes that man can live on leisure alone. In fact N would cease to increase at some point because of lack of food (Q) per head would lead to starvation. Moreover, this feedback of low Q on the size of the labour force would in a poverty-stricken community show itself also in a reduction of labour efficiency, so that the total number of hours worked (L) would produce a smaller (Q). The model has many limitations which are obvious. It also has this less obvious limitation that it is really applicable only to the environmental problems of the wealthier countries where the feedback of Q on health and efficiency may be neglected.

Index